THE COMPLETE ENCYCLOPEDIA OF
TREES AND SHRUBS

THE COMPLETE ENCYCLOPEDIA OF

TREES AND SHRUBS

All you need to know about growing trees and shrubs

NICO VERMEULEN

REBO PUBLISHERS

© 1997 Rebo International b.v., Lisse, The Netherlands

Text: Hanneke van Dijk
Photographs: George M. Otter
Cover design: Minkowsky Graphics, Enkhuizen
Redaction and production: TextCase, Groningen
Typesetting and production: Signia, Winschoten

ISBN 90 366 1583 6

Contents

Preface

It is not easy to regard a tree as just a plant. Trees have their own character and there are those who regard them as animated beings. The stately bearing, and long lives of trees supports such notions. A tree which we plant will soon grow taller than us and probably live longer than we do. In these matters, trees clearly have the better of us.

In nature too, shrubs, but especially trees, are the survivors. In contrast to most other plants, they do not die back each year to the ground. Their wooden skeletons remains standing. This enables them to keep space for themselves, and gives them a head-start on the other plants when the winter is over.

This ability of trees also ensures diversity: these large wooden plants form the backbone of the landscape and of our gardens. They provide height and shape in summer and winter, so that we can plan our gardens at three levels: herbage, shrubs, and trees.

This encyclopaedia is primarily intended to assist gardeners in choosing suitable trees and shrubs. To give the best possible impression of the various trees, many photographs have been included. The combined information provides a clear picture of the most important characteristics of the trees and shrubs – their growth habit and distinguishing details.

The international binomial system has been adhered to for the botanical name of the genera and species of the plants in this book. The common name is also given where applicable. Where a tree or shrub has previously been known under different genera or species names, this will be indicated by syn. (for synonymous with) followed by the alternative name. Related sub species are indicated by subsp., varitas (or varieties) are shown by var. and forms by f.

Nico Vermeulen

Left: an avenue with beautiful old plane trees

1 Introduction

Tree or shrub?

The experts do not agree about what is a tree and what a shrub. Some arboriculturists call all wooden plants that remain below five metres a shrub, others only refer to a plant as a tree when it has a definite trunk.

The type of soil and position often have enormous influence upon the growth habit and the eventual height.

Common sense has been used in this encyclopaedia for the subdivision of trees and shrubs to make finding them as easy as possible. The starting point has been what people generally regard as trees or shrubs. Many climbing plants are also woody plants but they are not dealt with here because this book deals solely with plants which can stand unsupported.

What is wood?

Immediately after germination, all plants are alike. They push their way to the surface of the ground. The space here is quickly fully occupied so that plants which can raise themselves above the green carpet have an advantage. Above, there is space, light and air. Trees are the champions in the 'high flying' stakes. In the primeval forest, the forest giants stick out tens of metres above the other plants. To climb so high, adaptation is necessary: an extensive root system anchors the tree in the ground. Tropical trees in swampy ground often form aerial roots which act as supports rather like the buttresses of a cathedral.

Some perennials also have sturdy stems and can grow as high as a shrub in a single season but in our climate, this growth dies back and has to start from the ground once more the following spring.

Trees and shrubs have a different means of survival. They do not have to constantly compete for space. The growth remains upright outside the growing season, so that the new leaves shoot high above the ground. The growth of trees or shrubs we call branches, except for the main growth stem –

Left: Quercus robur or English oak as magnificent focal point of a delightful landscape

that is thicker and bears the tree – which is known as the trunk.

By looking at a cross-section sawn through a branch or trunk, it is apparent that the structure is more complicated than with the average plant. On the outside of the trunk is the protective outer layer or bark. Inside this is the phloem which transports nutrients and water between the leaves – which absorb energy and process nutrients with the help of sunlight – to other parts of the tree and the roots.

Behind the phloem there is a layer that cannot be seen with the naked eye. It is the cambium. This layer is only the thickness of a single cell yet it is responsible for the thickening growth of the trunk. Wood is formed on the inside of the cambium, bark or cork is formed on the outside. Inside the cambium, the sapwood or young wood is formed containing capillary cells which pump water and nutrients from the roots to the crown of the tree. The sapwood is consequently very moist and alive.

This contrasts with the centre of the trunk where the heartwood is found. Here too there were once capillary cells but these have been crushed together as the trunk has become thicker and the old wood has died off. Its only function now is to provide strength for the tree.

A tree for every garden

The environment where there are ample trees is far better than that where there are none. Trees and shrubs release oxygen, transpire moisture, and capture many floating particles in the air. None of these processes can be seen yet they are all of benefit to our health.

What we can see is the shadow beneath a tree, the falling leaves, and the seeds that germinate. The disadvantages are therefore visible but the advantages are not. The advantages are such that every garden should have at least one tree.

If yours is a small garden, restrict yourself to a small tree. In this encyclopaedia you will find them grouped together. Should there really be too little space for a tree, there is an even wider choice of wonderful ornamental shrubs.

The right place for a tree

In choosing the right place to plant a tree in a garden, there are a number of considerations that have to be borne in mind.

- How tall will the mature tree become and where will the shade be, in the morning, the afternoon, and during the evening?
- Is the chosen type evergreen or deciduous? An evergreen will cast much longer shadows during the winter.
- Will the tree also shade the neighbour's garden? In this case, discuss the best position with your neighbour.
- Plant trees at least 2m (6ft 6in) and shrubs at least 1½m (5ft) distance away from any boundary.
- If the tree provides pleasantly diffused light, plant it against the sun. If the tree is chosen for its beautiful autumn colouring or richly toned fruits, place it so that the light falls on it.
- Plant a deciduous tree a little distance from the house in front of a south facing window. When the sun is high, sufficient light will shine through the window, whilst during the winter (when the sun is low) it will play through the tree.
- With a western or eastern facing window it is best to plant a tree fairly close to the house so that the early morning and evening sun will shine through the branches.
- Never plant a tree close to underground services or drainage pipes. There is always the danger that the ground will have to be excavated for access to the services.

Planting trees and shrubs

Good preparation is important when it comes to planting a tree or shrub.

There is the choice of the right type, selection of the best position – so that it does not cause an obstruction later – and checking the condition of the soil (see Soil types and Watering). Then you buy the tree. Do this by preference in the autumn (as soon as possible after the leaves have fallen) or in early spring (before the buds burst). It is possible to buy container grown trees which can, in principle, be planted at any time. The spring and autumn are still the best planting times, bearing in mind the problems that tree roots have in a container (see Container grown specimens).

If you buy a tree, buy also tree stakes and bands to support the young tree. The method for planting a tree or shrub is as follows. First, dig a large hole, then turn the soil over at the bottom of the hole to loosen it and make sure that the root ball will fit. Remember that the hole must be deeper and wider than the root system when it has been removed from the restriction of its packing. If the roots are packed in hessian sacking, they are likely to spring open quite a bit when loosened.

Once the holes have been made for the tree stake, the tree can be planted. One person holds the tree, the other removes the packing surrounding the root ball, opens up the roots so that they can spread in the planting hole, and fills the bottom of the hole to provide support for the roots. Consolidate the earth by pouring a bucket of water into the hole.

Make sure that the tree is planted at the same depth as it was grown in the nursery. This can usually be seen from discoloration around the trunk.

Fill the rest of the planting hole with earth, making sure that the soil penetrates between the roots (if necessary by pouring more water into the hole). Fill the hole to well over the brim and then carefully tread the soil in.

Attach any tree band loosely around the tree and fix it to the stake. If the soil sinks in, fill it again with earth but not higher than the surrounding ground. Keep the ground for about a metre (a yard) around the base of the tree free of plants that could compete with the roots during the first growing season. Sprinkle a fine mulch of compost, shredded prunings, or wood chips around the base to retain moisture.

Container grown specimens

By buying trees and shrubs in plastic containers and sacks, it is possible to plant them in any season. There is a hidden disadvantage with this method of packing, especially when the roots have been enclosed in the container for a long time, when they start to grow spirally around the edge. After planting, growth continues in the same direction so that the roots of container grown trees and shrubs spread out less quickly. On top of this, the spiralling roots gradually thicken and press on each other immediately beneath the trunk. This can lead to the sudden death of the specimen.

For this reason, it is best to plant at the correct time of the year with specimens in 'old-fashioned' packaging that have loosely packed root balls.

Support for young trees

Recently planted trees are usually supported until their roots have established themselves. The opinions of arboriculturists are divided on the question. Some believe that support in the private garden is unnecessary and that a tree will more quickly establish its roots if left unsupported. Others plead for one long stake about 2m (6ft 6in) against the tree on the side of the prevailing stronger winds, which is from the south-west in much of Britain.

Finally there are those who recommend three knee high stakes placed in a circle at least 50cm (20in) from the tree. Support bands are fixed to the top of these stakes and around the tree. The lower support position is said to aid the quicker establishment of the roots.

Transplanting of trees and shrubs

Young trees and shrubs can usually be transplanted or moved quite easily. Try to take as much soil as possible with the tree. To move a hedge, dig a trench beside the hedge first so that the individual plants can be tilted in order to free them with plenty of soil.

Older trees and shrubs are much more difficult to move. Even trees which seem very tough, such as birch can suffer when they lose the mould on their roots with which they have a symbiotic relationship.

If you are determined to move a larger tree or shrub, first dig a deep trench around a large portion of the root clump (it will need to be a manageable size). Fill in this trench with loose soil or peat. Any roots which it has been to cut will make new shoots within the root clump. After a year, the root ball can be moved. This method provides a tree with he best chance of surviving transplantation.

After planting

The period following planting or moving a tree or shrub is quite exciting – will the specimen survive? Young plants have the greatest chance of survival. They have few roots and most of them can be moved with the plant. Trees and shrubs have root systems that

Transplanting a hedge

spread out roughly to the same extent as the crown, so that it is difficult to take a large part of the root system with mature specimens when they are moved.

In the period following planting there is therefore a great chance that the leaves will transpire more water than the roots can provide, even when they are in moist ground. Conifers and other evergreens are especially prone to drying out. For this reason, always buy them with a good clump of soil and protect during the first year by surrounding with rush matting or similar protection. This reduces evaporation by wind and sun.

Deciduous trees require virtually no moisture during the time their branches are bare. These trees form tiny hair roots that absorb moisture from the soil even in fairly dry conditions. Once the leaves emerge on the tree or shrub in the spring, it is important not to let the soil dry out.

Diseases, pests, and growths

Little attention is given in this encyclopaedia to diseases. By following the guidance on appropriate growing conditions and location, any weakening of trees and shrubs should be avoided, so that disease is unlikely. The vegetation may well be eaten by animals but this is unlikely to do much real harm.

There are exceptions in respect of diseases, such as the infectious bacterial fireblight that affects trees in the *Rosaceae family*, such as apple, pear, and may. Dutch elm disease also affects otherwise healthy trees. There is no other remedy for both these diseases than removing and burning the complete tree.

Viral infections or fungi can cause growths that resemble bird's nests, known as witches broom. The growths cause a tight 'nest' of small branches to form. They are most commonly found on birch trees and can give them a fairy-tale appearance. This marginally reduces the vigour of the tree but is otherwise harmless. With conifers, this phenomenon is regarded positively, because it enables propagation through grafting.

Mistletoe is another growth that occurs. The mistletoe (*Viscum album*) is a parasitic plant whose roots enter the tree through fissures to

Betula pendula or silver birch with 'witches brooms'

tap the nutrients in the sapwood. This usually occurs with fruit trees, may, willow, and poplar. Mistletoe is most noticeable in the winter because of its greenness against the otherwise bare tree. The host tree has to share nutrients with the parasite but this is not a real problem for healthy specimens. If the tree becomes heavily laden with mistletoe, it runs the risk of its branches being snapped off by strong winds catching on the foliage of the mistletoe.

The mistletoe seeds are pressed against the trunk of the tree by birds cleaning their beaks.

Humans can sow the seed by making a small cut in a branch.

Apparent plagues of moths often cause panic. Worried citizens frequently telephone the parks and gardens departments of local councils to tell them that their shrubs are being stripped bare by the larvae or caterpillars. This may be larvae of the brown-tail moth (*Eupoctis chrysorrhoea*) which

Mistletoe (*Viscum album*) on a willow

cause a nasty irritation if touched, or one of the species of ermine moth (*Yponomeuta*) that gregariously gather together in tent like structures that festoon the affected tree. The caterpillars then pupate, protected against birds and other predators inside a chrysalis or cocoon . The stripped shrubs make a desolate sight. Fortunately the problem is only temporary. The pupae fall to the ground where they emerge. The shrubs quickly make new growth and are soon in leaf again.

Such pests do not usually kill a tree or shrub, making it unnecessary to use chemical insecticides. Indeed, insecticides can help to create problems with pests by destroying the

The ermine moth (*Yponomeuta*)

natural balance because they often destroy the predators of the pest as well. A natural equilibrium ensures that the gnawing beats do not reach plague proportions.

Storm damage

Some trees, such as *Robinia pseudoacacia*, or false acacia, have very brittle wood. Such trees are best planted where they will be sheltered by buildings or other trees. Those trees with branches that break easily are indicated in this encyclopaedia.

Other trees do not run a high risk of their branches breaking in a gale but they stand a higher risk of being blown over – it all depends upon the circumstances. An alder that grows next to streaming water which undermines its roots can fall without notice in even a moderate breeze.

Trees that naturally make deep roots can still be susceptible to winds under certain conditions – such as waterlogged soil or an unusually high water table.

Where a tree or shrub is planted, and its surroundings, play a significant role: a natural mixed wood is rarely damaged by storms yet it

Storm damage to spruce trees

is quite different with large-scale commercial woodlands. In this case, trees stand next to each other that are all of the same age. Such woodlands are prone to storm damage. Once the wind has created a breech, increasing numbers of trees fall before it. For evergreen trees, the risk is highest in autumn and winter. The tops of the uniform spruce are sometimes literally twisted off the trunk. The pine is blown over quite easily in commercial forests yet in natural circumstances it is one of the most wind resistant trees there are. Pines can withstand many hard winters standing fully exposed even in the shifting sands of dunes.

Soil types

Most trees and shrubs are not sensitive about the type of soil in which they grow. Where trees do require specific conditions, this is indicated in the entries. There are trees and shrubs that prefer lime-rich, alkaline soils and others that require acidic conditions. It is therefore important to know the type of soil in which a specimen is to be planted.

Peat rich soil such as former marshland or fen is always acidic. Marl contains lime and is therefore alkaline. To assess the alkalinity or acidity of these soils is straightforward. This is less clear with other types of soil. With sandy soils, loam, or clay it is less obvious. Loam can often be acidic but certainly not always. Clay can be alkaline but not in every situation, and there are both alkaline and neutral sandy soils. Geologists and botanist can tell much about the ground beneath you. The geologist knows how it came into existence. The botanist will recognise the soil type through the wild plants that grow there. The botanist will also be able to tell much about the structure of the soil, its humus content, the nutrients present or lack of them, and whether the soil has ever been disturbed.

This can all be ascertained by a soil survey but such a costly exercise rarely yields anything of true value. It is more useful to know your soil's pH level. This can be done easily with a do-it-yourself kit available in shops and garden centres.

Water management

The deeper layers of soil can be of greater importance with trees and shrubs than they are with perennials and annuals. A high water table in the winter can rot the roots. Water can also remain trapped in an impervious layer. This does not just mean the more obvious clay, rock or certain loams, because even some sandy soils prove impervious to water. This is because the sub-soil contains a dense layer of sand compressed to stone (usually red-brown in colour). When this is sufficiently close to the surface to cause real problems, it can be broken up by an excavator.

In most circumstances it is simpler to dig a deep hole by hand, that breaks through this layer of sub-soil, in the place where the trees or shrub is to be planted. The impatient gardener can even create wet conditions by bringing in new soil. Moisture does not seep quite as we might imagine. It can often become trapped between two layers with different structures, even though the ground may appear porous. Try to avoid creating different strata in the soil. When introducing new soil, mix it well with the existing ground.

Tree wounds

Shrubs branch out and usually are quite capable of healing themselves. A damaged tree trunk looks rather more serious yet trees are normally quite capable of healing themselves. New insights into arboriculture have led to recognition that some well-intentioned treatments can be harmful. In the past, wounds were cut back, rotten wood was cut away and large wounds were coated with special treatments. Today, the experts prefer to leave well alone.

The wound should be undisturbed if possible. Do not prune back damaged wood or cut out rotten growth, nor should you make drainage holes or ever fill hollows (and certainly never with cement since this only encourages the rotting process). Wound coating treatments do not help the tree to heal itself. The tree itself protects itself again further rot and infection.

The rise of tree surgeons means that more and more old trees are tidied up. This is fine when its is a matter of really old monumental trees which are inherent to the character of their

Lime tree filled with masonry

location. Such an ancient tree is irreplaceable because it takes many years before a newly planted tree will grow into a mature oak or lime of such character. Unfortunately the treatment is often extended to trees that naturally have much shorter life cycles, such as poplars and willows. The expensive treatment can only make a very small difference to the life span of such trees, because they do not have the ability to withstand disease or pests. It is better to let nature take its course with them. Leave the dead tree standing as long as possible,

provided there is no risk of it falling, to provide hollows and hiding or nesting places for all manner of creatures.

Preventing damage

Try to prevent damage to trees as much as possible. Put poles in the ground to protect trees where cars are parked, do not use a tree as a place to fix netting or wire since this can eventually be grown over, harming the flow of sap, and use non-ferrous nails to fix nesting boxes to a tree.

Bleeding

SSome types of tree are very prone to bleeding. When they are pruned at the wrong time of the year, sap gushes from any wound. In the most serious cases, the tree bleeds to death. Pruning in the spring (even when done before the leaves are out) can lead to serious bleeding with these trees.
Never prune the following types of tree between mid-December and the end of June:

maple (*Acer*), walnut (*Juglans*), yellow wood (*Cladrastis*), horse chestnut (*Aesculus*), and sweet chestnut (*Castanea*).

Pruning

Most types of tree have a typical shape to their crown. Limes, for example, form an upside down heart shape and Italian poplars form columns. When we are aware of how high a tree grows and how far it will spread and take this into account when planting, it is not necessary to prune them. The tree flourishes better because pruning is not good for a tree.
The exception to this rule is mature trees which carry a substantial weight on the ends of their branches when the trunk is becoming weaker. Such trees (often old fruit trees) benefit from lightening their load, which can extend their life.

Fruit trees are virtually always pruned, not because this is necessary for the tree, but because fruit grows better in airy surroundings without shadow. In addition, the shoots with blossom can be left and those without cut

15

away to improve the fruiting. A fruit tree is shaped right from the outset. The shape is determined by manner of the graft and the root stock used (strong or slow growing). In the past only trees with tall trunks (standards) were used by commercial fruit growers but then by means of an intermediate form with which the branches almost sprang from the ground without a trunk, they arrived at the trees with short trunks that are used today. They are often grown as spindlebushes in a line. The standard with its taller trunk is more attractive for a private garden because it is possible to walk beneath the tree and sit under its shade.

The first stage is the most important one: deciding which branches are to form the main frame. Choose three or four branches that do not cross each other and, if possible, that each point in a different direction – preferably with each of them placed at a third or a quarter of a circle. The other branches do not have to be removed immediately. They can first be encouraged to blossom by (preferably in the

The twigs are thinned out on an old pear tree

Only twigs a hand's length apart from each other are left

An old apple tree before pruning

Pruning an old neglected apple tree

The same tree after pruning

autumn) bending them down and holding them in position with a rope. Fruit trees on standard stems only bear fruit after a number of years but the branches which are bent down will blossom earlier. Once the other branches blossom, the branches which have been bent lower can be removed.

It is not possible to go into the whole business of pruning and forming the shape of a tree here. There are specialist books on the subject.

Practice is the best teacher, especially as every tree is different and often does not resemble the schematic drawings in books. There are also practical courses available on pruning fruit trees.

Other branches are removed completely or shortened

Thicker branches are sawn off

17

Pruning a young apple tree

Binding to encourage blossoming for a young pear tree

Topiary

Topiary work is done on trees and shrubs that have dense growth habit where the structure of the branches can no longer be seen. By continuously clipping out new growth, the shoots branch out further to fill every space with green. The most used genera for topiary are box (*Buxus sempervirens*) and yew (*Taxus*), together with many different coniferous trees. Outstanding examples of topiary are to be found at the Tulcán cemetery in

Ecuador. Many of the examples are animal figures which are significant in Indian culture. I have never seen better examples of topiary anywhere else in the world.

Grafting

The special characteristics of particular trees and shrubs that occur spontaneously are not reproduced by seeds from these specimens. The unusual shape of a cork-screw hazel can

Topiary work in a cemetery at Tulcán in Ecuador

Topiary work in a cemetery at Tulcán in Ecuador

only be reproduced by vegetative propagation (and not by sexual reproduction). Vegetative propagation can be done in a number of ways: by encouraging underground runners to form new plants, by staking a branch to the ground so that it forms its own roots, through cuttings, and by grafting.

Fruit trees with histories dating back for centuries, but of which it is no longer known how they came to acquire their beneficial properties, are also propagated by grafting.

3. The bark is raised

Depending upon the required growth habit for the tree, either vigorous growing or slow growing root stock is chosen. The graft is then made low down or higher up in accordance with the desired form of tree required.
T-budding and chip-budding are special methods of grafting by which instead of grafting a branch, just the bud is grafted. The best time to do this is mid-summer when the weather is dry but not too hot. The photos here show the procedure for T-budding:

1. Make a longitudinal cut with a sharp grafting knife in the rootstock.

2. Cut a short transverse cut at the top of the first cut.

4. A bud is cut out in a wedge form

5. The woody heart is removed

6. The scion is pushed behind the bark

7. Flaps of bark are bound around the graft

8. Attach a label to the stem

The importance to the Earth of trees

Trees form forests in which animals live. Nowhere are there more animal species than in the tropical rain forests. This wild life cannot exist without the trees, so that trees are tremendously important to the continued variety of life on Earth. The tropical rain forest is being rapidly felled, leading to the daily extinction of species of flora and fauna.

It is arrogant of us to point an accusing finger at the developing countries where trees are being felled. Our countries too were forest at the beginning of time and our riches are in part due to the clearing of the forests. What is more some of the felling of the tropical rain forest is in answer to our demand for tropical hardwood. Buying this timber leads to plundering nature's treasures. Do not buy tropical timber, unless the merchant can convince you, with proof, that it is specially grown – but beware, there is very little such timber from renewable plantations.

Transport of timber in Costa Rica

3. Prise open the flaps of bark with the grafting knife (a true grafting knife has a blunt rear edge that will not break the flaps).

4. Remove all leaves from the scion and then cut out the bud about 1cm (³/₈in) above and below the bud with a slanting cut.

5. The blade of the knife can be left in the cut but pull the scion free by hand. It should come away easily.

6. Push the remaining bud and bark in the incision in the rootstock, making sure the bud is the same way up as it was on the plant from which the scion was taken.

7. Bind the graft with plastic tape so that only the bud is uncovered.

8. Attach the name of the genus and species straight away.

Once the graft has taken and the bud has shooted, the rootstock above the graft can be removed by pruning.

2. Tall trees

Trees that grow taller than 10m (33ft)

Acer griseum

PAPERBARK MAPLE

Acer griseum

The mahogany-coloured bark peels into paper thin strips which hang attractively in flaps. The tree originates from central China and is fully hardy. When cultivated, this tree grows to about 12m (40ft) high and it is therefore suitable for the medium-sized garden. It is well worth planting because this is one of the most beautiful maples. The leaves turn a gorgeous shade of crimson and scarlet. Unfortunately its seeds do not germinate readily so there is a very limited supply.

Left: *Tilia tomentosa* 'Pendula'

Acer macrophyllum

OREGON MAPLE

Acer macrophyllum

The Oregon maple is large in every respect: its leaves are easily 20cm (8in) wide and when growing in the United States and Canada, the tree can reach 30m (100ft). In Europe this is usually more like 12m (40ft).

The lengthy flower clusters are succeeded by winged seeds, each about 5cm (2in) long. This tree grows rapidly and without problems but has a less impressive autumn ornamental display in Europe than in its native soil.

Acer platanoides

NORWAY MAPLE

Acer platanoides

The large green leaf of the Norway maple, superficially resembles that of the plane. Beneath this tree there will be dappled shade. It eventually grows quite easily to 20m (65ft) tall and can reach 30m (100ft). This species grows wild in much of Europe it has also been planted in many parks.

The flower clusters that appear in April are far more eye-catching than those of the sycamore. The five-lobed leaves turn miraculously bright yellow, orange, fiery red, and deep red in autumn. If collected and dried, the leaves will retain their colour for a long time.

Acer pseudoplatanus

SYCAMORE

The leaf of the sycamore, which originates from central and Southern Europe – just like that of the Norway maple – looks like the

Acer pseudoplatanus

Trunk and bark of *Acer pseudoplatanus*

plane or *Platanus*, hence its *pseudoplatantus* name.
The bark peels off in crisp flakes but does not have the appearance of the patchy bark of the plane tree. The sycamore grows between 20-30m (65-100ft) tall and it is often planted in avenues and in parks.

The autumn colouring is less spectacular than the Norway maple but it has given rise to many different cultivars that bear remarkable leaves.

Acer pseudoplatanus 'Atropurpureum'
syn. *A. p.* 'Purpureum Spaethii'

Acer pseudoplatanus 'Atropurpureum'

The underside of the leaf of the 'Atropurpureum' is purple throughout the summer and the upper side is the deepest imaginable green. These dark colours are retained by this 25m (82ft) tree in the autumn. It is very dark beneath such a sombre maple. This is partially relieved by the cheerful sight of the coloured wings of the seeds, yet I am astounded that such a tree is so widely planted.

Acer pseudoplatanus 'Leopoldii'

Acer pseudoplatanus 'Leopoldii'

Leaves of *Acer pseudoplatanus* 'Leopoldii'

The leaves of 'Leopoldii' are at first tinged with pink but then change to light green, that is speckled and splashed with creamy-white to pale yellow. Plenty of light gets through the canopy of this tree, which can reach heights of 20m (65ft). It is particularly effective planted in enclosed parks or woods where 'Leopoldii' creates an open feeling to the space.

Acer saccharinum syn. *A. dasycarpum*

SILVER MAPLE

Acer saccharinum

Leaves of *Acer saccharinum*

When the wind ruffles the leaves of the silver maple, their undersides sparkle. In eastern parts of the United States, this tree grows to heights of 40m (130ft). In cultivation, it grows to about 20m (65ft). The autumn colouring is yellow and orange.

Acer saccharinum 'Laciniatum Wieri' is the most widely cultivated form of silver maple. The leaf is deeply divided into sharply cut lobes and is silvery-white beneath. The leaves are borne on horizontally spreading branches that often hang gracefully down. This tree needs a sheltered position because its branches are easily broken.

Aesculus 'Digitata'

Aesculus 'Digitata'

The compound palmate leaves of 'Digitata', which is a cultivar of the buckeye or horse chestnut, are dark green, with noticeably long leaflets. 'Digitata' grows less vigorously than the common buckeye or horse chestnut and it creates a somewhat shapeless form. The tree, which grows to about 10m (33ft) is virtually only to be found in arboretums.

Aesculus flava syn. *A. octandra*

SWEET BUCKEYE

Aesculus flava

The sweet buckeye is a classic tree for parks and estates. Its leaves are virtually yellow but they change to a superb orange-red in autumn. The leaves consist of five or seven compound palmate leaflets. The flowers appear in May to June and are somewhat tubular, closely resembling those of *Aesculus glabra*. Brown fruits without prickles, that usually contain two chestnuts, are formed from the fruiting buds. The sweet buckeye grows into an elegantly-formed broad tree, which can reach about 20m (65ft) in height.

Aesculus glabra

OHIO BUCKEYE

Aesculus glabra

The Ohio buckeye varies little from the sweet buckeye. The fruit is somewhat more prickly and the leaf has less down on it and the bark is somewhat rougher.

This American chestnut is just as pleasing a tree for parks or large gardens as its cousin. It

Leaves and flowers of *Aesculus glabra*

Flower cluster of *Aesculus hippocastanum*

grows about 20m (65ft) tall and has a crown measuring about 10m (33ft) in diameter.

Aesculus hippocastanum

Aesculus hippocastanum

Aesculus hippocastanum

COMMON HORSE CHESTNUT

When the horse chestnut blooms in May, it looks as though the tree is covered with candles. The flower clusters bear white flowers with yellow and red flecks. It buzzes with bees and
other insects. The flowers are followed by the well-known prickly fruit shells. A large single brown seed, that is the chestnut or conker, falls from each of these in the autumn.
Despite the tree's Balkan origin it has now

spread throughout Europe, thanks to its graceful leaves and blossoms. Almost nothing grows beneath a horse chestnut and the tree's odour is none too popular. The horse chestnut will grow 30m (100ft) tall in the long run and it has an exceptionally broad crown.

Aesculus 'Laciniata'

Aesculus 'Laciniata'

The leaf of this type of horse chestnut looks as though it is ailing. Sometimes the leaves consist of little more than the veins with irregular incised form. This rarity is only likely to be encountered in an arboretum as it is rarely grown elsewhere – perhaps because it grows less vigorously than the common horse chestnut. Its height is about 15m (50ft).

Ailanthus altissima

TREE OF HEAVEN

Although the tree of heaven can grow to 30m (100ft) it has a delicate appearance due to its attractive branches and feathery foliage. In July it bears greenish-yellow flower plumes,

Ailanthus altissima

Bark and trunk of *Ailanthus altissima*

Branches of *Ailanthus altissima*

Alnus cordata

followed in autumn by abundant winged fruits on female plants . This Chinese tree self-seeds itself freely. The young saplings grow very rapidly, with exceptionally large leaves, that can be up to 1m (3ft 3in) long. Because of frost damage, the tree usually grows as a bushy shrub at first. When the ends of the twigs are frost-burned, new shoots are formed. Careful pruning will more quickly lead to an elegant tree being formed, to enable its splendidly marked bark to be seen more readily. Because this tree grows freely in almost any reasonably drained ground – even in a polluted urban atmosphere – it is frequently planted in urban parks. It is less suitable for planting in avenues because of its many roots.

Alnus cordata

ITALIAN ALDER

An attractive medium-sized to large tree with heart-shaped leaves. Its leaves are rather small, dark green and lustrous and they often remain on the tree until the end of the year.

The tree grows to 15m (50ft) and has an open, conical-shaped crown. The female seeds are exceptionally long (the longest of all alders)

and they appear in late winter. At this time, the tall alders swarm with seed eating birds such as goldfinch, siskin, and long-tailed tit that pluck the seeds from the tree. The Italian alder grows on any soil, including drier types.

Alnus glutinosa

COMMON ALDER

The native alder has always grown beside rivers and in marshy areas but it will also

Branches of *Alnus glutinosa*

Alder trees in winter

Betula costata

thrive in soil with normal levels of moisture, growing to 20m (65ft). The alder is widely found in the landscape forming thickets beside rivers, brooks and drainage channels, or as windbreaks, where they are trimmed to form tall hedges.

Because pruning does not harm them, this tree can also be planted in gardens. The rounded leaves, that throw deep shadows, often have scooped tips. In the summer, the leaves are often almost eaten entirely by larvae and beetles of the *elzenhaantje*, a black, shiny beetle, leaving just the veins. It is not necessary to do anything. The tree recovers for the second half of the summer.

Early in spring, often in March, yellow catkins hang in profusion. They are laden with pollen to impregnate the female blossoms. These form winged-seeds which decorate the tree throughout the winter, giving it an attractive appearance. The alder is rather like a jewel in winter.

Betula costata

The branches of this large birch – it grows 25m (82ft) high – point upwards at an angle, giving it a somewhat more austere appearance than the stylish *Betula pendula*.
The bark on the trunk and branches is quite beautiful though, which is why it is fairly widely planted in parks and arboretums. Some of the bands of bark are creamy white with orange and pink markings. The leaves are yellow in autumn. The tree closely resembles *Betula ermanii*, with which is often confused.

Betula davurica

A slender birch with a coarse character due to the loose flaps of bark on its trunk and the large bright green leaves. In cultivation, the tree rarely grows taller than 15m (50ft). The slender frame makes it quite suitable for private gardens, where this hardy northern Chinese species is regrettably rarely seen.

Betula davurica

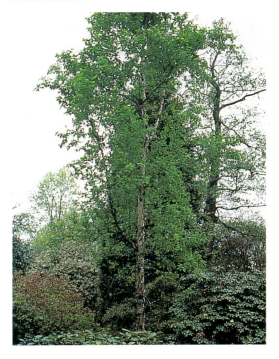

Betula ermanii 'Blush'

Betula ermanii

ERMAN'S BIRCH

Trunk of *Betula ermanii* 'Blush'

This species, with its magnificent trunk, originates from Eastern Asia. The bark peels off in thin curls to reveal new layers of yellow, orange, and pale pink. *Betula ermanii* is to be found from Sakhalin to Korea and it has different growth habits dependent upon its location. The tree will eventually grow to 25m (82ft) tall. The branches point upwards at an angle and form a broad crown.

Betula maximowicziana

MONARCH BIRCH

Betula maximowicziana

The leaves of this, originally Japanese, birch are exceptionally large at about 10cm (4in). In the autumn, the leaves are golden yellow, often with red veining. After the leaves have fallen, the russet branches and twigs sparkle in the low winter sunlight. The tree grows rapidly, reaching 30m (100ft) and it throws deeper shadow than the common birch.

Betula nigra

RED BIRCH, RIVER BIRCH

Betula nigra

Bark of *Betula nigra*

Bark of *Betula papyrifera*

The red birch or river birch originates in North America. It has rather dark bark, which peels in large curling sheets. The branches grow low down on the trunk to form an open pleasing crown. The leaves turn a pretty yellow in autumn. This is a beautiful tree for moist ground in both gardens and parks. It eventually grows to 20m (65ft) tall.

Betula papyrifera

PAPER BIRCH, CANOE BIRCH

The North American Indians used the water-proof bark of the paper birch to clad their canoes with. The tree is delightfully attractive with its paper-thin peeling bark. These trees grow with more than one trunk so that in spite of their slender habit, they are generally too large for most gardens. They reach 30m (100ft) in height.

Betula pendula syn. *B. alba*, *B. verrecosa*

SILVER BIRCH

Although the silver birch can eventually grow to 20m (65ft) it is widely planted in gardens.

Betula pendula

Bark of *Betula pendula*

The silver-white bark, weeping branches, catkins which appear in spring, and the light, rustling leaves that change colour to golden yellow in autumn, make this one of the most popular trees. The shade beneath the silver birch is light so that there is sufficient light for other plants (and people). A disadvantage of the silver birch is that it is very thirsty, drying out the soil surrounding it. Plant the silver birch in a position where it can mature fully. Should pruning become necessary, do it in late summer or autumn. The sap stream starts to flow again in mid-December and it will seep from the wounds. A birch can even 'bleed' to death. Some people intentionally bore holes into birches to tap their sap. It is consumed as a healthy, fresh, sweet drink, and also used as a cosmetic. The bore-hole needs to be stopped up after use with a suitable cork.

Betula platyphylla

The leaves of this birch, which originates from

Betula platyphylla (subsp. *platyphylla*)

Manchuria in China, emerge about three weeks earlier than those of other birches. The tree grows with a slender habit to 20m (65ft) with an open crown, which allows plenty of light to penetrate to the garden below. The leaves are a wonderful yellow in autumn.

Betula pubescens

WHITE BIRCH

Betula pubescens 'Urticifolia'

The white birch is often confused with the silver birch (*Betula pendula*). There are also hybrids of the two native species of birch. The new leaves and young shoots of the white birch feel soft to the touch. The branches of the white birch do not hang down in the same manner as *B. pendula*. While *B. pendula* will grow well in dry soil, the white birch prefers moist ground such as marshes or river banks. It grows to 20m (65ft).

Betula utilis var. *jacquemontii*

HIMALAYAN BIRCH

An outstanding birch that deserves a place in the garden. Generally offered for sale under the name *Betula jacquemontii*. The branches fork out from the marvellous white trunk fairly low down and then grow sharply upwards to form a broad crown that reaches 20m (65ft). The leaves turn golden yellow in autumn.
The varietas *jacquemontii* is completely hardy but the species itself (*Betula utilis*) is considered less hardy despite its origins.

Carpinus betulus

HORNBEAM

A hornbeam can grow to 20m (65ft) to form a beautiful tree with a pointed crown. The leaves start to turn colour quickly in the autumn but they do not fall for much longer.

The autumn brown leaves remain on the branches of young trees in the manner of beech. Hornbeam is also widely used like beech for hedges and arbours. By cutting back

Leaves of *Carpinus betulus* covered in frost

Hedge of *Carpinus betulus*

Carpinus betulus

two or three times during the growing season, hornbeam will form a dense hedge completely covered with leaves in which birds like to hide.

Carpinus japonica

Female catkins about 5cm (2in) long form in the late summer on this Japanese hornbeam. They consist of small leaves folded over each other that contain small nuts.

Carpinus japonica

The leaves have a very clear herringbone pattern of 20 to 24 pairs of veins. These attractive veins, the catkins, and its open growth habit, make this extremely hardy Japanese tree very graceful.

Castanea sativa

SPANISH CHESTNUT, SWEET CHESTNUT

Two or three nuts with soft shells are borne inside very prickly outer cases. The chestnuts can be eaten raw but are delicious when hot. The tree originates from Southern Europe, Asia Minor, and North Africa, but was spread widely northwards by the Romans because of its delicious nuts.

Elongated, sharply toothed leaves are borne on this tree, that can grow to 30m (100ft). The leaves turn yellow in autumn when the tree emits its characteristic autumn scent that signifies the presence of the nuts, even when they cannot be seen.

Specialist tree collections often include special forms such as *Castanea sativa* 'Albo margi-

Castanea sativa

Castanea sativa

nata' (also known as *C. sativa* 'Argenteova-riegata'). This has attractive leaves with creamy-white edges.

Castanea sativa 'Asplenifolia' has very unusual leaves in which the leaflets can be deeply serrated or grow like ribbons with irregular protrusions. These often bear variegated leaves.

Castanae sativa 'Albomarginata'

Castanae sativa 'Asplenifolia'

Cercidiphyllum japonicum

Cercidiphyllum japonicum

The *Cercidiphyllum japonicum* usually branches out close to the ground to form a broad columnar shape filled with attractive foliage. In spring the leaves first appear coloured purple before changing to light green. In autumn they are exuberant yellow, orange, and red. The leaves also give off an aroma resembling caramelised sugar or candy floss.

The tree originates in South-East Asia and is fully hardy, although new foliage can be damaged by late frosts. In the wild they often grow to 30m (100ft) but in cultivation they usually reach no higher than 15m (50ft). Because of its erect growth habit it is suitable for use as background planting in the medium to large garden.

Cornus controversa

DOGWOOD

The leaves of the dogwood change colour quickly in the autumn and then remain on the tree for a long time after. The branches grow outwards in an attractive horizontal manner. In late spring to early summer, the tree is

Cornus controversa

Davidia involucrata

Cornus controversa 'Variegata'

clothed in cream-white flowers which are followed in autumn by small, blue-black fruits. The tree grows in layers, higher and higher, eventually reaching 15m (50ft).
Cornus controversa 'Variegata' has varigated leaves with irregular silver-white to pale yellow margins.

Davidia involucrata

DOVE TREE, GHOST TREE, POCKET HANDKERCHIEF TREE

Davidia involucrata

Leaves of *Davidia involucrata*

In late spring and early summer Davidia involucrata is festooned with white bracts from which its common names are derived because the bracts surrounding the barely noticeable flowers give the appearance of white doves or pure white handkerchiefs. The two flower bracts that surround the globular flower cluster are of different shapes. The largest of them can grow as big as 20cm (8in). Unfortunately the tree does not flower before it is about ten years old. It has a fairly upright growth habit and reaches 15-20m (50-65ft). The leaves resemble an unfurled hazel leaf and they become warm yellow to orange in the autumn. Plant Davidia involucrata where it is protected from the wind, in rich, moisture-retaining soil, preferably clay. Immature specimens are prone to frost damage in severe winters.

Bursting leaves of *Fagus sylvatica*

Beech arbour of *Fagus sylvatica*

Fagus sylvatica

COMMON BEECH

Any piece of fertile ground, especially if it is lime rich, that is left untilled would eventually grow into a beech wood. This takes longer

Foot of *Fagus sylvatica*

than the span of a human life of course but once developed, nothing much else grows in a beech wood. This majestic tree that can eventually grow 40m (130ft) tall blankets out the light so that few plants grow beneath it.
Today though the beech suffers badly from the effects of pollution such as acid rain and poor air quality. This leads to less abundant foliage which lets more sun through to their trunks – which is harmful for them – and moulds and fungi gain a foothold. For these reason, increasing numbers of these magnificent tall trees are dying well before the ends of their natural lives, which should be counted in hundreds of years. Young beech trees make excellent hedges. Because they grow slowly, they only need pruning about twice each year although more frequent clipping will cause the hedge to form more dense growth. Through thoughtful pruning they can be trained into ingenious shapes. Arbours are back in vogue because of the attraction of walking through a green tunnel. Beeches are ideal for forming into arbours, because of their stately character that is perfect for this formal garden feature, that has long been associated with grand houses and estates. The arbour is not entirely bare in winter because some of the brown autumn-coloured leaves remain throughout the winter. There are many different forms of beech, that can be found and admired in arboretums and parks.

Fagus sylvatica 'Purpurea' group

COPPER BEECH

The leaves of this beech first appear as pinkish-red foliage in about May and become steadily darker throughout the summer until they turn purple and subsequently brown-green. This tall tree that grows to 40m (130ft)

Fagus sylvatica 'Atropunicea'

WEEPING BEECH

The branches of this tree grow horizontally and then upwards rather like the trumpeting trunk of an elephant. This tree, that grows to about 30m (100ft) high is more likely to be chosen out of curiosity than for its beauty. The twigs at the ends of the "elephant's trunks" hang down and can be so long that they form a green "veil".

Fagus sylvatica 'Quercifolia'

Fagus sylvatica 'Quercifolia'

lets very little light pass through its canopy so that it is remarkably dark and cool in summer beneath this tree. The form occurs naturally in nature and can be propagated from seed. About half of the germinated seedlings will have the pinkish-red foliage. Many different shades from russet to almost black-brown have been selected through cultivation.

Fagus sylvatica 'Pendula'

Fagus sylvatica 'Pendula'

Trunk of *Fagus sylvatica* 'Quercifolia'

The translation of the botanical name of this genus is "oak-leaved beech". The tree is very slow growing but will eventually reach 30m (100ft) high. The bark is equally smooth as the common beech but the spreading branches bear four-lobed leaves. The margins of these have coarse serrations.

Fraxinus excelsior

COMMON ASH

Fraxinus excelsior

The robust looking ash is actually a rather vulnerable tree. It cannot stand dry ground conditions, sea breezes, or air pollution. The preferred position for the ash is a well-drained lime rich soil from which the roots can freely derive oxygen. The young tree grows rigidly erect and has meagre foliage that drops in the autumn without noticeable change in colour. The leaves open relatively late in spring from black buds that are characteristic of this species. Each leaf consists of seven to eleven leaflets. On face value, not a first choice of tree, but look at a mature specimen that has grown to about 40m (130ft) tall, with its broad spread crown and branches pointing in every

Tak van *Fraxinus excelsior*

direction. The foliage permits sufficient light through its canopy to create a delightful, softly lit scene beneath this magnificent giant. Elongated fruits hang in trusses on female and dual gender trees after the leaves have fallen. They remain on the tree until the following summer.

Fraxinus excelsior 'Aurea Pendula'

WEEPING ASH

Fraxinus excelsior 'Aurea Pendula'

Although this golden weeping species of ash will eventually grow to 15m (50ft), it remains under 5m (16ft) for a long time. This means that it is suitable for smaller gardens.

Golden yellow leaves burst in the spring against twigs of a similar colour. The branches hang down in sweeping arcs to give the typical parasol form of this wonderful, but weak-growing, weeping ash.

Fraxinus excelsior 'Jaspidea'

Fraxinus excelsior 'Jaspidea'

This type of ash grows strongly upright to about 20m (65ft) tall. The young shoots are golden yellow, often with green stripes. The leaves are plain green in summer but during August they gradually become lustrous and slightly yellow, turning to bright yellow in September. The leaves fall quickly, making this one of the first trees to herald autumn. The new growth formed that summer remains yellow for some time.

Fraxinus excelsior 'Jaspidea'

Ginkgo biloba

This is the sole remaining species of this once large genus of trees, long since extinct. Sometimes called "a living fossil", it was part of a family that flourished 180 million years ago.

For a long time the Ginkgo was known solely in cultivation as a tree to be found at Japanese temples. It was introduced to Europe in 1727. Subsequently it was discovered that there were still specimens growing wild in the mountains of eastern China's Chekiang province.

This species has much to offer as a tree for parks and large gardens. It has irregular conical form to 40m (130ft) tall. The leaf looks like a fan with parallel veins. The foliage is bright yellow in autumn and the leaves fall quickly but decay slowly. They lend themselves to being dried and pressed. The male trees are most commonly planted because, although the fruits of the female are edible, they give off a powerful stench during ripening. The fruits are considered a delicacy in Eastern Asia.

Ginkgo biloba

Ginkgo biloba 'Variegata'

Leaves of *Ginkgo biloba* 'Variegata'

The species was added quite recently to the conifer group of trees. A number of cultivars are available that are grown from seed, such as: *Ginkgo biloba* 'Variegata', which has yellow-green leaves with green veins which could (with a bit of imagination) be considered "striped".

The forms with a more compact habit are more suitable for gardens: *Ginkgo biloba* 'Autumn Gold' which grows about 12m (40ft) tall. The leaves turn clear golden yellow in autumn. The height of Ginkgo biloba 'Horizontalis'

depends entirely upon the nature of the graft. The branches grow horizontally as ground cover but also form a parasol of spreading branches.

Ginkgo biloba 'Pendula' looks like 'Horizontalis', but is more graceful with its weeping branches.

Gleditsia macracantha

The trunk of this tree, which is 15m (50ft) tall when mature, is covered with sharp thorns. The branches are also covered with prickles but by contrast, the leaves are charmingly feathered with eight to fourteen leaflets. *Gleditsia macracantha* looks very much like *Gleditsia triacanthos* in appearance, which can occasionally be seen growing in parks.

Gleditsia triacanthos

HONEY LOCUST

The branches of the honey locust buzz with insects during the summer months. They busy themselves visiting the small trusses of yellow-

Gleditsia macracantha

Gleditsia triacanthos

green florets that have the aromatic scent of gingerbread. The flowers bloom in June and July This thorny North American tree has an erect growth habit and grows in cultivation about 25m (82ft) tall. The branches bend gracefully, bearing their feathery, light green leaves. Although this tree is planted in some parks, it deserves to be planted more widely, including in private gardens, but by preference on lighter, sandy soils.

The florets of *Gleditsia triacanthos*

Leaves of *Gleditsia triacanthos*

Gleditsia triacanthos 'Sunburst'

The golden-leaved honey locust is being increasingly planted in gardens. This is not just because of its foliage, that bursts golden yellow but changes to green-yellow during the season, but also because of its growth habit. The tree grows quickly but does not get taller than 12m (40ft). The branches spread attractively.

Plant it as a lone standing specimen so that you can fully appreciate its beauty.

Gleditsia triacanthos 'Sunburst'

Juglans regia

WALNUT

Juglans regia

A walnut tree on your property is said to bring luck. This robust tree of some 30m (100ft) is certainly only suitable for those with sufficient space because the crown must be allowed to fully develop. There is less shade beneath a walnut than most trees of similar stature. The leaves open somewhat later than normal and the tree also has a less densely packed frame of branches that many other trees, so that more light is able to penetrate. The bark of other than mature trees is smooth and silver grey. In autumn, the ripe walnuts drop off the tree, often still in their outer shells. The fruit is only borne by trees older than about ten years. The walnut grows somewhat meagrely in the first few years after planting. Mature trees too will often go a summer without fruiting, especially when late frosts have damaged the blossom in April or May. Leaves that have just burst can also be frost damaged too. The walnut prefers rich, deep, well worked soil because of its tap root, and thrives best on drained alkaline soil.

Kalopanax septemlobus

Kalopanax septemlobus var. *maximowiczii*

Leaves of *Kalopanax septemlobus* var. *maximowiczii*

This Asian type will only be encountered in gardens with specialised tree collections. The thin, spine-covered branches bear very large hand-shaped leaves that can be as big as 20cm (8in). The tree creates a tropical feel even though it is sufficiently hardy for all but the coldest parts of Europe. In the forests of Asia *Kalopanax* grows to 30m (100ft) but it remains significantly smaller in Europe.

Kalopanax septemlobus var. *maximowiczii* has extremely large, deeply lobed leaves than have hairs on their undersides. Presumably these were prickles in an early stage of evolution.

Liriodendron tulipifera

TULIP TREE

Flower of *Liriodendron tulipifera*

Autumn leaves of *Liriodendron tulipifera*

Liriodendron tulipifera 'Integrifolium'

The flowers of the tulip tree are larger than the average tulip and yet despite this, they are less noticeable. The yellow-green and orange colours are usually rather drab in Europe. The flowers, which have a delightful fragrance, are hidden behind foliage. Only mature trees of at least 20 years will blossom, in June to July. The trees blossom more readily in warmer summers than cool ones.

The leaves are the real attraction of this tree from the eastern parts of North America: they resemble an opening tulip. In the autumn the leaves change colour to a delightful bright yellow. The tree will grow rapidly in fertile, moist (but not wet) soil, to reach a height of 50m (164ft).

Liriodendron tulipifera 'Integrifolium'

Old plane trees

Liriodendron tulipifera 'Integifolium' has leaves with flattened side lobes that make it almost rectangular. A young, ordinary tulip tree has similar leaves. As the tree matures, the lobes become more pronounced.

Platanus x *acerifolia* syn. *P. acerifolia*

LONDON PLANE

The common plane tree is most probably a result of crossing the eastern *Platanus orientalis* with the western *Platanus occidentalis*. The latter tree originates in North America.
The hybrid *Platanus x hispanica* has widely differing characteristics and there are also many different varieties. This tree grows to 30m (100ft) tall and has a broad crown. The leaves usually have five serrated lobes, resembling the maple from which a former name of *P.acerifolia* (or maple leaved). The leaves do not appear until late spring. The tree's canopy lets plenty of sunlight through so that there is pleasant diffused light under a plane tree. This is one of the reasons why they are so widely planted in towns and cities. A second reason is that they can withstand polluted air.

The most noticeable characteristic of the trees is the bark which flakes off the trunk.
The bark flakes off particularly abundantly in dry years. The tree also loses some of its leaves

Platanus with a loudspeaker

Autumn leaves of *Platanus* x *acerifolia*

Platanus x *acerifolia*

Platanus orientalis

ORIENTAL PLANE

Platanus orientalis

when the summer is dry, to prevent evaporation. The replacement layer of bark under the flaking bark is green. The green bark takes over the role of photosynthesis from the leaves.

Planes can be readily pruned. By training horizontal branches a bower or arbour can be formed to shade a terrace.

Platanus x *acerifolia* 'Pyramidalis'

Platanus x *acerifolia* 'Pyramidalis'

The branches of this form of plane initially grow upwards. The leaves have three to five lobes that are less deeply formed.
They are frequently used for planting as avenues because the lower branches do not hang down and the crown is less broad. In common with other planes, the 'Pyramidalis' can be readily pruned and will become 30m (100ft) tall.

The Turkish poet Nazim Hikmet wrote: "A plane makes a gravestone above my grave unnecessary." Throughout southern Italy, Greece, and the coastal areas of Turkey and the Middle-East, the oriental plane is native and can be found in important positions in villages and towns. The life of the community unfolds beneath the gentle shade of this friendly tree.

The leaves are deeply lobed and the bark of the young tree peals off in scales. The branches of old trees – which can grow to 30m (100ft) tall– are rough. The oriental plane is rarely planted in northern and Central Europe because it is sensitive to frost, but it can be considered hardy in north-west Europe.

Platanus orientalis 'Digitata'

This version of the eastern plane has unusually deeply lobed leaves that resemble fingers. The edge of these "fingers" are fairly smooth, without the serrations that are normal with eastern planes. Grows to 30m (100ft) tall and is hardy in north-west Europe.

Platanus orientalis 'Digitata'

Platanus orientalis 'Digitata'

Leaves of *Platanus orientalis* 'Digitata'

Populus balsamifera

Populus balsamifera

BALSAM POPLAR

When the leaves of the balsam poplar open in spring the entire surroundings of the tree are filled with a balsamic fragrance.

The black buds and the dark green leaves shine and are coated with resin, which exudes the aroma. The balsam poplar grows rapidly into a tall but fairly narrow tree, which generally reach 20m (65m) high when mature, but can grow to 30m (100ft). Shoots often form at the base of the tree to create bush like growth.

Populus x *berolinensis*

SIBERIAN BALSAM POPLAR

This hybrid resulting from crossing *Populus laurifolia* with the black poplar (*Populus nigra*) is renowned for its hardy nature. The

Populus balsamifera

narrow tree grows to about 20m (65ft) tall and its leaves open quite early. It is one of the better poplars for timber production and is widely planted in parks.

Populus x canadensis

This name is given to a large group of hybrid black poplars resulting from crossing *Populus deltoides* and *Populus nigra*. The trees in this group have widely differing characteristics: some have hairs on the fine branches while, with others, the twigs are bare. The leaves are light green to dark green and either triangular or elongated. There is also wide variation in the colour of the trunks and of the frame of the trees, although the trunk and branches of all the trees in this group are noticeably rounded. The autumn colour is yellow. The trees in this group mature at about 30m (100ft) and they are principally planted for timber.

Populus x canescens

Populus x berolinensis

Populus x canescens

GREY POPLAR

It is difficult to tell the grey poplar apart from the white form (*Populus alba*). There are suggestions that *P. x canescens* results from crossing *P. alba* with *P. tremula*. The young leaves are covered with a white down. With the grey poplar, this disappears fairly quickly so that the leaves appear green, while the leaves of *P. alba* remain whiter.

There are also differences in the texture of the bark of the two forms, with *P. alba* remaining smoother longer. The bark of *P. alba* is also characterised by small square patches. The bark of the grey poplar becomes rough much more quickly.

Both forms of poplar grow rapidly and are at their most attractive in open landscape or on the coast, where the wind rustles their green-white leaves. In windy positions, they grow to 20m (65ft) but will reach 30m (100ft) in sheltered locations.

Populus nigra

BLACK POPLAR

The trunk of a mature black poplar can easily grow to 30m (100ft) tall and have a diameter of 2m (6ft 6in) across. The trunk is characteristically burred. The heavy trunk and branches have to bear a relatively large crown for a poplar. The leaves of the European native varieties are oval to square and slightly

Trunks of *Populus nigra*

Populus nigra 'Italica'

transparent at their edges. True black poplars are mainly to be seen as mature trees on country estates and in parks because commercial foresters prefer the timber from the hybrids created from crossing it with *Populus deltoides*.

Populus nigra 'Italica', or Lombardy poplar is the most instantly recognisable form, forming tall thin columns that are nothing like the normal black poplars. The leaves are smaller and they appear several weeks sooner than other black poplars. They were introduced from Lombardy in Italy in the eighteenth century.

Populus tremula

ASPEN

The trunks of young aspen are noticeably silver grey. The tree will grow quickly in any soil to 15m (50ft) tall and can reach 30m (100ft). Although the leaves are nothing special – they are prominently toothed – the slender leaf stalks are rigid and form an aerofoil which causes the leaves to tremble and quiver in even the lightest of winds. The leaves are quite hard and make quite a rustling sound.

Trunk of the *Populus tremula*

Prunus avium

Prunus avium

GEAN, WILD CHERRY

The trunk and bark of *Prunus avium*

The wild cherry needs hardly any introduction. It is the most important ancestor of the domesticated cherry. The trees grow to

White blossom on *Prunus avium*

15-20m (50-65ft) with upward slanting branches. At first, the trunk is shiny brown with horizontal stripes but later this becomes rough. Clusters of white flowers blossom towards the end of April, when the elongated serrated leaves also appear. The cherries are ripe by June. They are eagerly eaten by starlings and blackbirds so that if the tree will need protecting with netting if you wish to pick them. The leaves become a wonderful yellow to red-orange in autumn.

Many different edible cherry varieties have been hybridised by crossing wild cherry with the bush form sour cherry (*Prunus cerasus*).

Pterocarya fraxinifolia

CAUCASIAN WING NUT

The short stem of the wing nut is very thick and short with deeply furrowed bark. The thick branches shoot from low on the tree and in almost any direction. The leaves are up to 60cm (24in) long and are consist of twelve to twenty-four leaflets. In summer, the tree hangs with catkins about 50cm (20in) long. The green nuts are piled on top of each other. The tree is yellow in autumn and grows to 25m (82ft) tall with a spread of 20m (65ft), which is why it is mainly only seen in parks.

Pterocarya fraxinifolia

The trunk of *Pterocarya fraxinifolia*

The catkins of *Pterocarya fraxinifolia*

Pterocarya rhoifolia

JAPANESE WING NUT

The Japanese wing nut closely resembles the Caucasian variety from Western Asia. The bunches of nuts and the leaves of the Japanese variety are slightly shorter and the buds are surrounded by protective leaves. Because of its large overall size – 25m (65ft) high and 15m

Pterocarya rhoifolia

Quercus frainetto

(50ft) wide – it is mainly restricted to parks and arboretums.

Quercus dentata

Quercus dentata

This is one of the more suitable Asian oaks. Although the trees can grow to 20m (65ft), they usually only reach half that height. The tree does have a broad crown. The parchment-like leaves – that are generally about 15cm (6in) but can be double that length – are a particular feature in summer. The leaves are heavily covered with hairs, particularly on the underside. In autumn, the leaves turn brown but remain on the tree for a long time together with the ochre coloured acorns, that later turn brown. These are characteristically short and broad and are half-enclosed in the cup. The tree is also sometimes known as the emperor's oak.

Quercus frainetto

HUNGARIAN OAK

The short-stemmed leaf of the Hungarian oak is deeply cleft and the lobes sometimes cross over each other. Young trees bear particularly freakish large leaves that can be 20cm (8in) long. The leaves turn brown in autumn. This tree grows quickly to about 25m (82ft) tall and it has a regular, rounded crown. Although it originates in south-eastern Europe, the tree is completely hardy. It is widely planted as a attractive specimen in parks. It is suitable for dry and chalky ground.

Quercus x hispanica

LUCOMBE OAK

This naturally occurring hybrid of the turkey oak (*Q. cerris*) and cork oak retains its leaves until the New Year. In mild winters, the elongated, lobed leaves turn green-yellow with brown margins. After severe frosts, the leaves become brown. The old leaves can remain until the new ones unfurl in June. When mature, these trees – that originate in Southern and South-Eastern Europe – are about 30m (100ft) tall. They are also hardy in more northerly latitudes.The characteristics arising from the crossing vary because they are often propagated from seed, causing different dominant inherited properties of the parents and ancestors to be reproduced in the seedlings.

Generally, the cups of the acorns of this lovely ornamental tree are covered with moss-like covering in the same manner as the turkey oak (*Q. cerris*). The bark is fairly deeply fissured, but to a lesser extent than the cork oak.

Quercus x *hispanica*

The trunk of *Quercus* x *hispanica*

Quercus x *libanerris* 'Rotterdam'

Catkins of *Quercus* x *libanerris* 'Rotterdam'

Quercus x *libanerris* 'Rotterdam'

The light-green leaves of *Quercus* x *libanerris* 'Rotterdam' have sharply-serrated teeth. The male catkins dangle between them in May. *Quercus* x *libanerris* 'Trompenberg' is a hybrid created by crossing the turkey oak (*Q. cerris*) and the Lebanon oak (*Q. libani*). It resembles the first of these and has lobed leaves with the characteristic mossy covering around the acorn cups.

Quercus petraea

SESSILE OAK

The sessile oak is one of the two native British oaks and it closely resembles the other – *Q. robur*). The lobes of the leaves of this species are often more regular than the common or English oak and the leaves are generally about 12cm (4½in) long. In ideal conditions, both species can grow 45m (150ft) tall. Natural hybrids of the two species occur with many varieties.

Quercus petraea 'Mespilifolia'

Quercus petraea 'Mespilifolia'

This is a widely differing variety of the sessile oak. The slender tree bears elongated leaves that can be as large as 18cm (7in) and have soft, wavy-lobed margins.

Quercus robur

COMMON OAK, ENGLISH OAK

The common, or English oak, is a native species and is far more widespread than the sessile oak. Unlike other trees, the common oak can establish its deep roots even in light, sandy soils. Those very deep roots cause oaks to be struck by lightning more readily than other species because they form a good earth connection with the groundwater. Some farmers plant them intentionally as lightning conductors. Further back in history, the Germans regarded the tree as the god of thunder.
The oaks from those times have all now died,

Quercus petraea 'Mespilifolia'

Quercus petraea 'Mespilifolia'

but the last of them will not have been long dead, because oaks can, according to estimates, live for 1,500 years. They are amazingly resilient and tough, will withstand the wind when they are on well drained soil and they grow with a low profile to the wind in unsheltered positions. When the oak grows in a favourable position, it can become 45m (150ft) tall with a broad crown consisting of whimsically arranged branches. Such a huge tree provides a home to many animals – more than any other tree. This is why far more oaks

The Leaves of *Quercus robur*

should be planted, particularly as various governments provide grants to encourage tree planting. The main factor that prevents more of them from being planted is their extremely slow rate of growth. The trees are only sufficiently mature to be felled for timber after 100 years. The common oak grows on any type of soil except deep peat and marshy ground. The leaves are susceptible to mildew.

Quercus robur

Quercus robur 'Cristata'

Quercus robur 'Cristata'

This variety of common oak has unusually short, curled leaves that sit in dense clusters on the end of the branches.

Quercus rubra

RED OAK

The leaves of the red oak are between 10-20cm (4-8in) and they have sharply cleft lobes. They change colour to glorious orange to brown in the autumn and are often cut for decoration,

Quercus rubra

especially for use with seasonal chrysanthemums. The young specimens of the red oak – that originates from North America – grow fairly quickly and because they can withstand quite a bit of shade, they are often grown as under-planting by foresters. Where the straight, grey trunk manages to climb above the other trees, it will quickly spread its upwards growing branches and compete with the native species. They grow to 30m (100ft) tall but can reach 45m (150ft). The acorns, that do not ripen until the year after their first appearance, will germinate throughout Western Europe so that the red oak is gradually becoming regarded as a "weed" in forests and nature reserves

Quercus suber

Quercus suber

CORK OAK
The cork oak cannot withstand prolonged severe frosts and consequently, it can only survive winters in the west of England, Ireland, and southern Europe. This evergreen, that grows to 10-20m (33-65ft) high, loses its bark about every ten years. This bark layer is several centimetres thick and very springy and is the source of all products made from cork.

Robinia pseudoacacia

FALSE ACACIA
It is strange that this tree should ever be mistaken for an acacia because it is not in the slightest bit related. Perhaps the prickles on the branches and feathery foliage set people on the wrong track. The leaves sit whimsically on the tree that grow to 20m (65ft) tall. The trunk and branches are deeply furrowed and nuthatches use the notches to grip nuts with in order to open them.
In June, the tree bears clusters of fragrant

Bark of *Quercus suber*

Robinia pseudoacacia

The leaves of *Robinia pseudoacacia*

The trunk of *Robinia pseudoacacia*

leaves are made up out of at least nineteen leaflets. The are separated from the twig by a long stem. The leaves are green and clustered together, just like myrtle.

Robinia pseudoacacia 'Myrtifolia'

white butterfly-like flowers. These develop into brown pods in autumn. Although the tree originates from eastern parts of the United States, it has self-seeded itself in the wild throughout Europe on well-drained loam, and on alkaline sandy soil.

Poor soil ensures the best cultivation because in fertile ground the twigs of these trees snap off at the first wind, hail, or snowfall. They are usually found at the edges of woods, sheltered from strong winds but where they can get adequate light, which is another prerequisite. *Robinia* conveys nitrogen from the atmosphere to its roots, making the soil surrounding it more fertile. This often leads to rampant stinging nettles and similar weeds taking hold. The soil beneath its deep roots is depleted of any nutrients.

Robinia is sometimes cultivated to form a globular crown upon a standard stem. It is best to select a sheltered position for these varieties too, especially if the soil is damp or fertile, to prevent branches breaking off.

Robinia pseudoacacia 'Myrtifolia' is one of many varieties in cultivation that have different characteristics. With 'Myrtifolia', the

Salix alba

WHITE WILLOW

The white willow is one of the easiest willows to recognise in the landscape. The tree grows to about 20m (65ft) and it has orange-brown young branches and characteristic grey-green leaves (the colour is derived from the silk-like hairs on the leaves).

The flowering is not particularly noticeable. White willows are the tree for low-lying wet ground. In common with other willows, they are extraordinarily easy to propagate. Saw off a long, straight branch early in the spring before the leaves have come out, and remove any side shoots. Make a hole in the ground (with a post-hole borer for ease), and stick the branch in the ground. The odds are very high that the branch will root to create a new willow tree.

Old pollarded examples of *Salix alba*

Salix alba (white willow)

Willows were often grown as a convenient form of renewable timber on farms, where they were pollarded and then harvested every few years to provide fencing, bean sticks, and firewood.

The true species white willow is fairly rare. Willows cross readily with each other. Hybrids of the white willow and crack willow (*Salix fragilis*) are fairly common and there are more hybrids in nature than the pure *S. alba*.

Salix x *sepulcralis* 'Chrysocoma'

WEEPING WILLOW

Salix sepulcralis 'Chrysocoma'

Salix sepulcralis 'Chrysocoma'

The weeping willow is without doubt one of the most romantic trees, especially when growing next to water. In these conditions, it will grow to 20m (65ft) tall and spread almost as big across. The golden yellow branches hang down perpendicularly with their elongated light green leaves.

Sophora japonica

JAPANESE PAGODA TREE

Sophora japonica

Sophora japonica

The Japanese pagoda tree is much appreciated for its later flowering. Creamy-white butterfly-like clusters of flowers adorn the tree in August-September. The tree grows about 25m (82ft) high. The trees need to be about thirty years old before they will blossom. This is why they are mainly restricted to parks and arboretums. Despite this, the young tree does have feathery light green leaves that are highly decorative, although they can be damaged by late spring frosts. A mature tree is fully hardy. The Japanese pagoda tree thrives best in a warm position and will tolerate drought and poor soil.

Sorbus alnifolia

Sorbus alnifolia

The leaves of this *Sorbus* turn orange-red in autumn. This is the main attraction of this rarely planted tree. It grows in any position without a problem, eventually achieving heights of 20m (65ft) and it has a rounded crown. Clusters of white flowers appear at the ends of the branches in May. Each inflorescence contains at least ten florets, each about 1cm ($^3/_8$in) wide. They form yellow or orange egg-shaped berries during the summer.

Tilia

LIME, LINDEN

Limes grow in North America, Europe and Asia. They are among the most popular trees, due to the uniform shape of their crown, the attractive, often heart-shaped leaves, and sweetly-aromatic blossoms that attract many bees. The lime is often planted on its own as a specimen tree to show the tree to full advantage. Many commemorative trees are limes. They can be readily pruned and are frequently grown around farms as sunshades, where they are trained to form a living structure. This only provides shade during the hotter part of the year because the leaves appear quite late and fall early. Limes prefer soil that retains moisture but not waterlogged ground. The preference is for an alkaline soil but they will also thrive on acid soils. Try to give them some protection from strong winds. Limes can be heavily pruned and trained if required.

Tilia americana

AMERICAN LIME, BASSWOOD

The American lime looks less graceful and has less uniform growth than most of the other

Tilia americana

The leaves and blossoms of *Tilia americana*

species of lime. They originate from the eastern parts of the United States and grow to 20m (65ft) tall in Europe. The young green branches bear dark green leaves that are light green on their undersides. The leaves are quite large at 15cm (6in). They can even be 20cm (8in) on the suckers around the roots. Butter yellow, fragrant flowers blossom in June to July and they attract many insects. Later in the summer, fruits form in clusters that tend to be hidden from view. Care is similar as *Tilia* but extra care is needed to protect this species from strong winds that will cause the soil and leaves to dry out.

Tilia cordata

SMALL-LEAVED LIME

The small-leaved lime grows in widely scattered parts of Europe, including Britain, Spain, and Sweden, yet not in many of the countries in between. The tree eventually reaches about 25m (82ft) in height and usually forms a rounded crown. The leaves are rounded heart-shapes that are relatively small at 5cm

Leaves of *Tilia cordata* 'Rancho'

(2in) long and wide. The upper side of the leaves are dark green and the undersides light green. For growing conditions and care, see *Tilia*. *Tilia cordata* 'De Groot' is a cultivated weeping variety with a broad, upright crown that is attractively formed with dense foliage. *Tilia cordata* 'Rancho' is a cultivated form registered to a specific grower and protected by law. It too forms a broad, upright crown. This tree grows to at least 10m (33ft) tall and 5m (16ft 6in) wide.

Tilia cordata 'De Groot'

Tilia x vulgaris syn. *T. x europaea*

COMMON LIME

The common lime resulted from natural crossing between *Tilia cordata* (the small-leaved lime) and *Tilia platyphyllos* (the broad-leaved lime). The leaves of this hybrid species are somewhere between the two parents in size, averaging 7cm (2^1/$_2$in). The upper side of the leaves is shiny and dark green, the underside is light green. Scented pale-yellow flowers blossom in clusters, of five to ten flowers, in June to July.

This tree can grow to 40m (130ft) tall and it produces an abundance of suckers. A further disadvantage is the preference aphids have for

Tilia x *europaea*

Tilia x *europaea* 'Wratislaviensis'

this particular lime. They excrete excess sugars as a sticky substance known as honeydew that drips onto any cars or garden furniture beneath them. Furthermore, the leaves become black with mildew that grows on the honeydew. For growing conditions and care, see *Tilia*. *Tilia x europaea* 'Wratislaviensis' was discovered by accident in 1898. It is a variety in which the leaves first appear yellow before turning yellow-green.

Leaves of *Tilia* x *europaea* 'Wratislaviensis'

Tilia 'Euchlora' syn., *T. x euchlora*

CAUCASIAN LIME, CRIMEAN LIME

Tilia x *europaea* 'Euchlora'

The Caucasian or Crimean lime is worthy of separate mention. It is frequently planted in avenues because it is quite resistant to disease and plagues of insects. Aphids, that cause so much problem with their honeydew with the common lime, are not attracted to this species. The tree does not grow much taller than 20m (65ft), forming a broad upright crown. The branches tend to hang down. The oval leaves form opposite each other on the stem and are lustrous dark green. The undersides of the leaves are light green. Sweet smelling blossoms hang down in trusses in July. Bees are attracted to them but the nectar can sometimes be toxic for them and many dead bees can then be found beneath this tree. For growing conditions and care, see *Tilia*.

Tilia mongolica

Tilia mongolica

MONGOLIAN LIME

This tree makes you look twice. At first it looks as though it is a giant vine with its young leaves that resemble those of a vine, first appearing pink on red stems, and its buds that resemble young grapes. The tree does not grow taller than 20m (65ft) and usually stays much lower. Its branches spread out horizontally. It flowers in June. The seeds will only form in very hot summers. A highly recommended tree.

Tilia tomentosa

Autumn leaves of *Tilia tomentosa* 'Pendula'

Tilia tomentosa

EUROPEAN WHITE LIME, SILVER LIME

The white or silver lime has outstanding resistance to polluted air and it is therefore frequently planted in towns and cities. The most noticeable characteristic of this tree, that is 25m (82ft) tall when mature, is the silver-felted underside of its leaves. These are about 9cm (3½in) long and they are dark green on the upper side. Strongly fragrant flowers appear in June to July but their nectar is toxic for bees. Originating in South-East Asia and

Leaves of *Tilia tomentosa* 'Brabant'

neighbouring countries, this lime only produces seeds in very hot summers.

Tilia tomentosa 'Brabant' is a variety with a broad upright crown on a relatively tall trunk. *Tilia tomentosa* 'Pendula' is the weeping silver lime that originates from Hungary. Because it is so different to the other *T. tomentosa* varieties, it is also known as *Tilia* 'Petiolaris'. The leaves are borne on extremely long stems. In autumn, the leaves turn bright yellow. This is when the fruits ripen. These are quite different to fruits of the other white or silver limes. They resemble miniature melons.

Ulmus x *hollandica*

DUTCH ELM

In spite of its name, this hybrid arising out of crossing *Ulmus glabra* with *Ulmus minor* (syn. *Ulmus carpinifolia*), was not the source of the Dutch elm disease which has so changed the landscape. The disease did not originate in Holland, but it was Dutch scientists who discovered the cause of the disease (see also at *Ulmus* i in the chapter on low trees). Many of this hybrid's varieties are prone to attack by the disease so make sure that only resistant varieties are planted, such as *U.* x *hollandica* 'Groeneveld' and 'Dampieri

Ulmus x *hollandica*

Seeds of *Ulmus* x *hollandica*

Zelkova carpinifolia

The *Zelkova* and *Ulmus genera* are closely related, making these trees cousins of the elm, so that in theory they too could suffer from Dutch elm disease. In practice this rarely occurs. Zelkova carpinifolia grows very slowly to eventually reach about 30m (100ft) tall. The tree forms a long trunk from which upwards growing branches shoot. The branches seem to press inwards onto the crown but this is natural to the species. This tree thrives on any soil provided it is not too dry.

Zelkova serrata

The branches shoot from low down on the trunk with this species and they spread themselves to form a broad, fan-shaped crown up to 25m (82ft) high. This is a favourite species for bonsai enthusiasts, who restrict the growth to form miniature mature trees. Young trees can be prone to frost damage in locations away from the coast. The leaves are an elongated, ovoid form with serrations. In the autumn the leaves change colour to a superb yellow or orange.

Aurea'. The Dutch elm is a magnificent tree. Depending upon the chosen variety, it can grow to 12-40m (40-130ft) tall. The leaves are usually broad, ovoid shape, 6-12cm (2^1/$_2$-4^1/$_2$in) long. They are dark green on the upper side without hairs. The trees blossom at the end of March and the flowers are succeeded by winged seeds. Elms prefer a sunny position or partial shade. The tree forms deep roots in moist or dry soil provided the water table is not too high. In this latter case, the roots remain shallow and the tree is likely to be blown over.

Zelkova serrata (left) and *Zelkova carpinifolia* (right)

3. Low trees

Trees that do not grow taller than 10m (33ft)

Acer campestre

FIELD MAPLE, HEDGE MAPLE

Acer campestre

The field or hedge maple is native to large parts of Europe. It grows mainly on lime rich or chalky soil and in the wild reaches 20m (65ft) high. In cultivation they rarely exceed 10m (33ft). The tree will also thrive in neutral to slightly acidic soil. When grown in gardens, they are usually kept as a bush or grown as a hedge. This species grows rapidly and will need trimming four times every season in a mixed hedge to give the other shrubs a chance. The autumn colour is bright yellow.

Acer campestre 'Postelense'

When the leaves of 'Postelense' first open they are an eye-catching golden yellow. During the course of the summer, they gradually turn yellow-green. This is a mop-headed small tree or small shrub of about 3m (10ft) with spreading branches. The leaf colour looks its best in the sun but the leaves are inclined to wilt, so it is best to choose a position out of the midday sun.

Acer campestre 'Red Shine'

The new leaves of 'Red Shine' first emerge mauve but change to dark red and then dark green during the summer. This species will

Left: *Acer campestre* 'Postelense'

Acer campestre 'Red Shine'

grow as a free-standing tree to a maximum of 4m (13ft), but because of its strong and dense growth, it also makes an excellent tall hedge.

Acer campestre ssp. *leiocarpon*

The sub-species *A. c. leoocarpon* differs very little from *A. campestre*. The leaves of *A. c. leiocarpon* emerge yellow-green but quickly turn dark green and they have fine hairs on them. Many authorities no longer recognise this as a sub-species, including the standard work *Maples of the World* by D. M. van Gelderen.

Acer campestre ssp. *leiocarpon*

Acer davidii ssp. grosseri

SLANGESCHORSESDOORN

Acer davidii ssp. *grosseri*

Trunk of *Acer davidii* ssp. *grosseri*

The bark of certain maples has clear longitudinal stripes or "snake-bark" as some call it. *Acer davidii* is the best known of them. It has red-tinged green bark with lengthwise white stripes. With the sub-species *grosseri*,

Acer japonicum 'Aconitifolium'

the trunk is green with white. The tree will grow eventually to 10m (33ft) tall, but it does so slowly. The branches spread fairly wide so it is more suitable for a medium to large garden. This species prefers slightly acidic soil but will still grow under less ideal circumstances. The tree is red in autumn.

Acer japonicum

Acer japonicum is often called the Japanese maple but this common name is now reserved for *Acer palmatum*. This species is capable of growing to 10m (33ft) tall but it is usually grown as a shrub with spreading branches. The many cultivated forms are popular garden plants, especially for gardens with an eastern touch to them. Its autumn colours are astounding.

Acer japonicum 'Aconitifolium' grows just as wide as it does tall, with robustly spreading branches. The leaves are deeply lobed and each lobe is also serrated. In autumn these turn bright orange and red, but sometimes also yellow and dark red.

Acer monspessulanum

At first glance, *Acer monospessulanum* looks rather like *Acer campestre* but when you break a leaf of this latter species (the field maple), milky-white sap oozes out. This does not occur with leaves from *A. monospessulanum*. The tree rarely grows taller than 10m (33ft) and frequently grows as a shrub. In its natural habitat in southern Europe and Asia Minor, it grows up to 20m (65ft) tall. In mild winters the leaves may remain on the tree.

Acer monspessulanum

Acer palmatum 'Seiryu'

JAPANESE MAPLE

Acer palmatum 'Seiryu'

Most Japanese maples form shrubs but the branches of 'Seiryu' growing upwards before spreading and the tree can be 5m (16ft 6in)

tall. The branches bear deeply lobed, fern-like leaves, that emerge light green. During the summer, the leaves darken and eventually become deep mauve before they fall. Highly recommended.

Acer palmatum 'Shishigashira'

JAPANESE MAPLE

Acer palmatum 'Shishigashira'

With its mass of upright-growing branches, *A. p.* 'Shishigashira' is a real maverick among the Japanese maples. It grows to about 4m (13ft) tall. The leaves are dark green and quite small at about 3cm (1¹/₂in). The leaves are tightly packed together and tightly curled, making the branches look as if they are covered with moss. They change colour quite late in autumn to purple with orange. This variety can be readily trimmed to desired shape.

Acer shirasawanum

This Japanese species is frequently confused with *Acer japonicum*. The branches spread and the tree forms a number of trunks to grow

Acer shirasawanum 'Aureum'

Acer shirasawanum 'Palmatifolium'

to not more than 7m (6ft 6in). The attractive leaves are bright red in autumn.

Acer shirasawanum 'Aureum' (syn. with *A. japonicum* 'Aureum') has yellow leaves with nine to eleven lobes. The tree illustrated is about 7m (23ft) and at about 135 years old it is one of the oldest examples in cultivation. This species grows slowly – particularly in its early years – and it is therefore suitable for smaller gardens.

Acer shirasawanum 'Palmatifolium' turns to brilliant yellow, orange, and red in autumn but the leaves soon fall. They are 10cm (4in) wide and have eleven pointed lobes. The tree grows as a shrub to about 5m (16.6in) high.

Acer tataricum subsp. *ginnala*

This tree forms numerous branches from its base and rarely grows higher than 6m (20ft), often growing as a shrub. The elongated leaves of 6cm (2½in) have a protruding central lobe. The leaf is usually tri-lobed but leaves without lobes also appear and the odd variegated leaf

Acer tataricum ssp. *ginnala*

is not unusual. The remaining leaves are green and they turn light red in autumn.

Acer tegmentosum

Acer tegmentosum

This "snake-bark" maple has a waxy coating on its trunk. This tree will grow to about 8m (26ft). The large leaves emerge very early in the spring, creating a risk of frost damage. They are about 15cm (6in) long. In all other respects this species, that originates from northern China and the neighbouring countries, is hardy. The bright green leaves turn yellow in autumn. Unfortunately, they are not easily propagated, so that they are very rare.

Aesculus pavia

RED BUCKEYE

Aesculus pavia

The young leaves, the flowers in May to June, and the autumn leaves of this species are all red. The leaves do, however, turn green in the summer but the tree is still highly attractive. The red buckeye originates from the southern parts of the United States but it is fully hardy in most of Europe. This low tree or tall shrub, that eventually grows to 5m (16ft 6in) tall, deserves to be planted more widely.

Amelanchier laevis

JUNEBERRY, SERVICEBERRY, SNOWY MESPILUS

Amelanchier laevis

Amelanchier laevis

White blossoms of Amelanchier laevis

There is frequently confusion at the highest levels between A. laevis and Amelanchier lamarckii (which in turn is often wrongly called A, canadensis). We should just be grateful for the juneberry. If I had to fell all but one of the trees in my garden, I would certainly save the juneberry.

The white blossoms emerge in April at the same time as the olive-coloured leaves. The flowers sparkle at the ends of the branches and these are succeeded in August by the ripening of the fruits from dark red to black. They are eagerly eaten by blackbirds and other birds and are also quite edible for humans.

In September and October, the leaves change to their magnificent autumn colouring – yellow with flickers of orange, gradually darkening to a fiery red. When the leaves are gone, the tree continues to look graceful. It can be pruned and cut back to any shape or form, or to form a shrub if required. Although they can eventually grow to 10m (33ft) tall, they generally remain at about 5m (16ft 6in). They can be kept shorter if required by pruning. This species is suitable for any soil type, but prefers a rich, moist soil.

Betula pendula 'Youngii'

YOUNG'S WEEPING BIRCH

Betula pendula 'Youngii'

Young's weeping birch has hanging branches. When grafted to a silver birch (see Tall trees), a mushroom-form with pendulous branches is created that does not grow more than about 2m (6ft 6in) taller than when grafted. This manageable height of 5-7m (16ft 6in-23ft) has made 'Youngii' one of the most popular birches for the garden.

Betula pendula 'Youngii'

Catalpa bignonioides

Catalpa bignonioides 'Aurea'

Catalpa bignonioides 'Aurea'

The flowers of *Catalpa bignonioides* 'Aurea'

The enormous leaves, magnificent broad crown, and abundant flowers in the middle of summer, make *Catalpa bignoniodes* one of the favourites for a larger garden. The tree can grow to 15m (50ft) high but most cultivated varieties remain below 10m (33ft). The broad crown that can spread to 8m (26ft) will only

Catalpa bignonioides 'Nana'

Cercis canadensis

fully develop when the tree is planted as a free-standing specimen. The enormous, light green leaves – that are 20cm (8in) long – only emerge towards the end of May. They fall quickly in October, without changing colour. The main flowering occurs in July, with delightful flowers in clusters. Following a hot summer, 30cm (12in) long seed pods will be formed that remain on the bare tree throughout the winter. Plant this species where it will be sheltered from the wind. It thrives best where there are hot summers. *Catalpa bignonioides* 'Aurea', or the golden Indian bean tree, grows to 8-10m (26-33ft) and has golden-yellow leaves in the spring that change during the summer to yellow-green and then in autumn to yellow.

Catalpa bignonioides 'Nana' is a true dwarf. On its own root stock, it does not grow taller than 2m (6ft 6in) and its leaves are considerably smaller than the main species. This miniature is often grafted on to a root stock so that it will form a densely packed globe, that is very suitable for smaller gardens.

Cercis canadensis

Cercis canadensis

AMERICAN REDBUD

The American redbud is stronger than its close relative the Judas tree. This tree is more common in the wild in the eastern forests of the United States than Canada, where it can grow to 12m (40ft). In Western Europe it only grows to 5-7m (16ft 6in-23ft) tall and then has a more spreading habit.

The pink flowers appear first at the end of April, followed by the heart-shaped leaves that have obtuse tips. The main flowering flush is in May. The flowers are succeeded in autumn by the long seed pods which hang on the tree for a long time after the leaves have turned yellow and fallen.

Young shrubs sometimes suffer from frost damage but this is rare in more mature specimens. The American redbud prefers an alkaline soil.

Cercis siliquastrum

JUDAS TREE

The Judas tree is a text book example of a tree that bears flowers on its trunk. This is something that occurs mainly with tropical trees. *Cercis siliquastrum* originates from

73

Cercis siliquastrum

Cornus alternifolia 'Argentea'

around the Mediterranean and is less hardy than *Cercis canadensis*, although it can survive in a maritime environment in North-west Europe, though it may lose its new growth some years to late frosts.

The Judas tree will eventually reach 7m (23ft) tall with its haphazardly spreading branches, in common with *C. canadensis*. The two species are best recognised by their leaves. The leaves of *C. canadensis* have obtuse tips, while *C. siliquastrum* is kidney-shaped, with a rounded end. It prefers alkaline soil.

Cornus alternifolia

The botanical name is derived from the alternate leaves on the leaf stems, which is unusual among *Cornus*. *Cornus alternifolia* prefers damp soil, where it will grow into a 7m (23ft) tall bushy tree with noticeable horizontal layering.

In May, bunches of white flowers appear, followed by blue-black fruits. *Cornus alternifolia* 'Argentea' has variegated yellow and white leaves and is a popular bushy tree for large gardens.

Cornus florida

EASTERN DOGWOOD

The purple autumn leaves of the eastern dogwood remain on the tree for some time. The new season's buds, enclosed during winter by bracts, also appear in late autumn. This tree does not grow taller than 5-10m (16ft 6in-33ft).

The flowers themselves, that appear in May,

are hardly noticeable, hidden as they are inside four large white bracts which eye-catching. The flowers turn into a cluster of red fruits in autumn.

Cornus f. rubra is a group of naturally-occurring related varieties that occurs in the eastern states of America, where *C. florida* grows wild as undergrowth in the forests. The *C. rubra* varieties have rosy-pink bracts.

Cornus florida

Cornus florida f. rubra

Flower bracts and flower of Cornus kousa

The bracts and flowers of *Cornus florida* f. *rubra*

Corna kousa at its autumn best

Cornus kousa

Cornus kousa

This small tree of between 5-7m (16ft 6in- 23ft) tall is a real jewel with many good characteristics. It grows with an open habit and lets plenty of sunlight through. In June to July, the more mature trees bear flowers on erect stalks. The flowers themselves are surrounded by four white bracts which are the eye-catchers. These are 3-5cm (11/2-2in) long In hot summers, each flower head develops bundles of fruit like small strawberries but carried in the manner of cherries.

Finally, there is the breathtaking red autumn colour of the leaves, that remain on the tree for

Fruit of *Cornus kousa*

Cornus nuttallii 'Monarch'

a long time. *Cornus kousa* originates from eastern Asia and is at its best planted clear of other trees and shrubs.

Cornus nuttallii 'Monarch'

Cornus nuttallii

WESTERN DOGWOOD

The flowers in May of *Cornus nuttallii* are not surrounded by the usual four flower bracts, but by five, or more usually six bracts. Each bract is about 5cm (2in) long. The scarlet fruits are clustered in bunches. Examples of this species in the wild grow to 25m (82ft) in the western part of the United States. The western dogwood does not grow taller than 7m (23ft) in Europe, where it tends towards more bushy growth. It is yellow to red in autumn. Late frosts can damage the flower bracts. This tree prefers neutral soil, in partial shade, where the air remains moist. It also needs ample warmth to thrive.

Cotinus obovatus

CHITTAMWOOD

Cotinus obovatus

Cotinus obovatus grows as a tree and will reach between 5-10m (16ft 6in- 33ft) tall. The plume-like inflorescences resemble wigs, and are only half the size of Cotinis coggygria (see below) but the autumn orange colouring is at least as intense. This species is fully hardy but prefers a warm position. The best known Cotinus is C. coggygria, also known as the smoke tree, that grows as a shrub to about 3m (10ft) tall, with a similar spread. This tree is best known for its large plume-like inflorescences. When the blossoms have fallen, the stems remain on the shrub like wigs. The red-leaved cultivated variety Cotinis coggygria 'Royal Purple' is the best-known form.

Crataegus calpodendron

Crataegus calpodendron

Flowers of Crataegus calpodendron

HAWTHORN, THORN
Haphazard crooked branches of Crataegus calpodendron bear 10cm (4in) wide trusses of white flowers in June. There are many different varieties of American hawthorn. This one bears its flowers embedded in the 10cm (4in) long leaves that turn bright orange and red in autumn. At this time the tree also hangs with oval to pear-shaped fruits but the drab orange

Crataegus calpodendron

of these is barely noticeable. It is strange that this marvellous, fully hardy hawthorn of about 5m (16ft 6in) high is rarely seen outside of specialist collections.

Crataegus laevigata syn. C.oxyacantha

ENGLISH HAWTHORN, MAY

Crataegus laevigata 'Paul's Scarlet'

There is little difference between Crataegus laevigata and Crataegus monogyna apart from the number of stems to the flower and number of seeds born per stem. C. laevigata has two to three flower stems and these then bear two to three seeds per berry, while C. monogyna has only one of both. Both blossom in May to June and are widely seen in the wild where they are native species, frequently grown as a hedge. They both prefer alkaline soils. See other details for C. monogyna at the next entry. Crataegus laevigata 'Paul's Scarlet' is the most popular cultivated form of the red hawthorn or may, with its double scarlet flowers. These can sometimes verge towards pinkish red, which is a throwback to the parent stock of this cultivar, discovered in 1858 (Crataegus laevigata 'Rubra Plena').

Flowers of *Crataegus laevigata* 'Paul's Scarlet'

Both forms will eventually grow to about 4m (13ft) tall but they can be pruned and trained to form a hedge or covering for a wall. All hawthorns are susceptible to fireblight, which is a much feared disease among fruit growers. Some experts suggest that C. l. 'Paul's Scarlet' and other varieties listed as C. laevigata are in reality hybrids resulting from crossing between it and C. monogyna.

Crataegus monogyna

Crataegus monogyna

Crataegus monogyna

COMMON HAWTHORN, MAY

Except in having just the single flower stem and single seed per berry, the common hawthorn varies little from *C. laevigata* (see previous entry). This species is the most commonly found as dense thorn hedge in gardens and punctuating the landscape. It will grow as a lone specimen to a tree of 5m (16ft 6in) tall. The blossoms in May and June are followed in autumn by orange-red berries that are much liked by birds and quickly eaten by them.

Crataegus monogyna 'Lasiocarpa'

Flowers of *Crataegus monogyna* 'Lasiocarpa'

Crataegus monogyna 'Lasiocarpa'

The fine hairs on both sides of its leaves make *C. m.* 'Lasiocarpa' look somewhat grey. The leaves are deeply lobed, adding to their decorative appeal. The blossoms that are about 2cm ($\frac{1}{2}$in) wide are borne in bunches of up to twelve flowers in June. The autumn fruits are orange-red. This broad-growing tree does not become taller than 5m (16ft 6in). It is rarely available.

Blossoms of *Crataegus* x *lavalleei*

Crataegus x *lavalleei*

Crataegus x *lavalleei*

This 5m (16ft 6in) high tree is seen too rarely in gardens, though it is fairly common in parks. It flowers abundantly in June with 2cm (1/2in) white blossoms that are borne in bunches together between the 10cm (4in) long leaves. The orange-red fruits remain on the tree throughout the autumn and winter. This is a hybrid species created by crossing with *Crataegus mexicana*. The pollen probably came from *Crataegus crus-galli*. This hybrid species is fully hardy and highly recommended.

Fagus sylvatica 'Purpurea Nana'

BEECH
The beech clearly belongs to the previous chapter on tall trees, where an entry for *Fagus sylvatica* will be found. This cultivated form is the one exception. In most instances, this small tree will not grow taller than 3m (10ft) in fifty years. The leaves are very dark, almost aubergine.

Fagus sylvatica 'Purpurea Nana'

Ficus carica

FIG

Ficus carica

The fig is a short tree from Southern Europe. Its beautiful deeply lobed leaves have served for centuries as modesty-covering for nudes in paintings and on statues. The figs are formed without any visible blossom, which occur within the fruit buds themselves. The fruiting results from a complex process involving a wasp (*blastophaga*) that lives in symbiosis with the species. Other species of fig will bear fruit without being pollinated.

The fig will only survive winter in northern European latitudes in a sheltered but warm position, preferably a south-facing wall. Once mature, they can withstand up to minus 15°C in such a position. The tree will eventually grow to 2-4m (6ft 6in-13ft) tall but they can be readily pruned.

Gleditsia ferox

Gleditsia ferox

The trunks of these small *Gleditsia* (for the rest see the chapter on Tall trees) bear spiky growths that harden into thorns. This tree grows upright to about 10m (33ft) tall. The leaves have handsome feathering but despite this, the species is rarely seen outside arboretums.

Halesia carolina

SNOWDROP TREE

If you need a small variety of *Halesia*, choose the true snowdrop tree. It is a bushy tree that grows to about 5m (16ft 6in) tall. The flowers are not larger than 1.5cm (¹/₂in) long. Apart from these two features, there is no different between *H. carolina* and *H. monticola*.

Halesia monticola

MOUNTAIN SNOWDROP TREE

Although the mountain snowdrop tree will grow as tall as 30m (100ft) in the United

Halesia monticola

Halesia monticola blossoms

States, it rarely exceeds 5-10m (16ft 6in-33ft) high in Europe until very mature. The first snowdrop-like white flowers appear in May at the same time as the leaves emerge. The flowers hang three-to-a-stem and are 2cm (¹/₂in) long.

Hemiptelea davidii

This member of the elm family does not normally grow taller than 10m (33ft), although it is capable of growing to 15m (50ft). The

Hemiptelea davidii

Foliage of *Hemiptelea davidii*

Bark of *Hemiptelea davidii*

branches have strong prickles that differentiates *Hemiptelea* from its close relative *Zelkova*. This shorter tree is fully hardy and will grow in almost any soil and so far as is known, is not susceptible to Dutch elm disease.

The serrated leaves, the small, winged fruits, the veined bark, and the attractive shape of the crown make *Hemiptelea* a desirable ornamental tree. Unfortunately, few know about it, so it is mainly to be found in arboretums.

Koelreuteria paniculata

Koelreuteria paniculata

This is a relatively unknown ornamental tree from China and Korea that rarely grows taller than 10m (33ft). The feathery foliage that emerges quite red in spring, is attractive all summer, and then changes to yellow in autumn. In July, the ends of the branches are filled with plumes bearing yellow flowers and these are sometimes followed by 5cm (2in)

Leaves of *Koelreuteria paniculata*

long, puffed up fruits.
In the countries of origin, the summers are hot. Place this tree therefore in a sheltered, warm position. It grows best on dry, poor soil, which slows growth but prevents branches breaking off. Mature specimens can withstand minus 20°C.

Laburnum alpinum 'Pendulum'

Laburnum alpinum

SCOTCH LABURNUM

This particular laburnum generally grows with a bushy habit in contrast with the better known common *laburnum*. This species, that originates in the Alps and other mountains of south-eastern Europe, can grow to a medium sized tree though reaching 5m (16ft 6in). In June, the tree is covered with 25cm (10in) long clusters of hanging yellow flowers. The blossom has a wonderful fragrance.
Laburnum alpinum 'Pendulum' is a slower-growing variety, with arched branches that is usually grafted to produce a weeping form. **These plants are poisonous if eaten.**

Laburnum anagyroides

COMMON LABURNUM

Laburnum anagyroides

The laburnum is a popular garden tree. This medium-sized tree grows between 4-7m (13-23ft) tall. From the middle of May, it is festooned with 10-20cm (4-8in) long pendent clusters of yellow blossoms. After flowering,

Flower clusters of *Laburnum anagyroides*

Laburnum x *wateri* 'Vossii'

the pea-like flowers turn to "propeller" seed cases containing black seeds. The three oval leaflets are not clustered very tightly together so that the common laburnum throws diffused shade.

If you feel able to take the risk to plant this poisonous plant in your garden, place it in a sunny position in well-drained soil. Laburnums prefer an alkaline soil but will also thrive in neutral to lightly acidic ground.

Laburnum x *wateri*

This is a hybrid resulting from crossing the *Scotch laburnum* with common *laburnum*. The resulting form has characteristics mid-way between both parents, but looks most like *L. anagyroides* although it flowers later and with longer flower clusters.

Through cultivation, other varieties have been created such as the outstanding *L. x. wateri* 'Vossii'. This bears up to 50cm (20in) long pendent clusters of golden yellow, fragrant blossoms in June.

Flower clusters of *Laburnum* x *wateri* 'Vossii'

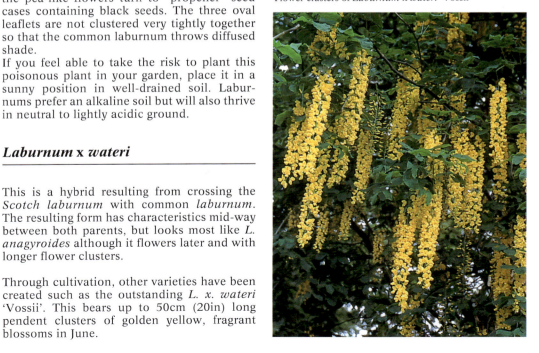

Maackia chinensis

Maackia chinensis

Each leaf of this tree, that bears pea-like flowers, consists of eleven to twelve leaflets which emerge at the end of spring. The leaves are covered with silvery hairs and they look superb against a dark background. In July and August, plumes of ivory white flowers appear at the ends of the branches, succeeded by 7cm (21/2in) long seed cases. *Maackia* grows fairly erect and in China, can grow to 20m (65ft). In Europe it does not exceed 10m (33ft). Plant this tree in a warm, sheltered position away from cold winds, and it will then survive frost of up to minus 20°C.

Magnolia

Magnolias are among the oldest flowering plants on Earth. Geologists have discovered fossils of the flowers, that are about 100 million years old, in rock strata. Beetles ensure the pollination of the magnolia (then and now).

The magnolia bears a mass of sweet-smelling flowers and it is this that has made the smaller varieties some of the most popular garden plants.

Magnolias often fail to thrive after planting because too little attention has been paid to the essentials for the plant's well-being. The tree must not be deeply planted to avoid the surface-level roots being smothered. Make sure that the top soil is not alkaline, has plenty of humus and is moisture retaining. Plant them in a position where they will be protected from late frosts (away from northern and eastern winds, and not in hollows where cold air gathers). Protect large-flowering varieties from the wind to prevent the flowers being damaged. Most varieties prefer a sunny position, where the wood can ripen in the summer, to make the tree less sensitive to frosts. Most magnolia will withstand frosts of minus 15°C, but even light frosts during blossoming will damage both the buds and flowers.

Magnolia 'Heaven Scent'

This is one of the Gresham hybrids, resulting from crossing various Chinese magnolias.

Magnolia 'Heavenly Scent'

'Heaven Scent' bears 12cm (4¹/₂in) diameter flowers in April to May that have a delightful honey perfume. The flowers are white inside but suffused to dark pink on the outside. This low-growing tree branches more or less from its base. For care and planting, see *Magnolia*.

Magnolia sieboldii

This extraordinary tree is virtually only seen in tree collections. It originates from Japan and

Bud of *Magnolia sieboldii*

Korea, where it grows in forests in the mountains. This is why *M. sieboldii*, in contrast with other magnolias, prefers partial shade and moist ground. The soil may be slightly alkaline. The pointed buds open in June and July to produce almost 10cm (4in) wide white flowers. Inside, the anthers and stigma are carmine.

These are only visible with more mature trees, because the flowers hang down, so that you need to be beneath them to look into the flowers. This tree grows with arching branches to about 10m (33ft) tall. For care and planting see *Magnolia*.

Magnolia stellata

Magnolia stellata

This magnolia, that has a star-shaped flower, is included in this chapter to make it easier to consult the general tips for magnolias. It is actually a slow-growing shrub that eventually reaches 3m (10ft) tall. In contrast with some other varieties, *M. stellata* is fully hardy. The flowers too, that appear in March to April, can withstand hard reasonably hard frosts. This species has a wonderful fragrance from its white flowers that are about 8cm (3¹/₂in) wide.

Magnolia x soulangiana

This hybrid, crossed between *Magnolia denudata* and *Magnolia liliiflora*, is one of the most popular magnolias. Sometimes they are loosely known as "tulip trees", but this name really applies to *Liriodendron*. The tree grows slowly, forming a broad, branching tree of about 5m (16ft 6in) although exceptionally it can become 10m (33ft) tall.

Magnolia x *soulangiana*

Magnolia x *soulangiana* 'Amabilis'

Magnolia x *soulangiana*

Magnolia x *soulangiana* 'Lennei'

white, tulip-form flowers appear on otherwise bare branches in March.

Magnolia x soulangiana 'Lennei' is one of the late-flowering varieties. The 10cm (4in) wide, virtually globular flowers are mauve on the outside and creamy-white inside. They appear profusely from April on this rapid-growing bushy tree, that spreads outwards.

Malus baccata

CRAB APPLE

The fruits of the crab apple grow no bigger than cherries and taste quite sharp. The crab apple, that originates from eastern Asia, is grown as an ornamental tree. It grows to 5-10m (16ft 6in-33ft) and bears white blossoms in April to May. The small round apples are yellow, flecked with red.
Malus baccata 'Gracilis' grows as a bush with pendent branches and is about 2m (6ft 6in) high. This superb shrub blossoms profusely in May with white flowers that emerge from pink buds. It is highly recommended.

The flowers emerge before there is a single leaf on the tree, often in April, but with cultivated varieties either earlier or later. Generally, they are more or less white, with a pink or red blush on the outside of the flowers. Both the buds and flowers can be lost to late frosts. For care see *Magnolia*.
Magnolia x soulangiana 'Amabilis' is one of the early-flowering varieties with white flowers. The bushy tree grows slowly with a rounded form to about 5m (16ft 6in) tall. The

Malus baccata 'Gracilis'

Malus baccata 'Gracilis'

Winter scene with *Malus domestica* 'Groninger Kroon'

Malus domestica

EATING APPLE

Blossoms of *Malus domestica* 'Court-Pendu'

Variety label attached to *M. d.* 'Herfst bloemzoet'

The edible species of apples came into existence so long ago that their origins are uncertain. Eating apples existed at least 8,500 years ago. It is thought that they were formed by the crossing of the native *Malus sylvestris* and the Asian *Malus pumila*, with the result that all eating apples are assigned to *M. domestica, sylvestris,* or *pumila*.

Over the years, increasing numbers of new varieties have been cultivated with improved taste. Since the inception of chemical spraying, too little regard is given to the susceptibility to disease, with the result that many popular varieties can only be grown successfully, free from disease, with repeated chemical treatment. Commercially grown apples gradually became toxic apples, leading

Pruned and trained *Malus domestica*

The ripening time and storage potential vary enormously between varieties. The specialist organisations that are seeking to reintroduce the older varieties will generally be happy to advise on which varieties to plant. Apples are grafted onto root stock which determines whether the new plant grows vigorously or more slowly.

The height at which the apple variety is grafted to its stock (see also chapter 1) also determines the form of growth of the new tree.

Commercial growers now almost exclusively grow cordon and spindlebush forms that remain low and can be picked without a ladder. These low stemmed trees are also available for the private garden and can be trained and pruned to any geometric form for a formal garden. In larger, more natural gardens, the standard is better suited. The branches form above head height, so that it is possible to walk beneath the tree. This also helps to ensure the survival of a disappearing element in the landscape, because these apple trees, standing tall on clear trunks, have largely disappeared from commercial orchards.

Apple trees prefer alkaline clay soil but will grow on any ground that is not too acidic, or poorly drained. They cannot cope with their roots being submersed in water and the pH of the soil needs to be 6 or higher. For pruning fruit trees, see chapter 1

to consumer resistance, that in turn caused chemical companies to develop more selective treatments. Now, there is increasing emphasis on natural control and disease resistance in the breeding of new varieties.

For those who wish to plant an apple tree, it is best to choose one of the old varieties that fruit without the need for chemical treatment. Enthusiasts for the older varieties have managed in recent years to rediscover an increasing number of specimens. Some of these have been rescued from old orchards.

When choosing a disease-resistant variety, take the soil and water needs into consideration. Varieties exist that have been specifically bred to cope with certain local circumstances.

Beyond that, it is a question of taste. Apples have properties that make them suitable for different purposes. Some are perfect for making an apple pie, another is perhaps better suited to making apple sauce, while yet another might make perfect apple juice, or be the perfect dessert apple.

Malus 'Flamenco'

This cultivated variety of cordons has extremely short side shoots and one main stem. This approach to apple trees existed as early as the nineteenth century but has been brought back under a variety of trade names. These trees are small enough – 1.5m (5ft) tall and 20cm (8in) wide – for anybody who only has a balcony to grow an apple tree in a pot.
Malus 'Flamenco' flowers from mid-May with pink-white blossoms. The dark red apples, that taste like a 'Cox', ripen in October, and can be stored for quite a long time.

Grow this container apple in rich, porous but clay-based soil. Grown in the ground, it is fully hardy but when grown in a pot the tree needs to be brought in during very severe frosts or protected with insulation.

Malus 'Flamenco'

Malus 'Hillieri'

This ornamental apple tree has its branches abundantly covered with pink blossoms and dark pink buds during May. *M.* 'Hillieri' is a selected cultivar of *Malus x scheideckeri* which is a densely branched low tree of about 5m (16ft 6in) high. 'Hillieri' flowers profusely and its autumn fruits, that are about 2cm (1/2in) in diameter, are yellow to orange.

Malus 'Makamik'

Malus 'Makamik'

Malus 'Hillieri'

The flowers of this ornamental apple are 5cm (2in) in diameter. They emerge on a tree which grows to 5m (16ft 6in) tall and that initially grows upright before spreading outwards at its crown. The flowers, that appear every year, are deep carmine but they change to pink, with a light fleck in the centre, as they age. In the autumn, orange to red fruits 2cm (1/2in) in diameter hang between green-bronze leaves.

Malus 'Profusion'

Malus 'Profusion'

Carmine blossoms emerge between the wine coloured leaves of *M.* 'Profusion' in May. This is the most popular flowering apple, and it closely resembles *Malus* 'Lemoinei'. This tree grows between 5-7m (16ft 6in-23ft) tall and has a broad crown. The leaves change to dark green during the course of the summer. In the autumn, the tree bears burgundy-coloured fruits.

Malus x *purpurea*

The new leaves, young growth, and the fruits of this hybrid are dark purple. The older growth and leaves later in summer are dark green. This hybrid arose in the nineteenth century by the crossing of *Malus atrosanguinea* and *Malus pumila* 'Niedzwetzkyana'. The tall, upright branches form a shrub or small tree of up to 4m (13ft) high. The purple blossoms flower in April.

Malus x *purpurea* 'Amisk' flowers alternate years with pink blossoms that emerge from carmine buds. The 2cm (1/2in) hips are dark red, sometimes with yellow, and they remain on the tree for quite some time.

Malus toringo var. *sargentii*

Malus toringo var. *sargentii*

Blossoms of *Malus toringo* var. *sargentii*

It is an unforgettable sight to see this attractive tree flower in May. The entire, broad tree, of 2-4m (6ft 6in-13ft), turns white with blossom. Unfortunately, this normally occurs only every other year. In the year between these flushes, it bears virtually no blossom. The leaves are dark green and they turn orange-yellow in autumn when dark red fruits also appear. These are only 1cm (3/8in) in diameter but they remain on the tree throughout the winter.

Mespilus germanica

MEDLAR
The medlar is one of the most beautiful small

Mespilus germanica

Blossoms of *Mespilus germanica*

trees for a garden, yet despite this, it is rarely planted. The tree grows to 3-5m (10-16ft 6in) tall, sometimes as a bush, but it can be kept as a tree with a trunk and a fine spreading crown, through pruning. The leaves are long and lustrous green, and they turn yellow to russet in autumn. The white, cupped flowers bloom in May to June at the end of the branches. They are about 4cm (1¹/₂in) in diameter. During the course of the summer, they develop into light-brown chunky fruits with hairs on. Once they have been broken down by the frost, they are edible. There is really only one disadvantage to the medlar: it is susceptible to fireblight, so that it is best not planted where there are fruit trees.

Morus alba

WHITE MULBERRY

Morus alba 'Pendula'

Although the white mulberry will grow eventually into a tree about 15m (50ft) tall, it is included in this chapter about lower trees because most varieties in cultivation remain under 10m (33ft) high, such as *Morus alba* 'Pendula'. The branches of this variety arch towards the ground. When grafted to a taller stem, this variety forms a weeping tree that in summer will provide a cupola of dark green leaves that are almost 20cm (8in) long. In China, silkworms feed on the leaves of this tree. The milk-white bunches of soft fruits ripen during the summer but these have little taste. For edible fruits, the black mulberry is a better choice.

Plant a mulberry in a sheltered, sunny position, because they appreciate hot summers. This tree needs well-drained, preferably very fertile soil. It is fully hardy. The leaves all fall immediately following the first autumn frost. It is one of the last trees in leaf in the spring, in May.

Morus nigra

BLACK MULBERRY

The black mulberry is planted more often than the white species, because the fruits develop more readily and taste better in the European climate. They resemble black raspberries. The skin of the mulberry is very easily damaged, so that they need to be picked carefully and eaten quickly. The wine coloured juice stains and is not easily removed by washing.

Where the summers are hot, the black mulberry will grow to a 15m (50ft) high tree. In Northern Europe, they are usually offered as

Weeping form of *Morus nigra*

Morus nigra

Morus nigra

Nothofagus antarctica

grafted specimens, from which the branches hang low. This form generally grows into a 3m (10ft) tall tree about 2m (6ft 6in) wide that also bears abundant fruit. For care, see *Morus alba*.

Nothofagus antarctica

SOUTHERN BEECH

In April when the leaves emerge, a wonderful balsamic fragrance is emitted by the southern beech. This is just one of the many good things

Nothofagus antartica as hedge

Parrotia persica

Parrotia persica

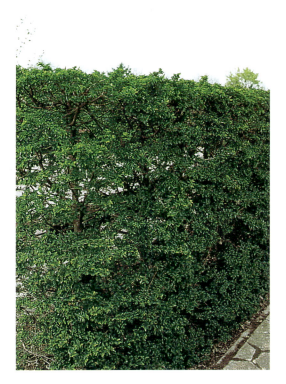

Nothofagus antarctica

Leaves of *Parrotia persica*

about this species. It originates from Tierra del Fuego on the southern, chilly tip of South America. The trunk at first surges upwards but then branches out to form a 5m (16ft 6in) high tree. The side branches have many twigs emanating from them in rows, in herring-bone fashion. The small, leathery leaves have undulating margins and they are golden yellow in autumn. This superb tree is mainly seen in botanical collections but its popularity is growing among gardeners.

The young leaves of *Parrotia persica* emerge salmon pink. The 8cm (3in) long leaves change to light green and then in autumn, they become yellow, orange, or red. In the early spring, before the leaves have emerged, the tree blossoms with red flowers that consist solely of stamens. The olive green bark of this

Bark of *Parrotia persica*

bushy tree – maximum height 10m (33ft) tall – peels off in flakes to reveal lighter green or cream patches rather like plane trees (see *Platanus*). This species prefers a warm, sunny position in fertile, well-drained soil.

Photinia villosa

The deciduous *Photinia* species are fully hardy, and this includes *Photinia villosa*, originating from Japan, China, and Korea. It

Photinia villosa

grows initially as a shrub and then into a medium-sized tree of about 5m (16ft 6in) high.

The leaves become spectacular orange-red in autumn, when the dark branches are also decorated with red fruits.

Planera aquatica

Planera aquatica

Planera aquatica

Although this species can grow to 12m (40ft) tall, it usually remains much lower and will fit in the average garden. The branches spread out and bear fairly transparent leaves that become a wonderful golden yellow in the autumn.

Although this tree originates from the United States, it is fully hardy in Western Europe. Despite this it is rarely offered, perhaps because it grows best in a non-maritime climate with hot summers. Plant it in very wet ground.

Prunus 'Accolade'

Prunus 'Accolade'

It is clear that the winter-flowering *Prunus subhirtella* provided the pollen for this hybrid. *Prunus* 'Accolade' can sometimes start blossoming in mid January. The main flowering flush is in April. The flowers are semi-double and distinctly pink. They make a marvellous sight on the leafless branches against a blue sky. The leaves are 10cm (4in) long, which it inherits from the "mother" plant, which was *Prunus sargentii*. The leaves have a red-orange colour in autumn.

This hybrid grows to about 6m (20ft) tall as a broad tree with spreading branches, that hang down slightly. The best results are achieved on moisture-retaining but well-drained soil in a sunny position.

Prunus domestica

PLUM, GAGE, DAMSON, BULLACE

Plum trees and their close relatives will grow to 12m (40ft) tall but this is not a problem for any garden because they can easily be kept pruned to a smaller form. This way, a tree is

Prunus domestica 'Victoria'

created entirely in keeping with the garden. The dark branches bear their white blossoms in April.

The plums appear during the course of the summer: depending upon the cultivated variety, they can be green, blue, yellow-orange, or reddish. There are legions of varieties with different characteristics, suited to different uses. Some are juicy dessert plums, or have fleshy fruit that is easily removed from the stone, and there are plums that are ideal for steeping in brandy.

Plum trees will grow in any soil that does not remain wet; their preference is for alkaline soil. Plums are best pruned immediately after harvesting the fruit – usually in August – when the leaves are still on the tree and the new wounds are less likely to be infected by silver leaf than during the winter.

Prunus domestica 'Victoria' is the best known cultivated variety, known as "Victoria plum" or "Queen Victoria". The skin is reddish coloured with firm, yellow flesh.

Prunus dulcis

COMMON ALMOND

Prunus dulcis

The almond tree flowers in March to April with unbelievably pretty pink blossoms, that fade to white. In warmer latitudes such as southern Europe, North Africa, Australia, and California, the broad, branching tree of 5-8m (16ft 6in-26ft) tall is grown for its nuts. The almond rarely fruits in Northern Europe, and since it is fairly susceptible to various diseases, it is not particularly recommended for planting in gardens. If you do want to try growing this tree though, place it in the warmest spot in the garden, well protected from northerly and easterly winds. *Prunus dulcis* 'Robijn' is the most suitable cultivar for cooler climates.

Prunus padus

BIRD CHERRY

Prunus padus

Blossoms of *Prunus padus*

The bird cherry is a native of western Europe. This bushy tree can grow to 15m (50ft) tall but generally remains beneath 10m (33ft) with branches fanning out. The dull green leaves emerge in early April, followed by 10cm (4in)

long clusters of white flowers that smell sweetly of almonds. These are replaced in summer by black berries that are much sought after by blackbirds.

This species has no particular planting requirements and it can withstand fairly extensive shade, although it will then flower less abundantly.

Prunus serrula

Bark of *Prunus serrula*

A Chinese tree of less than 10m (33ft) high that is planted mainly for its glistening bark. This is a marvellous red, and ribbons of bark peel from the trunk. The 2cm (1/2in) white flowers blossom amid the newly emerged leaves in April to May. This tree bears small red fruits in the autumn.

Prunus serrulata

CHINESE HILL CHERRY

During the first warm days, roughly around the end of April, the hill cherry is suddenly in full bloom. Clusters of pink or white flowers that are mainly double, hang from the ends of the

Prunus serrulata

widely spreading branches. After this short burst of blossoming, this tree has little else to offer except strong shadow, so it is best to choose one of the small cultivated varieties with a fine shape.

Prunus serrulata 'Kanzan' is the oldest of the Chinese hill cherries to be introduced to Europe. It is still one of the most favourable flowering cherries, forming a tree about 3m (10ft) tall on a broad trunk with a modest crown. The 5cm (2in) pink double flowers blossom around the end of April. There is a second colour display in autumn with the fiery red leaves.

Prunus serrulata 'Pink Perfection' is the favourite in many new housing developments because of its light-coloured appearance. This tree can grow to 9m (30ft). The light pink, 4cm (1¹/₂in) diameter, double flowers are born in thick bunches. More or less at the same time, the bronze-coloured leaves start to emerge. These later change to dark green and then orange to red in autumn.

Prunus serrulata 'Kanzan'

Prunus subhirtella 'Autumnalis'

A very attractive ornamental tree that branches from low on its trunk but that can be grown as a tree by pruning. It does not become taller than 9m (29ft 6in). The great attraction of this flowering cherry is that it flowers late in the year. The first white to pale pink blossoms can appear in November and they have a marvellous fragrance. In milder winters, without frosts or only light frost, it will flower throughout the winter. With a moderate frost, the blossoms will be lost but after the frosts, new buds appear and this tree will flower until March.

Pterostyrax hispida

EPAULETTE TREE

The epaulette tree gets its names because the plumes of blossom resemble the shoulder decorations of uniforms. It is principally the protruding stamens that create this impression, combined with the open nature of this fragrant flower. The blossoms do not appear until the tree is more than ten years

Prunus subhirtella 'Autumnalis'

Flowers of *Pterostyrax hispida*

old. By this time, they are about 5m (16ft 6in) tall with pendent branches. The bushy tree will eventually grow to 10m (33ft) tall. This species can withstand frosts up to minus 20°C, but the branches of immature trees are often damaged by frost.

Pyrus communis var. *sativa*

Pear tree in blossom (*Pyrus communis*)

Leaves and flowers of *Pterostyrax hispida*

COMMON PEAR

The dessert pear is virtually always grafted onto quince rootstock so that it does not grow taller than 10m (33ft). The trees have a distinct upright growth habit. This can be corrected by pruning and training the branches, so that pear trees can even be cultivated as a hedge. The popularity for growing pears as espaliers is increasing once more, where they are trained against a wall. The tree is festooned with white blossoms in May. Once the blossom has fallen, pears that can be either pear-shaped or more rounded are formed. There are countless varieties, including juicy dessert pears or ones that first need to be cooked.

Pear trees can live for 100 years. Careful pruning is essential (see under pruning in the introduction) to prevent a shapeless, gawky tree being formed. The tree recovers well from pruning. The soft wood from pears is highly regarded by wood carvers.

The pear is very susceptible to fireblight which can be recognised by the black-brown discolouration of the leaves. The infected tree needs to be felled immediately and burned.

Pyrus salicifolia

WILLOW-LEAVED PEAR

This ornamental pear will become about 7m (23ft) tall. Its leaves resemble those of willow – they are elongated and initially appear grey-green because of the fine downy hairs on them. Later in the season, the undersides remain grey but the uppers become dark green. Flower bracts containing eight cream florets blossom in April. These are followed by small, green but sour pears.

The weeping variety Pyrus salicifolia 'Pendula' is the principal ornamental form of willow-leaved pear in cultivation.

Quercus x brittonii

Two shorter oak trees grow in the eastern parts of the United States in similar areas. These are Quercus ilicifolia and Quercus marilandica, and these species cross of their own accord to form a low, bushy hybrid tree that grows to between 3-8m (10-26ft) tall. This is Quercus x brittonii. The male catkins dangle from its branches in May. The orbicular leaves are about 10cm (4in) long, leathery, and dark green on their upper side but lighter underneath.

Pyrus salicifolia 'Pendula'

Quercus x brittonii

Quercus robur 'Concordia'

This cultivar of the common or English oak grows to about 10m (33ft) tall with a crown of a similar breadth. The leaves emerge golden yellow in spring and retain this colour until the autumn. For further information, see Quercus robur (common oak) in chapter 2.

Quercus robur 'Concordia'

This species originates in the sheltered woods of the eastern parts of North America, so plant it out of the wind so that the leaves remain beautiful for longer in the autumn.

Robinia viscosa

Robinia viscosa

This marvellous tree from the eastern parts of North American becomes on average about 8m (26ft) tall with the occasional example reaching 12m (40ft). The densely packed branches form a broad crown. The young growth is covered with a sticky substance and

Rhus typhina

STAG'S-HORN SUMACH
The stag's-horn sumach is at its prettiest in the autumn when its feathery leaves become brilliant yellow and orange to red. At the same time, the plumes of fruit ripen that began to turn pinkish red around the end of July. During the winter, they usually remain on the otherwise bare branches and they change colour to deep purple.

The young shoots from the broadly spreading bushy tree – that eventually grows to 5m (16ft 6in) tall – are covered with fine downy hairs.

Rhus typhina

small prickles. The feathery foliage consists of thirteen to twenty-one leaflets per leaf. Lilac flowers, with yellow centres, bloom in June to August, in slightly pendent clusters.

Plant this tree in thin, well-drained soil in a position where it can get ample light but is sheltered from strong winds. When planted in very fertile or wet ground, the branches are prone to snap off. Some gardeners refer to robinias as acacias. This is not correct.

Salix babylonica 'Tortuosa'

Salix babylonica 'Tortuosa'

TWISTED WILLOW

This very attractive twisted willow looks wonderful growing beside a pond. The branches grow upwards in an irregular spiral. The elongated, light-green leaves are also bent. Stick a branch in the ground in spring, before the leaves emerge, and the chances are high that it will grow. Bear in mind that a twisted willow will eventually reach about 10m (33ft) tall with a crown packed full of twisted branches. It is often the case that this is when they are pruned but it is then too late because the tree will no longer look attractive and is best removed. It is only possible to maintain this tree in an acceptable form by pruning heavily every year.

Salix caprea

BOSWILG

The downy, silver female catkins that are offered for sale in the spring almost always come from the pussy willow as this species is popularly known in Britain. Goat willow, or great sallow form low trees or tall shrubs of 5-

Salix caprea 'Kilmarnock'

Salix caprea

8m (16ft 6in-26ft). The catkins are already forming on the tree in autumn but they appear fully in February, and blossom in March to

April. These catkins provide the first draw for the bees that need early pollen. After the downy catkins have appeared, broad oval leaves emerge on the red-brown to black branches. Once the leaves acquire their autumn yellow colouring, they drop. The pussy willow is also popularly known as the water willow, yet it prefers drier positions on the edges of woods, and open areas. Cultivated pussy willow is frequently grafted onto a different rootstock. These forms, that used to be known as *Salix caprea pendula*, are now known as *Salix caprea* 'Kilmarnock' with male catkins, and *Salix caprea* 'Weeping Sally' with female catkins. The branches arch towards the ground from the trunk and are festooned with catkins in the spring. They are widely used in the front gardens of new housing developments.

Sorbus aucuparia

MOUNTAIN ASH, ROWAN

The mountain ash or rowan was one of the first trees to colonise Western Europe at the end of the Ice Age. No other tree has branches that can so readily withstand severe frosts. What is more, this species can thrive on very poor and acidic soil, that is a characteristic of

Styrax japonicus

tundra landscape where the ice has recently retreated. The rowan blossoms in clusters of white flowers in May, shortly after the emergence of its feathery leaves. The flowers smell sweetly yet also somewhat musty. In autumn, they turn to orange berries that are eagerly fed on by starlings, blackbirds, thrushes, and redwings.

The rowan or mountain ash forms an attractive low ornamental tree or tall shrub, with its smooth, grey bark. It seldom grows taller than 10m (33ft).

Sorbus aucuparia

Styrax japonica

The ends of the branches of this species are decorated from the end of May to the end of June with small white flowers rather like snowdrops – they are in fact related. The branches of this short tree or tall shrub – that grows to about 5m (16ft 6in) tall – spread more or less horizontally. The leaves are shiny and green. The natural habitat for this species is the forests of South-East Asia, so it is happiest with a sheltered, warm position with moist air and soil. It is hardy and can withstand frosts to minus 20°C.

Syringa x hyacinthiflora

Syringa x hyacinthiflora

LILAC

A considerable number of hybrids resulting from crossing *Syringa oblata* with *Syringa vulgaris* are offered under this name. They are renowned for their early flowering, from the end of April. The flowers are clustered tightly together in panicles. Following the original crossing in 1976, the flowers were double – many others are single, such as those illustrated. The cherry red buds open to produce mauve-pink flowers, that have a strong but not heavy perfume. The bushy tree grows rapidly and quite upright. Prune about one third of the branches back low after flowering to encourage the tree to produce more branches, and to form a bushy tree of about 5m (16ft 6in) high. For further care information, see *Syringa vulgaris.*

Syringa vulgaris

COMMON LILAC

The wild lilac originates from the mountains of south-eastern Europe. For centuries, this bu-

Syringia vulgaris

shy tree has been a popular garden plant throughout the rest of Europe, with many hundreds of cultivated varieties stemming from *Syringa vulgaris.* Lilacs are particularly loved for their abundant flowering plumes or panicles in May, that also have a wonderful fragrance. Cut and brought indoors in a vase, they spread their fragrance of lilac blossom throughout the house. The bushy tree, that eventually grows to 7m (23ft) tall but usually stays much lower, grows well in almost any soil except extremely acidic. The branches grow both upright and spreading, to create usually an urn-shaped plant. The shape can be reasonably modified by pruning after flowering. The dead flowers on young shrubs are best removed to prevent seeds being formed, so that the plant can reserve its energy for growth. The leaves are usually heart-shaped. When not flowering, the lilac looks rather dull, so it is best to position it in the background. Over the centuries, the original wild form that blossoms with lilac or white flowers, has been cultivated to produce many new varieties with a range of colours: from purple, carmine, and pink, to pure white. The cultivated varieties also have different fragrances and varying forms of flower plumes.

Syringa vulgaris 'Belle de Nancy'

Syringa vulgaris 'Charles Joly'

Syringa vulgaris 'Belle de Nancy'

Mauve buds on elongated panicles open to produce double lilac-pink coloured flowers that spread a fresh, fragrance of lilac. This abundant flowering cultivar has be valued for more than a hundred years.

Syringa vulgaris 'Charles Joly'

This lilac is an upright growing bushy tree that flowers profusely with relatively small panicles. The double, dark purplish flowers are moderately fragrant. The curling inwards of the fairly large petals permits the lighter reverse side to be seen.

Syringa vulgaris 'Decaisne'

This is one of the most profusely blooming lilacs, with substantial panicles, filled with large single flowers, that during their emergence are strikingly blue. This cultivar emits a strong lilac fragrance.

Syringa vulgaris 'Decaisne'

Syringa vulgaris 'G.J. Baardse'

The panicles of this lilac are so long and heavy that they can easily hang on top of each other. They are densely covered with mauve flowers and have a remarkable sweet lilac fragrance.

Syringa vulgaris 'G.J. Baardse'

Syringa vulgaris 'Katherine Havemeyer'

Syringa vulgaris 'Katherine Havemeyer'

A vigorously growing, low tree with abundant panicles of double flowers, that can sometimes smother the green leaves. The petals of the double flowers are lobed, and can be lilac to mauve. The fragrance is a mixture of spices and lilac.

Syringa vulgaris 'Mrs. Edward Harding'

Syringa vulgaris 'Mrs. Edward Harding'

A very desirable cultivar with mauve, double flowers in perky, upright conical panicles. The innermost petals curl inwards, giving them a blurred appearance. During blooming, the flowers change colour to mauve. Their aroma is unfortunately weak. This cultivar grows vigorously.

Syringa vulgaris 'Miss Ellen Willmott'

Syringa vulgaris 'Miss Ellen Willmott'

The light green buds produce white, double flowers with a mild, fresh fragrance. The large flowers completely fill the informal panicles. Blossoms from mid May to beginning of June.

Syringa vulgaris 'Olivier de Serres'

The double flowers of this early cultivar emerge lavender from pink buds.

The panicles are large and abundantly filled, making this variety one of the most favourite lilacs, even though the young shrubs flower poorly. Has a strong, fresh fragrance.

Syringa vulgaris 'Paul Deschanel'

The thin panicles with purple to lavender double flowers stand erect on this very upright-growing bushy tree. Moderately fragrant.

Syringa vulgaris 'Paul Deschanel'

Syringa vulgaris 'Olivier de Serres'

Syringa vulgaris 'Primrose'

This 'Primrose' cultivar was the first, in 1949, to produce yellow flowers. In reality, the yellow is closer to cream. The flowers are weakly, but unpleasantly scented. The shrub grows nicely compact and weeping.

Syringa vulgaris 'Ruhm von Horstenstein'

A vigorous growing, abundant blooming lilac with short, multi-stemmed panicles bearing single, lilac flowers. Strong lilac fragrance.

Syringa vulgaris 'Rustica'

This relatively unknown cultivar deserves greater consideration because of its densely flowering panicles. The flowers emerge as pink flowers from pink buds. During flowering, the

Syringa vulgaris 'Primrose'

Syringa vulgaris 'Ruhm von Horstenstein'

light pink centre becomes apparent. Lightly, but pleasantly fragrant.

Ulmus glabra 'Pendula'

Syringa vulgaris 'Sensation'

This lilac deserves its name, because of the very striking two-tone flowers. Each carmine flower is fringed in silver-white. The cultivar came into existence in 1938 in The Netherlands and with its unusual two colours has remain something of a quirk. Some branches bear wholly white flowers.
A disadvantage of this cultivar is its light but somewhat musty scent.

Ulmus

ELM

The number of elm trees has been significantly decimated in the last thirty years or so through Dutch elm disease. A fungus blocks up the conductive tissues of the tree which can then only die. The fungus is transmitted to the tree by the elm bark beetle which lays its eggs under the bark. To prevent the disease from spreading, infected trees must be removed as quickly as possible and then burned or have

the bark removed and then be soaked in water. Until the disease has been eradicated, there is little point in planting elms, except for those that are known to be resistant. There are quite a few elms that do have resistance to the disease, although none that are totally resistant.

The following cultivars are recommended as having little susceptibility to the disease: *Ulmus* 'Clusius' (available since 1983); *Ulmus* 'Columella' (so far wholly resistant, was a seedling from *U.* 'Plantijn' in 1967, and commercially available since 1989); *Ulmus* 'Dodoens'; *Ulmus* 'Lobel'; *Ulmus* 'Plantijn'; *Ulmus* 'Recerta'; *Ulmus* 'Regal'; *Ulmus* 'Sapporo Autumn Gold'; and *Ulmus x hollandica* 'Groeneveld'. Plant elms always sufficiently far enough apart so that their roots cannot come into contact with each other, because the fungal disease is also spread via root contact.

Ulmus glabra

Ulmus glabra 'Camperdownii'

The most commonly planted cultivars of *Ulmus glabra* are the low growing, weeping forms. These seem to have little susceptibility to Dutch elm disease (see *Ulmus* above).

Ulmus glabra 'Pendula' is a weeping elm. The branches grow horizontally with weeping extremities that give this elm its weeping appearance. The tree grows to 10m (33ft) tall. *Ulmus glabra* 'Camperdownii' is smaller, with

branches that form a cupola reaching right down to the ground.

Elms grow best in a sunny position or in partial shade. The roots grow deeply in moisture-retaining or drier soils, provided the water table is not too high, because the elm will then form shallow roots and be liable to blow over.

Ulmus x *hollandica* 'Wredei'

A golden yellow leaved variety of the *U. x hollandica* (see this species in chapter 2). This

Ulmus x *hollandica* 'Wredei'

cultivar grows slowly and extremely upright to a maximum height of 10m (33ft). The newly emerged foliage is bright yellow. In the course of the season, this intensity is reduced until the tree bears yellow-green leaves in autumn.

The leaves are closely packed on the vertical branches and are somewhat arched and crooked. This cultivar is reasonably resistant to Dutch elm disease (see *Ulmus*).

4. Deciduous shrubs
Shrubs that lose their leaves in winter

Acer palmatum

JAPANESE MAPLE

Different varieties of *Acer palmatum* in autumn

No other variety of maple is planted as widely as the Japanese maple. In Japan, this grows as a bushy tree to about 8m (26ft) tall but the cultivated varieties almost all grow as shrubs. These can spread out significantly.

This growth habit, the attractive leaves, and the intense autumn colouring make varieties of Acer palmatum, with their oriental character, among the most popular shrubs in the garden.

Acer palmatum 'Bloodgood'

Acer palmatum 'Bloodgood' (left) and *Acer palmatum* (right).

Left: *Weigela praecox* 'Floreal'

Varieties of *Acer palmatum* in autumn colourings

Leaves of *Acer palmatum*

The leaves of this maple retain the same deep burgundy colour, almost tending to aubergine, right through from spring until they fall. This popular variety is an ideal dark background for colourful plants, particularly as this shrub grows upright to about 5m (16ft 6in) tall.

Leaves of *Acer palmatum*

Acer palmatum 'Dissectum'

Acer palmatum 'Dissectum'

A large number of commercially cultivated varieties are available within the 'Dissectum' group. With the true 'Dissectum', the leaves emerge at first yellow-green, become vibrant green, and then turn golden yellow in autumn. These trees bush out widely and generally grow no taller than 3m (10ft) tall.

Acer palmatum 'Dissectum Flavescens'

Acer palmatum 'Dissectum Flavescens'

There are cultivated forms within the 'Dissectum' group that have extremely deeply lobed leaves, the lobes of which are themselves so deeply serrated that they have they appear to be drawn from wire. The leaves of 'Dissectum Flavescens' are yellow-green, and the become yellow-orange in autumn. The shrub often has a single stem and takes on a weeping form. The maximum height is 5m (16ft 6in) tall.

Acer palmatum 'Ogon-sarasa'

Leaves of Acer palmatum 'Ogon-sarasa'

The leaves emerge somewhat reddish in spring but turn bronze-green during the season. This shrub branches out well into an attractive size and shape for the garden. Maximum height 5m (16ft 6in) tall.

Acer palmatum 'Orange Dream'

This is a remarkable Japanese maple that grows more upright than the general forms in cultivation. It will eventually grow to 8m (26ft) tall but the shrub remains attractive lower down because of its foliage . These open yellow-orange in spring and turn gradually to yellow-green in summer, and then to yellow for autumn.

Acer palmatum 'Orangeola'

This is a relatively new variety. It forms a cupola shape about 2m (6ft 6in) tall with drooping branches. The leaves reveal that it is a member of the 'Dissectum' group. The leaves first emerge somewhat reddish in spring but quickly turn yellow-green. They remain on the tree in autumn for quite some time.

Acer palmatum 'Orange Dream'

Acer palmatum 'Ornatum'

Acer palmatum 'Orangeola'

Acer palmatum 'Ornatum'

This is probably the most widely planted cultivated variety of Japanese maple. It belongs to the 'Dissectum' group, and it is frequently sold as 'Dissectum Ornatum' or 'Dissectum Atropurpureum'. The deeply dissected and divided leaves emerge purple, but lose much of the red during the course of the summer, to appear dark green – especially in shaded positions. It is golden yellow in autumn.

This shrub can grow to 4m (13ft) tall and spreads out to 5m (16ft 6in), but because it grows slowly, this will take several decades to achieve.

Acer palmatum 'Tsumagaki'

Acer palmatum 'Tsumagaki'

With its height when mature of 2m (6ft 6in), this Japanese maple is ideal for smaller gardens. The leaves are wonderfully coloured – golden yellow-green with red margins. The leaf stems are also a remarkable red. This is a real eye-catcher, that is unfortunately rarely offered for sale.

Acer sieboldianum 'Sode-no-uchi'

Acer sieboldianum 'Sode-no-uchi'

Although *Acer sieboldianum* can grow as a tree up to 10m (33ft) tall, the cultivar 'Sode-no-uchi' remains a smaller shrub. This slow growing shrub eventually reaches 2m (6ft 6in) so that it is suitable for smaller gardens. The small leaves are yellow-green all summer and turn yellow in autumn.

Actinidia kolomikta

This plant, just like the climbing *hydrangeas* and *Pyracantha*, is best know as a climber. Away from a wall, *Actinidia kolomikta* will establish its normal form, which is as an open shrub with arching branches, that usually grows no higher than 5m (16ft 6in).
The leaves are variegated, particularly with

Actinidia kolomikta

male plants. Sometimes only the tip of the leaf is white, in other cases a half or more of the leaf may be white and pink is also possible – especially where the plant is in a sunny position. An alkaline soil increases the variegation of the leaves.
Female plants bear 2cm ($\frac{1}{2}$in) long edible fruits in the autumn: *A. kolomikta* is after all a close relative of the kiwi or Chinese gooseberry. There needs to be a male plant close by to provide pollen for fertilisation. Young plants can be destroyed by cats because they are crazy about the scent from this plant.

Aesculus parviflora

This relative of the horse chestnut stands out for its later flowering. The wire-like flowers only appear in July and August, in 20-30cm (8-12in) long clusters along the stems. Occasionally *Aesculus parviflora* may grow into a small tree of up to 5m (16ft 6in) tall but it usually forms a shrub. The plant spreads outwards through underground runners that form new suckers, making it much wider than it is tall, with the flowering clusters born on the tops of shoots.

Amelanchier rotundifolia

JUNEBERRY, SERVICE BERRY, SNOWY MESPILUS

By contrast with the other species of this genera that are included in the chapter on shorter trees, the only European *Amelanchier* is a shrub that does not grow taller than 3m (10ft).
Amelanchier rotundifolia grows principally in the mountains of central and southern Europe.

Flower clusters of *Aesculus parviflora*

Amelanchier rotundifolia 'Helvetia'

In May, when the oval leaves are already on this broad shrub, the clusters of white flowers open. Blue-black berries are born in autumn that are eaten by birds.

The most suitable variety for gardens is the compact dwarf form *Amelanchier rotundifolia* 'Helvetia', which grows to 1-2m (3ft 4in-6ft 6in).

Amorpha fruticosa

Leaves of *Amorpha fruticosa*

Ear-formed cluster of *Amorpha fruticosa*

Amorpha nana

taller and wider. In this case, the main attraction is the feathery foliage with its string of oval leaflets. Give this airy, open shrub plenty of room – it grows about 3m (10ft) tall and about 5m (16ft 6in) in diameter – and plant it in moisture-retaining soil.

Amorpha nana

Amorpha nana

Amorpha fruticosa

FALSE INDIGO

The colonists to North America discovered that they could create an indigo-type die from *Amorpha* shrubs and they named it "indigo". During flowering in the middle of summer (end of June to August) clusters filled with tiny, deep purple florets appear on the ends of the stems. The yellow pollen contrasts strongly with the dark colour of the flowers. To ensure abundant flowering, plant this shrub in a sunny position. In partial shade, it will grow

This close relative of the false indigo is more suitable for most gardens than *Amorpha fruticosa*. The shrub barely grows taller than 1m (3ft 3in) and it is generally more compact in form. It flowers abundantly in June to July with its ear-formed clusters that are about 10cm (4in) long. The plant is filled with many fragrant florets that are violet with mauve pollen. The fine leaves are feathered and consist of countless small leaflets. *Amorpha* varieties grow best in humus-rich sandy soil that retains moisture.

Aronia x *prunifolia*

CHOKEBERRY

Aronia x *prunifolia*

Flowers of *Aronia* x *prunifolia*

The chokeberry is relatively little known without reason. In May to June, its branches are decorated with small white flowers and red pollen. It betrays its relationship with the mountain ash or rowan. During the summer, the flowers turn into red to red-black berries of about 1cm (3/8in) diameter, that are eagerly eaten by birds. The leaves are firm, even slightly leathery , and they become fiery red in autumn. This bright autumn colouring is a property of many trees and shrubs that originate from the United States, such as the chokeberry. Plant this shrub in moisture-retaining soil that does warm up too much in the sun. There are no further special requirements, although the chokeberry does not thrive in alkaline soil. It grows to about 3m (10ft) tall.

Berberis thunbergii 'Atropurpurea'

BARBERRY

Berberis thunbergii 'Atropurpurea'

Twigs of *Berberis thunbergii* 'Atropurpurea'

Green-leaved *Berberis* are rarely seen in gardens. The preference is generally to plant coloured shrubs such as 'Atropurpurea', whose leaves appear red-purple and remain so through out the summer. This is followed in autumn by orange, bright red, and deep scarlet. The branches are filled in May with small yellow and red flowers, that during the summer change into elongated red berries of about 1cm (3/8in). These are readily eaten by birds. The barberry can be pruned heavily. It can be pruned to form an impenetrable hedge. It grows to about 2m (6ft 6in) high.

Berberis thunbergii 'Aurea'

BARBERRY

Berberis thunbergii 'Aurea'

The yellow/red flowers of *Berberis thunbergii* 'Red Pillar'

Berberis vulgaris

COMMON BARBERRY
The common barberry grows wild in many

Berberis vulgaris

The golden-yellow form of *Berberis* grows extremely slowly to about 1m (3ft 3in) high and it is therefore suitable for use as a hedge. Those who really appreciate golden yellow should plant this variety where it gets plenty of light. In such a position, the foliage will be golden yellow to lemon yellow, although do not place directly in the full sunlight because the leaves tend to wilt. When shaded, this variety attempts to improve the process of photo-synthesis by making its leaves greener. Personally I prefer the yellow-green that results from shaded positions.

The yellow flowers of *Berberis vulgaris*

Berberis thunbergii 'Red Pillar'

The leaves of 'Red Pillar' are reddish brown, combined with green. This variety of Berberis thunbergii grows more upright to about 1.5m (5ft) tall. The shrub has cheerful yellow and red flowers hanging from it in May. Before the leaves fall in autumn, they have a bright autumn colour.

parts of Europe, Asia, and North Africa. It grows on any type of soil. This shrub will eventually grow to 2m (6ft 6in) tall, but will spread much wider than this because of the horizontally growth of its older branches. The yellow flowers in May are succeeded in the autumn by bright red, elongated berries that provide the principal attraction of this shrub.

Buddleja alternifolia

Buddleja alternifolia

The long branches arch gently and are covered in June to July by tufts of lilac flowers that bloom the entire length of the stems.
The shrub will eventually grow to 3m (10ft) tall and 4m (13ft) wide. Leave sufficient room for this plant, because pruning spoils the natural form of the plant. If pruning becomes inevitable, do so immediately after flowering. Pruning in the spring, as is customary with *Buddelja davidii*, will cause a season without flowering, because this occurs on the previous season's growth.
Buddleja alternifolia is fully hardy and will grow in virtually any soil. It does prefer a well-drained alkaline soil and a sunny position.

Buddleja davidii

BUTTERFLY BUSH

Of all *Buddleja*, *B. davidii* most deserves the common name butterfly bush, because its flower plumes are like a magnet to the butterflies in a garden. The butterflies stick their long roll-out tongues into the tubular flowers to extract nectar. These flowers appear on the ends of side shoots in profusion between July and August. By removing the plumes after flowering (to prevent them forming seeds) the smaller plumes on the side shoots flower more lavishly. The butterfly bush can be easily grown in every soil type. Plant it in as sunny a position as possible, because it will then produce the maximum nectar and the greatest numbers of butterflies will be drawn to it. After the end of any hard frosts in February and March, all the branches can be cut back hard in spring to about 30cm (1ft) from the ground. The plant makes substantial new growth and will flower the same season on its new shoots. If the shrub is not cut back, it will remain thin and weedy, climbing to about 5m (16ft 6in) tall and flower less profusely than a bushy shrub. The plant can grow to 2-3m (6ft 6in-10ft) tall in one season. *Buddelja davidii* bears lilac to mauve florets with orange in the mouth of the flower. In China, there are white examples growing wild. The many cultivated varieties include white, pink-red, purple, or lilac.

Buddleja davidii 'Nanho Blue'

The flowering plumes of this butterfly bush grow on the ends of widely spreading, flimsy

Flowering plumes of *Buddleja davidii* 'Nanho Blue'

branches. The shrub rarely grows taller then 1.5m (5ft). This variety is derived by selection from cultivars of *Buddelja davidii* var. *nanhoensis*, that has significantly smaller leaves and shorter flowering clusters.

The florets of 'Nanho Blue' are bluish-purple, and each floret has an orange throat.

Buddleja 'Lochinch'

Flower plumes of *Buddleja* 'Lochinch'

The 'Lochinch' variety was first cultivated in 1959. It is a hybrid resulting from crossing the less hardy species *Buddelja fallowiana* with, it is presumed, a variety of *Buddleja davidii*,

The result is a fine, compact shrub of about 2m (6ft 6in) high. The young leaves at the end of the branches are woolly and white, giving the plant a distinctly grey-green appearance. The flowering plumes appear from June and they are quite short but a wonderful lilac blue with a mild fragrance.

Buddleja x *weyeriana*

Flower plumes of *Buddleja* x *weyeriana*

This variety is a hybrid resulting from crossing *Buddleja davidii* with *Buddleja globosa*. The second of these has yellow flowers which are borne in ball-like clusters on the branches. It is only sufficiently hardy for growing close to the sea. The hybrid can withstand frosts of minus 20°C. A number of excellent cultivated varieties have been bred from this hybrid, such as 'Sungold', with orange-yellow flowers that are partially clustered together but which also form spears on the tips of branches. If pruned back each year, the shrub grows to 3m (10ft) tall.

Callicarpa bodinieri var. *giraldii* 'Profusion'

Berries on *Callicarpa bodinieri* var. *giraldii* 'Profusion'

This shrub, with its long name, is mainly grown for its violet coloured fruits. These appear in September to October in dense clusters around the branches. At the same time, the leaves take on their attractive autumn colouring. The rest of the year, the shrub is somewhat dull.

Calycanthus fertilis var. *laevigatus*

ALLPICE

In spite of its exotic appearance, allspice is fully hardy. The dark red of the flowers does

Flowers of *Calycanthus fertilis* var. *laevigatus*

Caragana arborescens 'Pendula'

not catch the eye and they do not open more fully then shown in the illustration. They appear in May to July and smell of ripening fruit. Calycanthus grows into an open shrub of about 2m (6ft 6in) tall.

Calycanthus floridus

CAROLINA ALLSPICE, COMMON SWEETSHRUB, STRAWBERRY BUSH

Flowers of *Calycanthus floridus*

This allspice exudes a wonderfully delicious aroma of clove. The leaves and branches are both aromatic, The semi-double, dark red flowers that appear between May and June, have an unmistakable aroma of strawberries.

Caragana arborescens 'Pendula'

From its origins, 'Pendula' is a creeping variety of *Caragana arborescens*, but it is virtually always grafted onto a stem to form a low weeping tree, 1-2m (3ft 3in-6ft 6in) high.

Flowers of *Caragana arborescens* 'Pendula'

The drooping branches bear lovely light green leaves. The yellow, pea-like flowers appear in May to June and these subsequently produce berries.

The cultivated variety *C. a.* 'Walker' has elongated leaves but closely resembles the growth habit of 'Pendula'.

121

Caryopteris x *clandonensis*

Caryopteris x *clandonensis* 'Heavenly Blue'

Flower cluster of *Ceanothus* x *delilianus* 'Gloire de Versailles'

In August, when most trees and shrubs have finished flowering, *Caryopteris* bursts into bloom. The ends of its grey-green leaved shoots bear clusters of purple flowers. This shrub grows from a small base to reach about 1m (3ft 3in) high. In winter, the greater part of the growth dies back in most areas of Europe and the entire plant is only sufficiently hardy to be grown near the coast. In other areas, try to plant it in a sheltered position on a south-facing wall.

Ceanothus x *delilianus* 'Gloire de Versailles'

CALIFORNIAN LILAC

In areas where it freezes more than minus 10°C, few Californian lilacs will survive. The old cultivated variety 'Gloire de Versailles' is one of the strongest, withstanding minus 15°C. Regardless of this, plant should still be sited in a sheltered, warm position; then you will be able to enjoy its deep blue clusters of flowers

from the start of autumn through to October. The leaves fall in autumn from this 1m (3ft 3in) shrub.

Cephalanthus *occidentalis*

BUTTON BUSH

Few shrubs combine so well with perennials as *Cephalanthus*. The shrub eventually grows to 5m (16ft 6in) tall but it remains shorter than

Cephalanthus occidentalis

Flowers of *Chaenomeles*

frequently has thorns, these plants are wildly grown in public open spaces. In autumn, these low shrubs bear hard yellow fruits that have a wonderful fragrance, that can be eaten once cooked. Any pruning should be done immediately after flowering, because next year's flowering buds quickly start to form.

Chaenomeles x *superba*

Flowers of *Chaenomeles* x *superba* 'Fascination'

this for a long time. Shrubs of the variety *Cephalanthus accidentalis pubescens* do not exceed 2m (6ft 6in) tall.

The branches are fairly red, the large leaves are yellow-green, and light-yellow fragrant flowers bloom closely together, like 2cm ($^{1}/_{2}$in) wide buttons, during the summer months. Plant this shrub in wet ground in a sunny position, because in the wild in North America, it grows in sunny swamps.

Chaenomeles

JAPONICA, QUINCE

These old names are still often mistakenly used for this genus of deciduous shrubs. 'Japonica' merely means "from Japan" and can be applied to many plants and *Cydonia* is now the genus of true quinces. This "quince" begins to flower as early as March, often before the leaves emerge. The three species of *Chaenomeles* originate from China and Japan. There are many hybrids created between the three species, from which tens of cultivars have been selected. Because it grows without difficulty, seems impervious to air pollution, and it

Chaenomeles x *superba* 'Jet Trail'

This is a hybrid resulting from crossing *Chaenomeles japonica* and *Chaenomeles speciosa*, from which the majority of varieties in cultivation have been bred. The main flowering flush is in April with white, salmon pink, brick red, orange, or dark red blooms.

Chaenomeles x superba 'Fascination' has vigorously spreading branches that give the 1m (3ft 3in) tall shrub an oriental character. This is reinforced by the erect scarlet flowers that grow in tiny clumps along the stem. The fruits resemble small yellow apples.

Chaenomeles x superba 'Jet Trail' flowers very abundantly with white blooms along the whole length of the previous year's growth. The shrub becomes about 1m (3ft 3in) high.

Clerodendrum trichotomum

KANSENBOOM

This strong growing large shrub can become about 7m (23ft) tall but usually remain lower than this with bushy growth. The lengthy branches bear leaves that are 10-20cm (4-8in) long. The red bracts, from which 3cm (1½in) wide white flowers emerge, do not appear until July. In fine summers, these are succeeded by

Bladder-like pods and the flowers of Colutea x media 'Copper Beauty'

Clerodendrum trichotomum

blue berries between the swollen calyces.

This shrub is only recommended for areas with a definite maritime climate, where frosts below minus 15°C are unlikely. Plant it in a sheltered spot where it will get plenty of sun.

Colutea x media

BLADDER SENNA

The bladder senna has much to offer: delightful blue-green foliage, orange-brown butterfly flowers from June, which immediately develop into blown-up bladder-like pods. The shrub becomes 2-3m (6ft 6in-

10ft) tall and it grows extremely well in dry ground. It can withstand frosts to minus 20°C without problems. It is therefore a mystery why this beautiful plant is not more widely planted, particularly in coastal areas.

Colutea x media 'Copper Beauty' is the most rewarding cultivated variety, due to its long and abundant flowering, after which the red "bladders" decorate the shrub right through until later autumn.

Coriaria sinica

Coriaria sinica

After a severe winter, the frosted branches of *Coriaria sinica* will need to be cut back. The shrub will then make new growth, bushing out with about 5cm (2in) long divided leaves on either side of its arched branches. The dark berries are borne in the autumn. Those shrubs which are not frost damaged can grow to 2m (6ft 6in) tall and at least as wide.
One of the few *Coriaria* that is planted in gardens is *Coriaria terminalis* var. *xanthocarpa*,

Berries of *Coriaria sinica*

which is sufficiently hardy for a maritime climate. The red branches bear trusses of yellow berries in the autumn.

Cornus alba

RED-BARKED DOGWOOD

The white berries of *Cornus alba*

There is little to admire with the red-barked dogwood in summer. It forms a dense bush about 3m (10ft) high. The leaves are borne on the branches evenly spaced opposite each other and are about 7cm (2½in) long. The shrub makes an ideal windbreak. In autumn

Cornus alba 'Sibirica'

the modest flowers develop into white berries The red colouring of the bark of the branches can only be seen when the leaves fall. The red bark looks superb all winter long and is particularly red with certain of the cultivated varieties.

Cornus alba 'Sibirica' is one of the bright red bark examples with its almost coral red branches. By pruning in the spring, much of the older wood (that gradually loses the red colouring) is removed and the shrub can produce new wood for the coming winter.

Cornus mas

CORNELIAN CHERRY

The sweet smelling blossom of the cornelian cherry opens as early as February, before there are even any leaves on the shrub. The bees busy themselves collecting the abundant nectar to be had from the flowers on this tall and broad shrub which can grow to 5m (16ft 6in) tall. The leaves do not appear until April, when the flowers are finishing. In southern Europe, the flowers are followed during the summer by elongated, red berries. Once they

Cornus mas in autumn

Cornus mas

Leaves of *Cornus mas*

Cornus sanguinea

EUROPEAN COMMON DOGWOOD, RED CORNEL

Cornus sanguinea

are dark red and soft to the touch, they are ripe enough to eat. They taste like fresh, sharp cherries. These are followed in autumn by the spectacle of the yellow, orange, and dark red leaves, that remain until the autumn winds.
The cornelian cherry can be readily pruned, which is why it is often grown as a hedge, but in this case it will rarely blossom, because the buds are formed on the previous season's growth. *Cornus mas* 'Elegantissima' is a variegated leaved variety, the leaves of which have broad yellow margins. Some leaves can be completely pale yellow.

The European common dogwood, or red cornel, is a native plant in chalky soils but will grow when planted in neutral or even slightly acidic soils. The plant forms a dense bushy growth. The leaves are copious and therefore this is a popular choice for windbreaks. The plant has little ornamental value, with the exception of the red autumn leaves. The clusters of flowers which bloom in autumn have little of interest, except for their somewhat musty smell, that attracts a host of insects.

Corylopsis pauciflora

The leaves of this eastern Asia species looks very much like that of hazel *(Corylus)* but they are not related. *Corylopsis pauciflora* flowers from the end of February, before the leaves emerge. The pale yellow flowers smell of almonds. They are gathered in small bunches

Leaves of *Cornus mas* 'Elegantissima'

Corylopsis pauciflora

but there are so many of them that the branches are covered. This species is regarded as the most abundant flowering of the entire genus.

The shrub will eventually grow to 1.5-2m (5-6ft 6in) tall and it thrives in any normal, not too dry garden soil. The leaves turn yellow in autumn. If the plant is sited in a sheltered position, you will be able to enjoy the autumn leaves somewhat longer.

Corylopsis spicata

The second best known *Corylopsis* grows somewhat taller than the previous species. Trusses of yellow flowers hang down from the shrub in March to April.

They have a fresh, sweet fragrance. The leaves emerge from the buds all wrinkled, after the flowering is over.

They look like hazel leaves and change colour to yellow to orange in autumn before they fall. The 2m (6ft 6in) tall shrub grows best on acid soil in a sheltered position, but will tolerate other conditions.

Flowers of *Corylopsis spicata*

Corylus avellana

COBNUT, EUROPEAN HAZEL

Corylus avellana

The hazel blossoms early, in February, with long yellow catkins. These are the male flowers that scatter pollen to the wind. The wind carries the pollen to the very small but attractive female flowers on other shrubs. In the autumn, hazel or cob nuts ripen on bushes that are a few years old.

This shrub is a mass of fine foliage all summer long – the leaves are about 8cm (3½in) long. The branches grow thick and spread out horizontally, eventually reaching about 5m (16ft 6in) high. The hazel or cobnut can withstand substantial shade. It will grow in virtually any soil but prefers humus rich, alkaline soil.

Corylus avellana 'Contorta'

CORKSCREW HAZEL

Back in 1863, a very strange hazel was found in England. The branches had grown all twisted, and the leaves too grew rolled up into

Corylus avellana 'Contorta'

Catkins of *Corylus avellana* 'Contorta'

themselves. This odd-ball is less vigorous growing than the common hazel, but it can reach 4m (13ft) tall.

The attractions of this shrub are really restricted to the winter, when its strange growth is seen in silhouette, and in the early spring, when yellow catkins dangle from the branches.

The cultivated varieties are sold grafted onto common hazel rootstock. Straight branches often shoot from the base of the shrub. Cut these back as close to base as possible if you want to retain the twisted growth.

The corkscrew hazel will grow in any soil but does best in alkaline, humus-rich soil. It can withstand a great deal of shade.

Cotoneaster frigidus

The arching branches of *Cotoneaster frigidus* create an elegant form of shrub that can become 5m (16ft 6in) tall but which usually remains lower than this. In June, clusters of white flowers appear between the oval leaves that are green and soft to the touch.

Cotoneaster frigidus

Cotoneaster horizontalis 'Robusta'

The shrub is covered in autumn with light red berries that remain for much of the winter. In very mild winters, some of the leaves do not fall.

Cotoneaster horizontalis

The side shoots are arranged herring-bone fashion on the main branches which arch towards the ground and spread out to provide ground cover. They can be trained as fans against a wall. In June, the branches are completely covered with small, white to slightly red flowers that attract bees in their droves, which ensures the fruiting. The branches are festooned in autumn with orange-red berries. The leaves turn to a dazzling orange or red for autumn too. *Cotoneaster horizontalus* 'Robusta' is one of the most widely planted cultivated varieties. It can grow to 1.5m (5ft) tall against a wall and very much wider. The leaves turn fiery red in autumn and remain on the shrub. The berries are light red.

Cotoneaster racemiflorus

The white flowers in June combine beautifully with the grey-green foliage of *Cotoneaster racemiflorus*. The branches spread themselves

Flower of *Cotoneaster frigidus*

Cotoneaster racemiflorus

Branches of *Cotoneaster racemiflorus*

and bend low, especially in autumn, when they hang with red fruit. The shrub becomes not greater than 3m (10ft) wide and usually remains shorter than this. Although they originate from around the Mediterranean and further east into the south-west of Asia, they are quite hardy.

Cydonia oblonga

QUINCE

In May, the fruiting buds on the ends of the branches of the quince start to swell. The leaves have already emerged. The white or pale

Cydonia oblonga 'Leskovacz'

pink blossoms – about 5cm (2in) wide – burst at the end of May or early June. These are succeeded by wonderfully fragrant, yellow, pear-shaped fruits that are about 5-10cm (2-4in) long. These will only ripen in sheltered warm positions, but in Asia Minor and the countries surrounding the Mediterranean, they are among the most important fruits there are. They can only be eaten after they have been cooked and can be used in many dishes. Even when the fruits do not ripen fully, the quince is worth planting for its beauty – which includes its strong yellow colour in autumn. The shrub spreads outwards but remains below 2m (6ft 6in) for a long time, though it can eventually reach 5m (16ft 6in) tall. It then forms a skeletal, wide bushy tree. The quince likes humus-rich, moisture-retaining soil. It is ideal for planting next to water.

Cytisus purgans

BROOM

The young branches of this broom remain green and bear bright yellow, intensely

Cytisus purgans

fragrant flowers in May. After flowering in June, a coarse brush-like form remains of notched stems, with virtually no leaves. If this 1m (3ft 3in) tall shrub is not pruned after flowering each year, then after a few years the base of it will become woody and bald. Prune in plenty of time therefore, and only cut back green wood, because the older wood does not shoot so readily, if at all. This plant is fully hardy but it likes a warm spot, if necessary in poor, dry soil.

Cytisus scoparius

Cytisus scoparius

COMMON BROOM
This species grows wild throughout most of Europe. In gardens, we can encounter count-less cultivated varieties from the *Scoparius* group. The yellow flowering varieties in particular have the most overwhelming fragrance when they are blooming. Do not, therefore, plant the strong, sweetly aromatic broom too close to your patio. Varieties with other colours: pink, carmine, dark red, and brown, have been cultivated by crossing with, in the main, *Cytisus multiflorus*. There are also white, and light yellow varieties, and even two-coloured brooms. They have few demands in respect of soil but have a slight preference for warm and sunny, dry positions, and rather poor soil, that should not be very alkaline. Under these circumstances they will retain their beauty longer. Broom can grow 2m (6ft 6in) tall. For pruning, see *Cytisus purgans*.

Daphne mezereum

MEZEREON
The well-known mezereon of cottage gardens does not exceed 1m (3ft 3in) high, which is

Daphne mezereum 'Rubra'

why it is so popular for front gardens. This *Daphne* blooms with pink flowers in March and April. Mezereon smells overwhelmingly like lilac and it is a real eye-catcher, because it flowers on leafless branches. The dull, elongated leaves emerge after flowering. The bright red berries suddenly appear in summer. These are very poisonous.
Daphne mezereum grows wild throughout much of Europe, preferring rich, alkaline soil and partial shade. In cultivation in the garden, the shrub has few demands, but do not plant it in a dry soil. Many cultivated varieties have been bred from the original species, most of which have darker pink to red flowers, or even white. An attractive, dark pink variety, with large and strongly fragrant flowers, is *Daphne mezereum* 'Rubra'.

Decaisnea fargesii

The feathery leaves of this shrub are almost 1m (3ft 3in) long and they create a tropical impression. The shrub originates from the west of China. The leaves will be damaged by late

132

Decaisnea fargesii

Fruits of *Decaisnea fargesii*

frosts, causing the stricken branches to form new growth.

This shrub will initially grow to about 2m (6ft 6in) tall but very mature specimens can reach 5m (16ft 6in). Small yellow-green flowers blossom in May and June from which elongated fruits quickly form. These are initially yellow-green too but by autumn, they are blue-black and about 10cm (4in) long. The fruits remain on the tree long after the golden yellow autumn leaves have fallen. Plant this shrub in a position where it is sheltered from the wind, in rich, moisture-retaining soil. This plant is not suitable for planting too far from coasts where more severe frosts can be expected.

Deutzia

BRUIDSBLOEM

Deutzia are among the most popular shrubs for gardens. They generally do not grow taller than 2m (6ft 6in) and flower profusely in June with white or pink flowers, that also smell wonderful. The sixty natural species originate mainly from eastern Asia. Most of them can only be differentiated by an expert using a microscope. The cultivated varieties are mainly planted in gardens. The majority of these were bred between 1880 and 1920 in France. Deutzia thrive best in moisture-retaining, rich soil, but they are not too fussy about how you treat them. Pruning becomes necessary after a few years. Cut back a few of the oldest stems right to the ground after flowering. The stimulates the shrub to form new shoots.

Deutzia gracilis 'Aurea'

Deutzia gracilis

BRUIDSBLOEM

From late May until early July, the approximately 1m (3ft 3in) long branches of *Deutzia gracilis* will be festooned with white flowers. The branches of this Japanese species bow their heads gracefully. Late frosts can damage the buds so that they produce only small flowers or the flowers do not open at all – the normal ones are about 2cm ($^{1}/_{2}$in) in diameter. *Deutzia gracilis* 'Aurea' has yellow-green foliage.

Flowers of *Deutzia* x *magnifica* 'Nancy'

Deutzia x magnifica

This is one of the many hybrids that originate from the French grower Lemoine of Nancy. He crossed *Deutzia scabra* with *Deutzia vilmorianiae,* resulting in dense, vigorously growing shrubs, which grow as tall as 3m (10ft) and bear double, white flowers in June to July. The cultivar *Deutzia x magnifica* 'Nancy' is a real eye-opener because of the large double flowers of white, that open fully to completely cover the tips of the branches.

Deutzia parviflora

Deutzia parviflora

The botanical name of this *Deutzia* indicates that the flowers are relatively small – they are slightly more than 1cm (3/8in) wide. The flowers grace the ends of the attractive branches in June. The shrub remains small at about 1m (3ft 3in). It is fully hardy, yet it is rarely offered for sale.

Deutzia x rosea

At the end of the nineteenth century, the French grower, Lemoine, crossed Deutzia gracilis with Deutzia purpurascens. The hybrid varieties that originate from this union

Deutzia x rosea 'Campanulata'

are among the most beautiful Deutzia plants to be found in any garden. *Deutzia x rosea* 'Campanulata' bears clusters of bell-shaped flowers that are about 2cm (1/2in) wide. The true charm of this at least 1m (3ft 3in) tall shrub comes from the combination of the white petals of the corolla with the suffused red of the calyx and stems. *Deutzia x rosea* 'Grandiflora' bears flowers with even more red in them than 'Campanulata'. The outside of the corolla is pink-red and the insides are more or less white. The shrub grows to about 1.5m (5ft) high. The flowers are about 3cm (1 1/2in) wide.

Deutzia x rosea 'Grandiflora'

Deutzia scabra

Deutzia scabra is one of the more rugged species of Deutzia. The branches have many side shoots and they grow robustly upright to reach about 2m (6ft 6in). It is perhaps the strongest *Deutzia,* and its flower buds are not troubled by frosts. The flowers open in mid June and continue well into July. *Deutzia scabra* 'Macropetala' has unusually long flower petals of 1.5cm ($1/2$in). These are white and they stand out against the dark green leaves, that are about 14cm ($5^1/2$in) long. This variety is rarely offered for sale.

Deutzia scabra 'Pride of Rochester' is the most popular cultivar. The double, white flowers, that can sometimes be flecked with pale pink on the outside, are borne in dense clusters on panicles.

Deutzia taiwanensis

This *Deutzia* grows as a 2m (6ft 6in) high shrub in the mountains of Taiwan. In Northwest Europe, this shrub is not hardy. Continuing temperatures below minus 15°C will cause frost damage. The plant has slender white flowers in plumes on the end of the branches in June.

Deutzia scabra 'Pride of Rochester'

Deutzia taiwanensis

Deutzia scabra 'Macropetala'

Flowers of *Diervilla sessifolia*

Diervilla sessifolia

Diervilla sessifolia

The leaves of this shrub are directly attached to the branches without stems (*sessifolia*), in a similar manner as Weigela. Green-yellow flowers are borne on the ends of the stems from June through to August. The shrub can be heavily cut back in the spring, because the flowers are formed on the new grown wood. This fully hardy plant originates from the United States and it becomes a little more than 1m (3ft 3in) tall and at least twice as wide.

Dipelta ventricosa

The tubular flowers of Dipelta smell wonderful. The 3cm (1½in) long flowers bloom in June to August. They are mauve on their outsides and white with yellow ochre inside. The shrub originates from the west of China where it can become 5m (16ft 6in) tall but it usually does not exceed 2m (6ft 6in). Pruning to keep the plant from becoming over mature can be done immediately after flowering by cutting several old branches right back to the base of the shrub.

Dipelta ventricosa

Flowers of *Dipelta ventricosa*

Elaeagnus multiflora

OLEASTER

Elaeagnus multiflora

Flowers of *Elaeagnus multiflora*

The long branches of this oleaster are festooned with bunches of flowers in April and May. They are butter yellow and they have a wonderful sweet fragrance that also attracts the bees. During summer, russet fruits replace the flowers. The young shoots of this shrub are covered in dark brown scales. The leaves are grey-green. The entire shrub does not become taller than 3m (10ft), but it becomes extremely broad.

Elaeagnus umbellata

Elaeagnus umbellata

This open shrub becomes 4m (13ft) tall and wide. The spreading branches bear thorns and, in summer, they carry extremely long, soft, and supple leaves for an oleaster. Clusters of two to three small flowers, that have little ornamental value, emerge at the nodes. It looks at its best beside water and grows preferably in wet soil.

Elaeagnus umbellata

Flowers of *Elaeagnus umbellata*

Enkianthus campanulatus

Enkianthus campanulatus

In clearings in the mountainous forests of Japan, grow tall shrubs with flowers that display an affinity with our bilberry. The flowers hang in clumps on wiry flower stems that emanate from the nodes of the newly emerged leaves. The creamy bells with pink stripes are almost 1cm (³/8in) wide. The leaves turn a fantastic red in autumn.

Enkianthus campanulatus usually grows to between 1-3m (3ft 3in-10ft) tall, depending upon its position. In a sunny, sheltered position, in rich, moisture-retaining soil, it will grow vigorously and healthily. It cannot tolerate an alkaline soil, and is sufficiently hardy to withstand frosts down to minus 20°C.

Euonymus alatus

KARDINAALSMUTS

The appendix alatus means "winged" and this refers to the branches of this bushy shrub, that can grow to 2m (6ft 6in) high with a similar spread. The wings in question are cork

Cork wings on *Eunonymus alatus*

"wings" that form on the twigs. There are usually four per twig. These are hidden in summer behind ovate leaves, that turn a magnificent red in autumn but then fall soon after. The greenish yellow flowers that appear in May to June do not catch the eye. This shrub grows in virtually any soil, in a sunny position or partial shade.

Euonymus alatus 'Compactus'

Euonymus alatus 'Compactus'

The low, broadly spreading growth of *Euonymus alatus* is further reinforced with this cultivar. The shrub does not exceed 1m (3ft 3in) high, but can spread to 3m (10ft). There are virtually no other differences. The leaves turn an even deeper red in autumn.

Euonymus europaeus 'Fructococcineus'

SPINDLE

Wood from the wild spindle was used for making spindles for spinning. It is also widely used throughout Europe in hedges and for windbreaks because of its rapid, dense growth

Fruits of *Euonymus europaeus* 'Fructococcineus'

– to about 5m (16ft 6in) high. The branches are noticeably green, slightly rectangular in section and have cork wings. Most people will fail to notice the summer flowering but the brilliant red fruits in late summer and autumn certainly catch the eye. The fruits somewhat resemble a cardinal's mitre and when they open, they reveal seeds contained in vivid orange skin that is very digestible for birds. This shrub can suffer from the voracious appetite of the caterpillars of ermine moths but they recover fully in later summer. The fruits of the 'Fructococcineus' cultivar are extremely brilliant red.

Euonymus phellomanus

Euonymus phellomanus

A fine type but with unpleasantly scented fruits. In late summer red fruits appear containing seeds packed in red membranes. The twigs bear cork "wings" and dark green ovate leaves about 10cm (4in) long. The shrub will eventually grow to about 5m (16ft 6in) tall.

Euonymus planipes

Euonymus planipes

Because of its abundance of fruit and magnificent autumn colour, this is one of the most rewarding species of *Euonymus*. The shrub will become about 5m (16ft 6in) tall and wide. The greenish flowers burst from red buds. Shrubs in gardens under the name *Euonymus sachalinensis* are in reality *E. planipes* with green flowers from red buds. The true *E. sachalinensis* has both red buds and flowers.

Exochorda x macrantha

Flowers of *Exochorda* x *macrantha* 'The Bride'

The branches of this hybrid initially grow upright but arch over increasingly as they become older. By this means a rounded shrub is formed, about 3m (10ft) high. The parents for this hybrid were *Exochorda korolkowi* and *Exochorda racemosa*. Both species originate from Asia and bear pure white flowers about 3cm (1½in) in diameter. The

Exochorda x *macrantha* 'The Bride'

hybrid flowers like them in May with large white blooms. *Exochorda x macrantha* 'The Bride' is the most rewarding variety for the garden because of its exceptionally abundant flowering. This shrub forms a cupola of arched branches with light-green leaves about 1.5m (5ft) tall, that is festooned in May with an overwhelmingly display of flowers. It is suitable for any soil and is fully hardy, but prefers to be placed in the full sun.

Forsythia x *intermedia*

It is impossible not to see *Forsythia* in April. Its branches are a mass of yellow flowers, that with daffodils, complete the spring picture. Yet I feel that this 2-3m (6ft 6in-10ft) high shrub is planted too widely. Outside its flowering period, Forsythia is an exceptionally dull shrub. The branches grow at first bolt upright before then arching over. The leaves are light green and darken during the summer.

Forsythia can be pruned but this must be done immediately after flowering or the following year's flowers will be poorer or lost completely.

Forsythia x *intermedia*

Forsythia x *intermedia*

Forsythia x intermedia 'Densiflora'

Flowers of *Forsythia* x *intermedia* 'Densiflora'

Forsythia x intermedia was first bred in 1978 by crossing *Forsythia suspensa* and *F. viridissima*. Many cultivars were quickly selected from this hybrid that appear widely in our gardens. *F. x i.* 'Spectablis' is the most widely cultivated variety and it does indeed flower spectacularly. There are often five or six petals per flower instead of the more usual four. The flowers of 'Densiflora' are relatively large at 3.5cm (1¹/₂in) but they appear less abundantly than 'Spectablis'.

Fothergilla gardenii

WITCH ALDER
This low-growing shrub from eastern parts of the United States deserves to be more widely planted. It is mainly to be seen in arboretums, although it will grow extremely well in open, sandy and peaty soils in which the branches of this more or less creeping shrub can spread

Fothergilla gardenii

Autumn leaves of *Fothergilla gardenii*

out. It grows to about 80cm (31¹/₂in) high. In April there are white flowers and their fragrance to enjoy. These consist of clusters of stamens. The leaves emerge after the flowers, and these are brilliant red in autumn.

Fothergilla major syn. *F. monticola*

Fothergilla major grows as a broad shrub that does not become taller than 3m (10ft). The

Fothergilla major

141

Flowers of *Fothergilla major*

Halimodendron halodendron

flowers in spring have a wonderful fragrance. They consist solely of clusters of stamens that form a ball shaped "flower". The autumn colouring with this species is also a major bonus. The leaves conjure up a palette from egg-yolk yellow, through pink-red, orange, or deep red. *Fothergilla* prefers shelter, in open, sandy or peaty soils, and it deserves to be more widely planted in gardens.

Halimodendron halodendron

SALT TREE

The branches of *Halimodendron* droop under the weight of the flower clusters in June and

Halimodendron halodendron

July. The fragrant mauve flowers, together with the fine, feathered leaves, provide the attraction of this 1.5m (5ft) high shrub. It is often grafted onto rootstock of other genera that bear pea-like flowers: *Caragana* or *Laburnum*. The roots are very susceptible to rot, particularly in wet winters.

Plant this inhabitant of the dry salt flats of Siberia and Central Asia in a sunny position on poor, dry, sandy soil. The plant can tolerate salt and it is therefore ideal for gardens on the coast.

Hamamelis

WITCH HAZEL

In the middle of winter, witch hazel manages to conjure up flowers on its bare branches. The ribbon-like flowers hang limply during severe frosts but then straighten themselves and continue flowering. The flowers have a wonderful fragrance. Apart from the autumn-flowering witch hazels, they begin to flower in mid December. Each of the cultivars flower for about one month, but because there are both early and late varieties, flowers can be enjoyed as late as March from later varieties such as 'Adios'. The leaves resemble those of hazel *(Corylus)*.

There are four species of witch hazel that grow wild: two from the United States, one from China, and one from Japan. The American species *H. virginiana* flowers in the autumn,

Hamamelis mollis

Hamamelis x intermedia

Hamamelis x intermedia

Coloured leaves of Hamamelis x intermedia

and the other American sort *H. vernalis* is a winter flowering species, that is deliciously fragrant. The best known witch hazel is undoubtedly *H. mollis,* with its clear yellow flowers. The petals of *H. japonica* closely resemble *H. mollis,* but they have a more crumpled appearance. The two Asian species have been crossed to form the hybrid *Hamamelis x intermedia.* As the botanical name suggests, the hybrid is literally "a cross between the two". They can be very variable, however, and through careful cultivation, numerous cultivars have eventually been selected that provide yellow, orange, or red flowers. These are the most rewarding witch hazels for the garden.

Care

Witch hazels grow by preference in moist soil, although *Hamamelis mollis, H. japonica,* and the hybrid *H. x intermedia* have a reasonable resistance to drought. These shrubs also prefer a slightly acidic soil, so that normal garden soil is fine. They cannot though withstand lime-rich soils. Bear in mind that the small flowering plant that you buy will in about twenty years grow into a shrub several meters (6-10ft) tall and about 5m (16ft 6in) in diameter. For plants that are going to be allowed to mature over fifty years, reserve a circle of about 10m (33ft). It is possible to prune after flowering but it is not advisable because the wounds do not heal readily and the natural grace of the shrub will be lost. Many witch hazels are grafted onto *H. virginiana.* The root stock can sometimes send out suckers that can be identified by their different foliage. Break or pull such a sucker off the stem of the root stock, whether it is above or below ground.

Many cultivars resulted from the hybrid *Hamamelis x intermedia* that was bred by crossing *Hamamelis japonica* with *Hamamelis mollis.* These now form some of the most loved varieties of witch hazel.

The creation of hybrids and selection of cultivars requires considerable patience, since a shrub will only demonstrate its true characteristics after about twenty years. Only then can the flowering colour and form be regarded as stable and the autumn colouring judged. In spite of these hurdles, new varieties are regularly introduced.

Hamamelis x intermedia 'Jelena'

'Jelena' is one of the most loved witch hazels. About 1925, several seedlings were discovered

143

Hamamelis x *intermedia* 'Jelena'

Hamamelis x *intermedia* 'Ruby Glow' in autumn finery

Flowers of *Hamamelis* x *intermedia* 'Jelena'

Flowers of *Hamamelis* x *intermedia* 'Ruby Glow'

at Kalmhout in Belgium beneath *Hamamelis japonica* var. *flavopurpurascens*. They flowered in about 1950 with a truly notable copper red colouring. The then owner, Robert de Belder, named the fortuitous hybrid after his wife.

'Jelena' spreads its branches and grows several meters (6-10ft) high and eventually about 10m (33ft) across. The main flowering is in January. For care, see *Hamamelis*.

Hamamelis x *intermedia* 'Ruby Glow'

The leaves of most varieties of *Hamamelis x intermedia* have wonderful autumn colours. Those of 'Ruby Glow' change in September from green to orange, and finally to yellow. In January the bare branches are filled with red flowers. The flowers wilt during frosts but once there is a thaw, they immediately perk up.

This shrub grows quite tall for a witch hazel, reaching 4m (13ft) at a fairly young age. For care, see *Hamamelis*.

The fruit of *Hamamelis* x *intermedia* 'Ruby Glow'

Hamamelis x *intermedia* 'Vesna'

The withered leaves from the previous season still hang on the branches of 'Vesna' when the new flowers begin to shoot in January. This would normally be seen as a disadvantage in a cultivar, yet the rich brown of the leaves is an excellent foil for the orange petals of the flowers, that emerge from burgundy calyces. This shrub has a fairly upright growth habit. For care, see *Hamamelis*.

144

Flowering and withered leaf of *Hamamelis* x *intermedia* 'Vesna'

Hamamelis japonica

JAPANESE WITCH HAZEL

The clearest difference between the Japanese witch hazel and *H. mollis* is in the form of the yellow strip-shaped petals of the ribbon flowers. Those of *H. japonica* are 2cm (¹/₂in) long, but they are wavy, twisted and curled. Those of *H. mollis* are stretched out.

The Japanese witch hazel has several forms, in terms of its growth habit. The specimen illustrated spreads mainly horizontally, and

Hamamelis japonica

even when extremely mature, rarely exceeds 3m (10ft) tall. Other forms can reach 5m (16ft 6in). For care, see *Hamamelis*.

Hamamelis mollis

CHINESE WITCH HAZEL

Flowers of *Hamamelis mollis*

This is the best known species of witch hazel. The golden yellow flowers spring into life from the beginning of January, but since the plants offered for sale are invariably cultivars, the flowering period can vary from shrub to shrub. Some of them still flower in March.

Fruits of *Hamamelis mollis*

The flowers exude a wonderful fragrance. By contrast with the curled ribbons of *H. japonica*, the flowers of *H. mollis* stretch out the relatively wide ribbons of their petals. The young shoots of *H. mollis* are covered with a white "down". The leaves turn yellow in autumn. For care, see *Hamamelis*.

Hamamelis mollis 'Pallida'

Flowers of *Hamamelis mollis* 'Pallida'

The flowers of 'Pallida' cheer up the dark winter days. The bright yellow stands out against grey skies. This brilliant, popular witch hazel also looks good against a background of evergreen shrubs. It remains a manageable size for quite a long time but will eventually grow to a 10m (33ft) wide shrub. Although known as a cultivar of *H. mollis,* some suggest that it is really a hybrid that should be classified as *H. x intermedia*.

Hamamelis virginiana

VIRGINIAN WITCH HAZEL

Flowers of *Hamamelis virginiana*

Hamamelis virginiana

The Virginian witch hazel flowers in autumn. The yellow autumn leaves are usually still on the shrub, so that the delicate yellow flowers can easily be overlooked. The gentle, sweet fragrance of them will attract you to the flowers though. This shrub grows vigorously with an open habit, rather more outwards than upwards. This species is often used to provide the root stock for other witch hazels. It needs moister ground than the Asian species. For further care, see *Hamamelis*.

Hydrangea petiolaris syn. *H. anomala subsp. petiolaris*

CLIMBING HYDRANGEA

The climbing hydrangea fastens itself on to walls and fences and can climb really high. When it is not supported though, an entirely different style of shrub is created. Then it is more or less a ground cover plant, with bunches of upright shoots that climb over each other. In June to July, these approximately 50cm (20in) high green hillocks are decorated with flattened clusters of flowers, or umbels. The small, green, fertile flowers are surrounded by a ring of sterile, white flowers. These attract insects to the heart of the cluster. This shrub is fully hardy and it grows best in humus-rich soil.

Hydrangea arborescens 'Annabelle'

'Annabelle' is a highly regarded Hydrangea. The colour of the flowers is almost invariably described as white or cream, but this only applies to the fully open flowers. When they first open and after the peak, there is a delightful green haze to them.

Flowering umbels of *Hydrangea petiolaris*

Hydrangea arborescens 'Annabelle'

The flowers appear in June on new wood that has grown the same year. This makes it possible to cut this shrub back each year to the ground. The new growth then reaches up to about hip height. This species has globular flower clusters or umbels about 20cm (8in) across, the weight of which makes the stems

arch over. Without pruning, the shrub adopts a more natural shape with smaller, but more flower clusters. Such a shrub will eventually grow to about 1.5m (5ft) high. It is fully hardy.

Hydrangea aspera subsp. sargentiana

The young leaf stems and undersides of the leaves of this notable *Hydrangea* are closely covered with orange-brown hairs, rather like the kiwi fruit plant. The upper side of the dark green leaves feels velvety to the touch. Unfortunately it does not remain this fine.

Flowers can be anticipated on the ends of the branches of this rather unkempt looking shrub from July to September. The reddish blue fertile florets, in the centre, are surrounded by a ring of white, sterile ray-florets.

Plant this *Hydrangea* in a sheltered, and partially shaded position, so that it will remain attractive for longer. This *Hydrangea* can withstand frosts of down to minus 20°C.

Hydrangea aspera ssp. *sargentiana*

Hydrangea heteromalla

Hydrangea heteromalla

This species originates from a wide area ranging from the *Himalayas* to the eastern parts of China and has many local varieties. Depending upon its growing position, this shrub will grow to between 2-7m (6ft 6in-23ft) tall. The 10-20cm (4-8in) leaves have a beautiful autumn colour. This *Hydrangea* mainly flowers in July with white to yellow fertile flowers, surrounded by a circle of eye-catching white, marginal ray-florets. This species is less susceptible to drought than most other forms of *Hydrangea*.

Hydrangea heteromalla 'Bretschneideri'

The 'Bretschneideri' variety was found in the mountains near Peking. It does not vary greatly from *Hydrangea heteromalla*. This is a variety that has marginal ray-florets (see *H. macrophylla* below), surrounding the fertile central flowers. The main flowering is in July. This shrub remains small in its spread and grows to about 3m (10ft) high. The leaves are smaller – at about 12cm (4¹/₂in) and whiter on their undersides than other *H. heteromalla* varieties. Fine autumn colouring. Fairly tolerant of dry conditions.

Hydrangea macrophylla

HORTENSIA

The *Hydrangea* varieties that are known as hortensias, together with those known as lacecaps, are derived principally from *H. macrophylla* or hybrids originating in part

Hydrangea heteromalla 'Bretschneideri'

Hydrangea macrophylla (lacecap)

Hydrangea macrophylla, growing wild on the Azores

Cultivated *Hydrangea macrophylla*

from this species. Many cultivars exist in both forms. *Hortensias* are the large globular flower clusters that consist entirely of sterile florets. The lacecaps are the cultivars of this genus (and hybrids) that have the larger circle of sterile ray-florets surrounding the fertile but less conspicuous florets in the centre of the flower clusters. The colour of the flowers with many cultivated varieties is dependant upon the amount of aluminium available in the soil for absorption. This is principally determined by the degree of acidity of the soil. The hortensias that grow wild on the very acidic volcanic soil in the Azores produce blue flowers. If a cutting from such a plant was introduced to more alkaline soil (a higher pH) then the plant would produce pink flowers. For blue flowers with some cultivated varieties, a pH of lower than 6 is necessary. Other cultivated varieties maintain their colour, flowering white, or orange, or the new varieties which change colour during flowering. The dead flower clusters of all these hortensias and lacecaps become attractive in autumn and can be used in dried flower arrangements. *Hydrangea macrophylla* flowers from the end of May to July at tip of wood formed the previous season. Pruning them in spring can lead to a year without flowers. This can also happen with frosts below minus 15°C which can damage the new growth. Always plant hortensias and lacecaps in humus rich, moist soil, preferably where they are sheltered from cold winter winds.

Hydrangea paniculata

Hydrangea paniculata 'Floribunda'

The pointed flower clusters of *Hydrangea paniculata* easily extend to 20cm (8in). If the shrub is cut back hard to the ground in the spring, the clusters or plumes are so big that they bend the stems bearing them (see also *H. arborescens* 'Annabelle'). If cut back, the shrub grows to about 1m (3ft 3in) tall, otherwise, it will grow to 4m (13ft). This is a classic cottage garden plant. It flowers in July to August and can be planted in the full sun.

Hydrangea quercifolia

HORTENSIA

The foliage is the principal attraction of this *Hydrangea*. The person who named it was given to think of the leaves of an oak tree, but these leaves are far larger at 15-20cm (6-8in) long. The leaves turn orange to dark red in autumn. The flowers are born on stretched out, somewhat untidy clusters with many unattractive fertile florets and few white sterile florets, that turn red later. The shrub grows to between 1-2m (3ft 3in-6ft 6in) high and it prefers a sheltered position at the edge of a wood in humus rich, moist soil.

Hydrangea quercifolia 'Snow Queen'

Hydrangea quercifolia 'Snow Queen' is a cultivated variety with more white, sterile florets.

Indigofera kirilowii

INDIGO

Indigofera kirilowii

Indigofera tinctoria was one of the most sought after plants because it was the source of blue dye. *Indigofera kirilowi* is one of the few species from this genus that is hardy. The shrub grows to about 50-100cm (20in-3ft 3in) high with slender stems and attractive feathered leaves. The heavy clumps of flowers appear from June. This species can withstand minus 20°C, but will in these circumstances lose all vegetative growth above ground. This is not a problem, because the flowers are formed on the same season's new wood. Try to ensure as warm a position as possible in fairly dry soil.

Jasminum nudiflorum

WINTER JASMINE

The winter jasmine flowers right in the middle of winter with wonderfully fragrant, yellow

Jasminum nudiflorum

Flowers of *Jasminum nudiflorum*

flowers. The are particularly eye-catching because they appear on otherwise bare branches. This shrub can become 3m (10ft) tall and wide but it usually remains lower than this, because its slender green branches droop under their own weight in all directions. Because of this unkempt growth, winter jasmine is usually planted against a wall, where it can be supported. With support it can manage 4m(13ft) tall or better. Winter jasmine flowers most profusely when it is planted in a sheltered, sunny position but it will cope with less ideal positions and any type of soil. This plant is sufficiently hardy for western Europe. The leaves in summer triple lobes and are about 2cm (1/2in) long. When not pruned, the shrub maintains its carefree appearance. If pruning is necessary, do it immediately after flowering because the flowers emerge on wood that was formed the previous summer.

Kerria japonica

The supple green branches of *Kerria japonica* are covered in April and May with 3-5cm (1¹/2-2in) yellow flowers, that resemble buttercups.

Kerria japonica

Kerria japonica 'Pleniflora'

Flowers of *Kerria japonica* 'Pleniflora'

The branches bend in every direction, so that this carefree-looking shrub rarely exceeds 2m (6ft 6in) high. During winter, the leafless branches remain green. *Kerria japonica* can be pruned after flowering, preferably by cutting older branches back to the base of the shrub. *Kerria propagates* itself through underground suckers. *Kerria japonica* 'Pleniflora' is the most widely cultivated variety. It is hardier and more robust that the original parent but its double flowers do not have the same charm of the buttercup like flowers of *Kerria japonica*.

Kolkwitzia amabilis

Kolkwitzia amabilis

Flowers of *Kolkwitzia amabilis*

BEAUTY BUSH

Weigela is a shrub that is generally used in gardens. *Kolkwitzia* though, which is much like it, is rarely seen and that is a shame, for the latter of these two Chinese shrubs is in every respect more elegant. The branches grow in arches from the base and can be 3m (10ft) tall and just as wide. In winter, the peeling bark catches the eye. In May and June, the shrub is festooned with delicate flowers that are about

1cm (³/₈in) in diameter. The flowers are suffused pink through white outside, with white elsewhere, except the ochre speckles in their throat. The shrub is fully hardy and it will grow in almost any soil, preferring lime rich ground. The shrub is kept renewed by each year cutting some of the older branches back to the base.

Leycesteria formosa

Leycesteria formosa

The deep mauve berries that appear on *Leycesteria formosa* in autumn are highly appreciated by pheasants. For this reason, gamekeepers plant this species in Britain and France, where it has also become naturalised. This 2m (6ft 6in) high shrub originates from the Himalayas. The hollow stems die back fully in a cold winter but the plant grows back again from its base. The shrub is suitable for planting in either a sunny or partially shaded position, preferably in fertile and humus rich soil.

Ligustrum obtusifolium

PRIVET

Ligustrum obtusifolium

This Japanese species of privet is quite similar to our native *Ligustrum vulgare* or common privet. In contrast with that species, *obtusifolium* has stumpy or obtuse leaves and grows with more of a spreading habit. This privet will grow to about 2m (6ft 6in) tall. In the summer it has short plumes of 1cm (³/₈in) long white flowers on the ends of the branches. These have a marvellous fresh fragrance that attracts many insects and bees. In autumn it has grey-black berries.

Ligustrum vulgare

Ligustrum vulgare

Ligustrum vulgare 'Aureum'

COMMON PRIVET

The native privet may be described as common but it is not the privet so widely grown as a hedge. Allowed to grow naturally, this privet will reach 5m (16ft 6in) but this indestructible shrub is usually trimmed regularly in gardens to keep it much smaller. Unfortunately, its role as a hedge plant has been virtually taken over by *Ligustrum ovalifolium*. This is a rather dull plant that retains some of its leaves in a normal winter. *Ligustrum vulgare* is a more elegant alternative. All the leaves fall in winter, but if the hedge is kept well trimmed, the common privet will form a dense mass of branches which cannot be seen through even when bare. The common privet makes a far denser hedge than *L. ovalifolium*. There are variegated varieties of *Ligustrum vulgare*, just as there are of *L. ovalifolium*. *Ligustrum vulgare* 'Aureum' has golden yellow to golden-green leaves so that it is commonly known as golden privet.

Lonicera maackii

Lonicera maackii

HONEYSUCKLE

The leaves of this unusual shrub-form honeysuckle hang in double rows from the branches. They are about 8cm (3¹/₂in) long. In June, 2cm (¹/₂in) long, white flowers bloom from the leaf nodes. The flowers are wonderfully fragrant and they change yellow during blooming. This shrub has virtually only horizontal stems which help it to create a graceful appearance, even though it can mature to 4m (13ft) tall and across. Although this species has no special requirements, it is relatively unknown and rarely planted in gardens.

Lonicera tatarica

This is perhaps the best known shrub species of honeysuckle. It has white to dark pink, fra-

Lonicera tatarica

Lonicera tatarica 'Arnold Red'

gracefully to about 3m (10ft) high and as broad across and is densely covered with blue-green leaves. The flowers of *Lonicera tatarica* 'Morden Orange' are white with a red blush on the outside. The 'Orange' in the name indicates the orange-coloured berries that decorate the branches when flowering is ended.

Myrica gale

Lonicera tatarica 'Morden Orange'

Myrica gale

BOG MYRTLE, SWEET GALE

A line of bog myrtles, or perhaps their more apt common name, sweet gales, spreads a wonderful balsamic fragrance in summer. The bog myrtle is a native species that grows as its name implies in wetlands and beside the water. It grows to about 1m (3ft 3in) tall. Its branches are covered in spring with long golden brown catkins, and then in autumn with resin covered fruits. This resin can be harvested for use in candle-making. The resulting candles burn with a delightful aromatic fragrance. Plant bog myrtle in acidic, wet peaty or sandy soil , and preferably beside water. They look best in an open, natural-looking garden.

grant flowers in May to June. The variation in both colour and growth habit is enormous.

With the exception of certain dwarf varieties, this shrub grows to about 4m (13ft) across and just as tall. This is a very robust, fully hardy shrub that thrives in almost any soil. *Lonicera tatarica* 'Arnold Red' has the darkest red flowers of all cultivated varieties. It grows

Philadelphus coronarius

MOCK ORANGE

Philadelphus coronarius

The flowers of the mock orange are richly fragrant. The cream blooms are borne on the drooping branches of this 2-3m (6ft 6in-10ft) tall shrub in June. The more the shrub matures, the further over the branches hang. *Philadelphus coronarius* is a very hardy shrub that has no special requirements for its cultivation except regular pruning in the right manner. This is necessary because the natural growth habit leads to a less attractive shrub and also to reduced flowering. Cut back the oldest branches immediately after flowering as close to the ground as possible. There are many cultivated varieties of *Philadelphus coronarius* with widely differing appearances.

Philadelphus 'Virginal'

In addition to single flowered varieties of mock orange, there are also double flowered varieties.
With these all (or most) of the stamens form a calyx. The result catches the eye more but with

Philadelphus 'Virginal'

most varieties the cost is a less fragrant flower with the double flowered varieties.

The exception to this is 'Virginal'. The 5cm (2in) wide white bells are semi- to fully-double but their fragrance is wonderful. The shrub grows with a coarse form to about 3m (10ft) high and has dark green leaves. For care and planting see *Philadelphus coronarius*.

Physocarpus malvaceus

Of the ten species of *Physocarpus*, nine originate from the United States including this

Physocarpus malvaceus

Fruiting form of *Physocarpus malvaceus*

Physocarpus opulifolius 'Dart's Gold'

Physocarpus opulifolius 'Luteus'

one. The low shrub, that grows no taller than 2m (6ft 6in) can withstand dry ground and has no other special requirements.

After the yellow leaves have emerged – they change to green during summer – clusters of white flowers appear in June, followed by pink-red bladder-like fruits. The volume of flowers and fruits is less than with *Physocarpus opulifolius.*

Physocarpus opulifolius

NINE BARK

The white, tinged with pink, flowers of nine bark remind one of *Spiraea*. The two come from the same family of *Rosaceae*. After the flowers have ended, pink-red fruits appear like blown-up bladders. The clusters or corymbs are about 4cm (1½in) in diameter, which is considerably larger than those of *Physocarpus malvaceus*. This is why 3m (10ft) high *opulifolius* is planted more often, even though it needs more moisture than malvaceus. In all other respects, this is a trouble-free plant, that

is frequently seen in parks and public open spaces.

Physocarpus opulifolius 'Dart's Gold' remains golden yellow all summer. This variety does not grow taller than 1.5m (5ft) so that it is ideal for smaller gardens.

Physocarpus opulifolius 'Luteus' has yellow foliage in spring but this changes to green during the summer.

Poncirus trifoliata

Poncirus trifoliata

Flowers of *Poncirus trifoliata*

JAPANESE BITTER ORANGE

Citrus fruit trees are grafted to stems of *Poncirus*, because of its vigorous growth and hardiness. For although *Poncirus* is a close relative of the orange and lemon, it can withstand Northern European winters. Indeed this large shrub that grows about 4m (13ft) high is very attractive in winter, with its bare green branches filled with flower buds like impressive green thorns. The sweetly fragrant white blossoms open in May, at the same time as the new light-green foliage, that together make a fantastic picture. Later in summer, the triple leaflets of the leaves turn darker green. The shrub bears green, then orange extremely sour oranges, that are inedible but very fragrant. Plant this shrub in well drained and well worked, fertile soil, in a sunny position.

Potentilla fruticosa

The shrubs of Potentilla originate from an enormously wide range of the globe: from

Potentilla fruticosa (cultivar)

Potentilla fruticosa (cultivar)

China to Europe, and certainly not forgetting North America. This low shrub has white flowers. With such a wide range of distribution is not surprising that there is considerable diversity with many local varieties that once were described as separate species. Through crossing and selection, at least 130 cultivated varieties have been bred. Potentilla fruticosa grows to between 50-100cm (20-39in) high and has arched branches on which grass green leaves consisting of three to five leaflets appear

Potentilla fruticosa 'Abbotswood'

Potentilla fruticosa 'Goldstar'

prefer moist ground in the wild, the generally do well in sunny positions where the soil is relatively dry. They make deep roots. *Potentilla fruticosa* 'Abbotswood' is generally regarded as the best of the white-flowering varieties. This shrub grows to about 80cm (31$^{1}/_{2}$in) tall and spreads to about 1m (3ft 3in). It has blue-green leaves to set off against the white flowers. *Potentilla fruticosa* 'Goldstar' remains lower than 1m (3ft 3in) high and has spreading branches. This cultivar blooms abundantly with 4-5cm (1$^{1}/_{2}$-2in) wide golden-yellow flowers.

Prunus nipponica 'Brillant'

Prunus nipponica 'Brillant'

for summer. Some of the cultivated varieties have attractive grey-green leaves with silk-like hairs. The shrub flowers non-stop from June to September, with continuing fresh flowers made up of five petals. Depending upon the variety, the flowers vary through, white, pale yellow, golden yellow, orange, and copper, to red. All the cultivated varieties are easy to grow and make very rewarding garden plants. They usually grow to about 1m (3ft 3in) tall and slightly wider, so that when planting in line, they make a fine soft rounded hedge that does not need clipping. Although these plants

This Japanese flowering cherry grows very slowly as a shrub rather than as a tree, eventually reaching 5m (16ft 6in). The 3cm (1½in) flowers blossom in April to May, hanging from attractive flower stems. The flowers are white to pink.

Prunus pumila var. depressa

SAND CHERRY

Prunus pumila var. *depressa*

The sand cherry grows on the sandy banks of North America lakes as a shrub as tall as a man. In Europe, the main variety sold is the creeping form *depressa*. This always remains under 30cm (1ft) high providing ground cover that has lovely white flowers between the newly emerging leaves in April to May. The foliage is initially grey-green and it turns to a brilliant red in autumn. There are also little red fruits to provide further interest. Give this creeper a sunny spot on light, well broken soil.

Prunus spinosa

BLACKTHORN, SLOE

Prunus spinosa

Flowers of *Prunus spinosa*

The blackthorn or sloe is a native shrub with virtually black, extensively thorn-clad branches. The shrub flowers suddenly with very pretty white blossoms on the bare branches. The leaves emerge later. At the end of summer the sloes appear, that are avidly eaten by birds but which can be used to make preserves or sloe gin. The blackthorn is a perfect plant to create a windbreak, barrier, or hedge. It can grow to 5m (16ft 6in) tall but can easily be pruned to whatever form is required. Prune immediately after flowering so that the next season's flower buds can be formed during the summer. The blackthorn prefers chalky soil in a sunny position but this extremely tough specimen will cope will less ideal situations.

Rhododendron 'Amoena'

AZALEA

Rhododendron 'Amoena'

This is one of the best known cultivars from *Rhododendron kaempferi*. The shrub will eventually grow to 2m (6ft 6in) tall and it has double, mauve flowers in May. Suitable for partial shade in moisture-retaining chalk-free soil.

Rhododendron molle subsp. japonicum syn. *R. japonicum*

Rhododendron molle subsp. japonicum

JAPANESE AZALEA
This sub species of *Rhododendron molle* closely resembles that sort but is more frequently used for creating hybrids. This shrub reaches between 1-2m (3ft 3in-6ft 6in) high and it flowers in May, before the leaves emerge. The flowers have no scent and they are salmon pink with orange. Cultivated varieties can have entirely different colours, but mainly between yellow and red, frequently with some orange. The long leaves have an attractive autumn colour before they fall.

Rhododendron kaempferi

JAPANESE AZALEA
This Japanese azalea is semi-evergreen, retaining some leaves at the ends of its branches but it loses the majority of its leaves in Northern Europe. The shrubs is covered in May with funnel-shaped flowers, singly or in clusters, on the ends of the branches. The flowering colour varies through carmine, pink, and orange, which can be bleached out by the sun. Plant them therefore in partial shade, in moisture-retaining lime-free soil.
Rhododendron kaempferi (that is also offered for sale under the name *R. obtusum*), reaches 1-2m (3ft 3in-6ft 6in) when mature. There are many cultivars, such as *R.* 'Amoena'. The varieties are offered with an added name but also just as *R. kaempferi* with the addition of "cultivar".

Rhododendron luteum

AZALEA
The yellow flowers of this azalea have a sweet fragrance. The leaves only start to emerge

Rhododendron kaempferi (cv.)

Rhododendron luteum

during flowering in May to June. This shrub can become 3m (10ft) tall, but it usually remains somewhat lower. This species originates from eastern Europe and Turkey. It is fully hardy. Although there is little to improve with this species, *R. luteum* is widely crossed.

Rhododendron 'Mollis Azalea'

AZALEA

Rhododendron 'Mollis Azalea'

Rhododendron molle is just one of the ancestors of the deciduous garden azaleas. The hybrids have in turn been cross-bred, leading to an enormous number of cultivated varieties. These deciduous shrubs flower in the spring with full clusters on the ends of the branches. The colours vary widely: through white, yellow, and orange, to red and pink. At the same time as the flowers or sometimes slightly later, the elongated, lively green leaves emerge. These shrubs are usually about 1-2m (3ft 3in-6ft 6in) when mature.

To bring some order into the mushrooming growth in cultivated varieties, they have been gathered together into groups, such as 'Mollis Azalea' and the popular 'Knaphill-Exbury Azaleas'.

It is best to buy them from the grower in spring when they are flowering, to prevent surprises, since the colours shown on the labels often turn out to be from different varieties. Azaleas from the 'Mollis' group are robust and prefer partial shade, although they can withstand the full sun. Grows well in normal or acidic ground and even where relatively dry.

Rhododendron 'Silvester'

JAPANSE AZALEA

'Silvester' is one of the abundant flowering compact Japanese azaleas. It was bred from

Rhododendron 'Silvester'

two other cultivated forms, 'Aladdin' and 'Amoena' in 1963. The pink flowers with their dark pink hearts appear as early as April on this broad shrub, that grows slowly to about 1m (3ft 3in) high. For care, see *R. kaempferi*.

Rhododendron viscosum

SWAMP AZALEA

Rhododendron viscosum 'Roseum'

The leaves of the marsh azalea begin to change from green to plum colour, red, and bright orange, in September. The leaves fall in October, leaving the shrub bare until the following May. This is when the wonderfully aromatic flowers bloom. The external parts of the flowers are covered with sticky hairs (*viscosum* means viscous). The flowers are white, except for the cultivar *R. viscosum* 'Roseum', which is pink.

This azalea originates from the swamps in the eastern parts of the United States and it thrives best on very wet, acidic soil. It will eventually grow to 2m (6ft 6in) and is fully hardy.

Ribes odoratum

BUFFALO CURRANT

Ribes odoratum

The aromatic yellow flowers of the "scented flowering currant" appear in April to May. The wonderful fragrance they spread has a hint of clove. The deeply lobed leaves turn a lovely yellow, orange, and dark red in autumn. This is a rewarding shrub for the garden that thrives in almost any soil that is not too dry. It can withstand shade. The yellow alpine currant, *Ribes aureum*, closely resembles *R. odoratum* and it is regularly confused with it. The difference is in the hairless young twigs of the true *R. aureum* and the suffusion of orange in its flowers. This species is also less strongly aromatic. Both species bear dark violet, pea-sized berries that taste very sour, and both species also have cultivated varieties with orange and yellow berries.

Ribes sanguineum

FLOWERING CURRANT

Ribes sanguineum (cultivar)

The flowers appear on the red flowering currant as early as April. Depending upon the cultivated variety, they are white, pale pink, pink, or red. Very gradually during the summer, the inedible blue-black berries are formed, usually with a white bloom on them. This shrub grows in any garden soil to a height of about 2m (6ft 6in).

Rosa

ROSE

Roses are such a major part of any garden that it is difficult to think of them as shrubs. Yet this is their origin throughout much of the northern hemisphere, including the United States, Europe, and Asia. This vast area has a wide range of growing conditions and yet there is general advice concerning the roses that are cultivated in Europe. They prefer an open and airy position, in well-worked, nutrient- and lime-rich soil. Roses will also do reasonably well on sandy soils, though are less successful on peat soil. They cannot cope with standing water around their roots. A few of the thousands of cultivated varieties of rose are given here. These are used as examples for their group.

Rosa

MINIATURE ROSE

Miniature roses have known periods of great popularity, followed by times when they have almost disappeared from sight. With their small flowers and bush height of 25-50cm (10-20in) they are really only suitable for small gardens, except when planted in large groups together. They are also sold as house plants in pots but will need planting out in the fresh air after a time, to revive them. Even outdoors, most of the varieties are susceptible to disease. The origins of the miniature roses is not certain. .It is possible that they originate from *Rosa chinensis*, that was cultivated long ago in China as miniature roses.

Rosa 'Baby Carnaval'

MINIATURE ROSE

This small rose has multi-coloured flowers, containing yellow, salmon pink, plain pink, and carmine. The bush grows to between 40-

Rosa 'Baby Carnaval' (below) with *Rosa* 'Excelsa' (standard)

50cm (16-20in) high and it flowers for a long time with slightly fragrant blooms. 'Baby Carnaval' arose at the beginning of the 1950s by cross-breeding *Rosa* 'Peon' (also known as 'Tom Thumb') with the floribunda rose 'Masquerade'.

Rosa 'Bobbie James'

This is an excellent rose for great effect. Provided the shoots are well supported, this rose can reach 9m (30ft) high and cover almost

Rosa 'Bobbie James'

as great a spread. It is therefore perfect for covering an ugly wall and ideal for climbing up a tree. From about the end of June, its branches are festooned for about three weeks with small, white heavily scented flowers with a delightful fragrance. The yellow stamens can clearly be seen in the semi-double flowers. The shrub bears masses of orange-red hips in autumn. The vigorous 'Bobbie James' is relatively resistant to disease.

Rosa 'Celestial'

Rosa 'Celestial'

The old garden roses have become popular again, in part due to the work of David Austin (see *Rosa* 'Leander'. Unfortunately many of the old garden roses are susceptible to disease. This is less the case with the alba varieties that combine resistance with large, often double-bloomed flowers in pastel shades. What is more, they have wonderful fragrances. 'Celestial' is an alba rose. The shrub grows to head height with blue-green foliage, and it has strongly scented, pale pink, double flowers. The flowering is short-lived, mainly in July. This rose is perfectly for a romantic garden, even in partial shade, and it combines well with clematis.

Rosa 'Excelsa'

This climbing "rambler" (see *Rosa* 'Paul's Himalayan Musk'), grows to about 5m (16ft 6in) high. *Rosa* 'Excelsa' is mainly cultivated as a standard, whereby a graft is made about 1m (3ft 3in) up the stem of the rootstock (see grafting in chapter 1). This makes it possible to under plant with other roses. The branches of 'Excelsa' hang down in "weeping form", and in July, they are covered with small double,

carmine flowers. After flowering, the young growth and dark green leaves are unfortunately often infected with mildew.

Rosa 'Francis E. Lester'

Rosa 'Francis E. Lester'

Rosa 'Francis E. Lester'

The flowers of this "rambler" (see *Rosa* 'Paul's Himalayan Musk') emerge like apple blossom.

The pink buds produce pale pink flowers that quickly change white. The flowers are delightfully aromatic. In autumn, this rose has countless orange hips. This strong grower will reach about 5m (16ft 6in) high and almost as broad across. By training and pruning, it lends itself well to forming rose arches, as a hedge, or for use with a pergola. It is relatively resistant to disease. 'Francis E. Lester' was a cultivar from the musk rose hybrid 'Kathleen'.

Rosa 'Havaps' syn. R. 'Poker'

Rosa 'Havaps'

Rosa 'Havaps' is a hybrid tea rose (see *Rosa* 'Macgaura') and is somewhat better known under the name *R.* 'Poker'. The hybrid tea roses are renowned for their susceptibility to disease but 'Havaps' is one of the newer generation with which the rose breeders have taken disease resistance into account. The flowers are big and broad, double, and pink. This strong bush rose grows to about 1m (3ft 3in).

Rosa 'Westerland' syn R. Korwest'

Disrespectfully, one might describe the colour of the fragrant flowers of *Rosa* 'Westerland' as orange. The colour palette of these blooms, with yellow ochre, and shades of pink, is far more refined than that. The colour can be influenced by the weather.
R. 'Westerland' belongs to the floribunda group (see *Rosa* 'Iceberg') but it is neither a bush rose or a climber. The 1.8m (6ft) rose is really between the two. It is a hybrid resulting from crossing *R.* 'Friedrich Wörlein' with *R.* 'Circus', that was introduced in 1969.

Rosa 'Korlawe'

Rosa 'Leander'

Rosa 'Leander' is one of the English roses, also known as Austin roses, after David Austin, who has developed them since about 1950. He was fascinated with the old garden roses with their delicate colours and open flowers but they only flowered for a short time. By crossing them with more recently bred varieties, the remontant, or continuous-flowering, English roses were created. They are typified by their open habit, that is perfect for a romantic garden.
R. 'Leander' is one of the stronger specimens from this group. It resulted from a selection from the robust *Rosa* 'Charles Austin', which it closely resembles. The main flowering flush occurs in later summer, with a lengthy, but less abundant period of flowering to follow. The apricot-coloured flowers are large and fully-double. They have a fruity fragrance. This bush becomes about 2m (6ft 6in) tall but it can also be grown as a climber, when it can reach 4m (13ft).

Rosa 'Leander'

Rosa 'Macgaura'

Rosa 'Macgaura'

This modern rose from New Zealand, is better known by the name R. 'Penthouse'. It has large flowers with very tightly packed pink petals. This scented rose, flowers all summer on the end of sturdy stems. This bush spreads broadly and to about 90cm (35in).
R. 'Macgaura' belongs to the most popular

group, the hybrid tea roses. These resulted from crossing old tea roses with their cleft buds and repeated flowering, with the scented remontant roses that produce large flowers and are strong growers. Unfortunately many hybrid tea roses are susceptible to disease.

Rosa 'Handel'

Rosa 'Handel'

The climbing rose, 'Handel' was bred by crossing R. 'Columbine' with R. 'Heidelberg'. The foliage is dark green against which by contrast the flowers have a frivolous colour : silver-white, with pink margins and yellow to salmon on the underside of the petals. It is lightly scented. This is a climbing floribunda (see R. 'Iceberg'), that can reach 3m (10ft) and flowers all summer long.

Rosa 'Mozart'

This rose is one of the musk roses that originate from *Rosa* moschata, that are not known in the wild, but which have been cultivated in Europe since time immemorial, not least because of their delightful musky

Rosa 'Mozart'

fragrance of the flowers. The flowers of *R.* 'Mozart' are borne in laden racemes, or clusters, on stems that bend under their weight. The single flowers are carmine with an almost white centre. They flower continuously from mid summer to autumn. This rose grows to about 1m (3ft 3in) high and lends itself for use as a hedge. It will grow on poor soil and it is fairly resistant to disease.

Rosa 'New Dawn'

This rose combines a rare combination of first class characteristics, making it the most widely

Rosa 'New Dawn'

planted of all climbing roses. *R.* 'New Dawn' flowers throughout summer until late in autumn with pale pink to pearl white, beautiful cupped flowers

This rose has a delightful, sweet fragrance. This strong plant will even survive on a north-facing wall, although it will flower less abundantly, and it has little problem from disease. Despite this, it grows slowly, reaching about 3m (10ft), and through pruning can be trained to whatever form is required, including a non-climbing shrub rose.

Rosa 'Paul's Himalayan Musk'

Rosa 'Paul's Himalayan Musk'

The precise origins of this rose are not known. It is classified as a musk rose but it also belongs to the group of "ramblers". Ramblers are a type of climbing rose with the special characteristics of abundant flowering for a short period. For several weeks in succession, the rambler is hidden behind a mass of flowers that hang down in great profusion from the ends of its stems.
R. 'Paul's Himalayan Musk' is festooned in July with pale pink flowers, that taken on a tinge of lavender. This rampant climber can quickly take over a tree or pergola of at least 10m (33ft) high and can spread outwards at least as far.

Rosa 'Poulcov'

Rosa 'Kent' is a ground cover form, with creeping growth. The notion that this prevents any weeds from growing is unfortunately not true. Despite this, this rose is widely planted in

Rosa 'Poulcov'

parks and public open spaces. This particular creeping rose is not rampant. The rose spreads about 1m (3ft 3in) and is about 50cm (20in) high. It flowers with semi-double white flowers from June until the first hard frosts. This rose can be grown in a pot or container to provide winter interest. The variety was first bred in 1987, but grows so well and flowers so long that it has since become one of the most popular roses.

Rosa pteragonis 'Cantabrigiensis'

Rosa pteragonis 'Cantabrigiensis'

Rosa pteragonis 'Cantabrigiensis' arose from an accidental crossing of two botanical roses in the botanical gardens in Cambridge. The likely parents are *Rosa xanthina forma hugonis* and *Rosa sericea*. Both belong to the *Pimpinellifoliae* group, to which the native rose, *Rosa pimpinellafolia* (or burnet rose), belongs. This group of roses from Europe and eastern Asia have unusual, attractive fern-like leaves. 'Cantabrigensis' flowers rather early for a rose at the end of May, with open, pale yellow flowers that are succeeded in autumn by small, orange-red hips. The stems initially grow upright, to about 2m (6ft 6in) and then turn horizontal. They are heavily thorned and have light green foliage.

Rosa rubus

Rosa rubus

The flowers of *Rosa rubus* are large and pink, with centres filled with bunches of stamens. After flowering, green hips are formed about 3cm (1½in) in diameter. They change colour in September to orange-red and draw the various finches and similar birds, that eat the seeds in the hips.

This does not prevent the rose from reproducing itself. Underground runners ensure new, dense growth. This rose grows more or less upright to reach about 1.5m (5ft). There are numerous cultivated varieties available to purchase.

Rosa rugosa

HEDGEHOG ROSE, JAPANESE ROSE, RAMANAS ROSE

The hedgehog rose blooms from June with large pink flowers.

Rosa rugosa

The centre of the flower is a mass of stamens. After the flowers have ended, this rose has large green hips, about 3cm (1¹/₄in) in diameter. These turn red-orange in September and are eagerly sought out by the greenfinches and other finches and birds that eat the seeds.

This does not prevent the rose from propagating itself. Underground runners ensure constant spreading of the growth. *Rosa rugosa* grows virtually erect to about 1.5m (5ft). There are numerous cultivated varieties available from garden centres in a range of colours, including white.

Rosa 'Iceberg' syn. *R.* 'Schneewittchen'

Rosa 'Iceberg'

Rosa 'Iceberg' remains one of the most gratifying floribunda roses. This group was created from crossing the polyantha roses with the hybrid tea roses. Floribunda roses flower profusely and for a long time, with more than one flower per stem. Floribunda roses are also extremely hardy.

R. 'Iceberg', bred by crossing R. 'Robin Hood' with R. 'Virgo', was introduced in 1958. It is frequently described as the best white floribunda rose, due to its large semi-double flowers, that have a slightly blue tinge towards the end of the season. The shiny, green leaves on this about 1m (3ft 3in) high bush, are susceptible to rust but the plant usually continues to grow unhindered.

Rubus deliciosus

Rubus 'Benenden'

Flowers of *Rubus* 'Benenden'

This urn-form shrub grows with profuse stems and shoots in the south-western parts of the United States. It has large, white flowers in the summer, followed by purple-black berries. A close relative is *Rubus trilobus* from Mexico. A cultivated variety resulting from cross-breeding these two species is sold as R. 'Beneden'. There is virtually no difference between the three of these species and hybrid. All three of them grow as a 3m (10ft) high shrub that at first glance looks like a white rose. The flowers are 5cm (2in) in diameter. This shrub has arching stems that bear no thorns. It is fully hardy and suitable for virtually any soil.

Rubus odoratus

FLOWERING RASPBERRY

Rubus odoratus

Flowers of *Rubus odoratus*

A difficult spot in the garden with dry soil and partial shade will quickly be filled by the red-flowering raspberry, that grows to 3m (10ft) tall with arching stems and large green leaves. The wonderfully fragrant, pink-red flowers appear in June and July. Each flower is about 5cm (2in) in diameter. *Rubus odoratus* 'Albus' has white flowers. The orange-red fruits are not edible. The shrub makes root runners so that it constantly spreads wider.

Rubus spectabilis

SALMONBERRY

The salmonberry flowers in April to May with shaking pink-red flowers on a shrub that grows to 1-2m (3ft 3in-6ft 6in) tall. The species originates from the United States but is so content growing in north-west Europe that it has become one of those cultivated species that now grows wild. This, combined with its somewhat rampant growth, is the only disadvantage of the salmonberry.

Rubus spectabilis

Salix cinerea

GREY SALLOW

A tall, shrub-like willow at the water's edge, that bears catkins in April, is often the grey sallow, since this is the most common shrub species of willow. Confusion is possible with the 2m tall *Salix aurita*. These two species looked very much like each other and they cross with each other quite readily, leading to a wide range of natural hybrids. The true grey sallow grows to about 5m (16ft 6in) tall and has larger leaves, that are 10cm (4in) long and 4cm (1^1/$_2$in) wide, while *S. aurita* are merely 6cm (2^1/$_2$in) long by 3cm (1^1/$_2$in). Both species have two small supporting leaflets or "ears" on the leaf stem. These are both trouble-free plants in any wet soil.

Salix helvetica

Willows do not only grow in wet, low-lying terrain, they also grow in the mountains. *Salix helvetica* even grows above the tree line. This 1m (3ft 3in) tall mature shrub grows this

Salix cinerea

Salix helvetica

high up, in full sunlight. It protects itself from the full strength of the sun by coating its leaves with furry-white "down", that gives the shrub a grey appearance. This robust species must be planted in the full sun but otherwise will grow on any soil, even on drier ground.

Salix integra 'Hakuro-nishiki'

Salix integra 'Hakuro-nishiki'

Those who like variegated leaves will make a good choice with this Japanese cultivated willow. These are usually grown on a standard root stock. The leaves are arranged opposite each other on the leaf stems which is unusual for willows. This cultivated variety has elongated, light-green leaves that are unevenly stippled with white. There can also be a pale pink tinge to them. This easy to grow plant normally reaches 2m (6ft 6in) high when grafted as a standard. It remains most attractive when the branches are cut back each winter, or in other words is pollarded.

Sambucus nigra

Sambucus nigra

Berries of *Sambucus nigra*

Sambucus nigra 'Guincho Purple'

Sambucus nigra 'Aurea'

Sambucus nigra 'Laciniata'

COMMON ELDER

The elder is widely spread by birds that eat its berries in autumn and then pass the seeds in their droppings. This works well for the elder, because they thrive where there is ample nitrogen in the soil and so they therefore grow most readily in places where fertiliser has been used or the soil is rich in nitrogen for other reasons – such as a chicken run, where fertiliser has been spilled at the edges of fields, or where flood waters have deposited plenty of organic material. The coarse leaves, that consist of five to seven leaflets, emerge in April. The cream umbels of white flowers follow at the end of May with the distinctive elderflower scent. When these are not picked to make elderflower wine or some of the other delicacies that are possible with them, they turn into clusters of dark black berries. In addition to the deeply staining die, these contain the seed. Flocks of starlings, that have just started to migrate, often descend in

172

multitudes upon the elder and get plastered on the berries because of the alcohol and yeasts formed by the over-ripe fruit.

The elder only grows for a few decades before it stops flowering and declines. The broad shrub has then reached about 5m (16f 6in), except in windy areas, where it remains lower. There are attractive cultivated varieties for gardens:

Sambucus nigra 'Aurea' has golden-yellow foliage. *Sambucus nigra* 'Auromarginata' has irregular, golden-yellow leaf margins, and *Sambucus nigra* 'Guincho Purple' has purple-brown leaves. It is also known under the name *S. n.* 'Purpurea'.

Finally, there is *Sambucus nigra* 'Laciniata' that has deeply lobed leaves in which the leaflets too are deeply incised, to give it the appearance of parsley and of a strongly-branched shrub.

Sambucus racemosa

RED-BERRIED ELDER

Sambucus racemosa 'Plumosa Aurea'

While the common elder prefers soil that is high in nutrients and either clay or chalky, the red-berried elder is found growing wild in acidic, sandy and peaty soil. Used as cover for game birds in Britain, this species has been cultivated for many centuries.

The yellow florets appear on the shrub in April to May at the same time as the new leaves. They form conical plumes that by August have become clusters of orange-red berries.

Sambucus racemosa 'Plumosa Aurea' is a fine cultivar for the garden. It has deeply toothed leaflets with unusually serrated margins. The leaves emerge golden yellow and will remain fairly yellow for some time if in the sun, bit in shade, the leaves quickly turn green.

Sorbaria kirilowii syn. *S. arborea*

Sorbaria kirilowii

Sorbaria flowers in the second half of the summer with striking plumes of cream flowers borne on the ends of its branches. These branches can reach up to 7m (23ft) high and they also bear leaves that are feathery with opposing leaflets that are about 8cm (3½in) long overall. Protect the foliage from strong winds and plant this species by preference in the sun, in moisture-retaining, fertile soil. This shrub sends out root suckers.

Spiraea x *cinerea* 'Grefsheim'

With *Spiraea x cinerea*, the stems which grew the previous year, will be hidden from view behind clumps of white blossoms along their entire length in April to May. The arched form of the branches is accentuated by this appearance.

Spiraea x *cinerea* 'Grefsheim' as a hedge

Spiraea japonica 'Anthony Waterer'

Spiraea japonica 'Goldflame'

The cultivated variety 'Grefsheim' originates from Norway. Its is extremely hardy and it makes an ideal low, broad hedge. Eventually, 'Grefsheim' can become 2m (6ft 6in) tall but it usually remains much lower. It can be kept compact through trimming immediately after flowering. Set aside room for a plant at least 1m (3ft 3in) high and about 1.5m (5ft) wide. For further information about care and planting, see *Spiraea japonica*.

Spiraea japonica

This is the best known *Spiraea*, that bears 30cm (1ft) wide clusters of pink-red flowers in the summer, but there are numerous cultivated varieties from dark red to pink and white. Depending upon the variety, this shrub becomes 50cm-1.5m (20in-5ft) tall. They are not fussy about growing conditions and will survive even under the most unfavourable circumstances. They flower abundantly in a sunny position and prefer moisture-retaining but well-worked and drained soil. They are fully hardy.

Spiraea japonica flowers on the wood that was formed the previous season, so pruning is best done immediately after flowering. Regularly cut back some of the oldest branches to the ground.

Spiraea japonica 'Anthony Waterer'

This very old cultivated variety from 1875, remains one of the most popular *Spiraea* cultivars. It grows to about 80cm (31½in) and bears broad terminal clusters of carmine flowers. White or variegated leaves sometimes appear among the otherwise green leaves.

Spiraea japonica 'Goldflame'

The leaves of *S. j.* 'Goldflame' first emerge pink-red but then gradually change via orange and yellow to pale green. The dark pink flowers appear in late summer in panicles. The black tubular fruits remain on the ends of the branches until the next spring.

Spiraea japonica 'Nana'

These knee-high shrubs grow mainly widthways. In summer, they are covered in carmine blossoms that fade to white with time.

They spread a light, fresh fragrance that attracts many insects and bees. Highly recommended.

Spiraea japonica 'Nana'

Spiraea media

Spiraea media

The branches of *Spiraea media* can hardly be seen in April to May for the garlands of white blossoms that festoon them. The shrub grows to about 1.5m (5ft) high and is extremely hardy. It will flower more profusely in a sunny position than elsewhere but it has no other special requirements, which is why it is widely planted in parks and public open spaces.

Spiraea salicifolia

The branches of this *Spiraea* grow almost upright until the shrub is mature at about 2m (6ft 6in); then they hang horizontally. The leaves are covered with fine, down-like hairs that makes the plant look grey-green. In July and August, the ends of the branches bear plumes of pink flowers.

The plant makes many suckers from its roots and can become rampant. It can tolerate little lime in the soil. For further care, see *Spiraea japonica*.

Spiraea salicifolia

Staphylea colchica

BLADDERNUT

Fruiting bladders of *Staphylea colchica*

The bladdernut blossoms at the end of May with white flowers but the real interest in this 4m (13ft) high shrub is yet to come. Fairly soon after the blossoms, green fruiting bladders are formed, that look somewhat like an upside-down jester's hat. These eventually grow to

175

doornbosii 'Taiga' with a lilac blush. All the snowberry varieties mentioned here form shrubs of 1-2m (3ft 3in-6ft 6in) with high arching stems and almost circular, dark-green leaves opposite each other. These plants can withstand considerable shade and are therefore suitable for planting under trees. Very hardy, prefers moist, humus-rich soil.

Syringa microphylla 'Superba'

Syringa microphylla 'Superba'

about 8cm (3^1/$_2$in) long. The shrub has leaves of apple green consisting of three to five leaflets. Plant the bladdernut in fertile, moisture-retaining soil, and in the sun, where the bladder fruits will turn slightly red, or in partial shade. Zet de pimpernoot bij voorkeur op rijke, vochthoudende grond in de zon (de vruchtblazen zullen daar enigszins rood aanlopen) of in gedeeltelijke schaduw.

Symphoricarpos albus var. *laevigatus*

SNOWBERRY

The white fruits of the snowberry provide much pleasure in late summer. Children pick them and throw them at the ground or stamp on them to make them explode. They are also good for blowing through a tube.

For those who find the berries too white, there is a cultivated variety of *Symphoricarpos x doornbosii*, such as *Symphoricarpos x doornbosii* 'Magic Berry', with lilac berries, *Symphoricarpos x doornbosii* 'Mother of Pearl', with a pink blush, or *Symphoricarpos x*

LILAC

The botanical name *"microphylla"* indicates that this abundantly flowering lilac has small leaves. These are only 1cm (3/8 in) long and they are clustered together at the ends of the thin branches. The shrub becomes 1-2m (3ft 3in-6ft 6in) high and because it thrives under almost any circumstances, it is widely planted in parks and public open spaces. In gardens, its fairly free-form growth looks rather untidy.

Syringa pinnatifolia

Syringa pinnatifolia

LILAC

The leaves are the main focal point of this lilac. The pinnate leaves are about 7cm (2¹/₂in) long and formed from nine to eleven leaflets. The leaves are borne on branches that grow upwards at an angle. These can reach 3m (10ft) tall. The white flowers appear in small clusters but they do not really catch the eye, hence this plant is rarely seen in gardens.

Tamarix ramosissima

TAMARISK

The branches of the tamarisk resemble those of a conifer. The very fine, scale-like leaves are

Tamarix ramosissima 'Rosea'

borne on flexible twigs. The shrubs naturally grow close to the coast, where they can withstand the strongest winds, salt in the air and the soil, and survive in the driest of soils. Further inland, they need more moisture. In these circumstances plant them in as warm and sheltered a position as possible, because although fully hardy, this shrub will flower more abundantly following a hot summer.

The dirty pink flowers bloom in summer like stretched-out catkins. Those of *Tamarix ramosissima* 'Rosea' are strikingly pink-red. The spent flowers are flesh coloured.

Ulmus parvifolia 'Geisha'

CHINESE ELM

Ulmus parvifolia 'Geisha'

This is the variegated leaf and miniature variety of Chinese elm. The leaves are strikingly leathery and small, borne on the branches almost without a leaf stem. The Chinese elm can grow to 20m (65ft), but 'Geisha' is slow growing and bushy, so that it rarely exceeds 2m (6ft 6in). The leaves first appear cream coloured in spring but change during the season to yellow-green. This shrub is not susceptible to Dutch elm disease (see *Ulmus* in chapter 3).

Vaccinium corymbosum

HIGH BUSH BLUEBERRY

Vaccinium corymbosum

Flowers of *Vaccinium corymbosum*

The American high bush blueberry, as its name suggests does not remain close to the ground like its European related species of bilberry. Instead, it grows to about 2m (6ft 6in) high. Urn-shaped blossoms dangle from this shrub in May, that are slightly suffused with pink.

The blueberries are about 1cm (³/8in) in diameter and taste delicious. They are grown in marshy areas in the United States. The orange to red autumn colouring of the leaves in autumn is an especially fine garden feature.

This shrub is only suitable for moisture-retaining, lime-free soils, that do not have to be marshland.

Viburnum x bodnantense

Viburnum x bodnantense

Of all the winter-flowering shrubs, *Viburnum x bodnantense* is one of the most gratifying. The first white and pink flowers can open as early as November. They are gathered in ball-like clumps on the new wood of the otherwise bare shrub and they spread a delightful fragrance. If the temperature drops below minus 10°C, the flowers will be lost but as soon as it warms up again, new buds open. This happens throughout the winter until the end of March. Each mild period is used to flower. The shrub grows erect with upright branches to about 3m (10ft). It has oval leaves about 10cm (4in) long.

Viburnum x carlcephalum

Viburnum x carlcephalum

Each flowering cluster of this hybrid – resulting from cross-breeding *Viburnum carlesii* with *Viburnum macrocephalum* bears about 100 florets. The clusters are about 15cm (6in) wide and they are borne on the ends of the branches. The flowers appear in May from apple blossom pink buds. The flowers smell of clove, but less strongly than *Viburnum carlesii*. This species flowers more reliably than the capricious *V. x carlcephalum*. Plant this fully hardy, open habit shrub in fertile soil. It grows to about 2m (6ft 6in) high and 3m (10ft) across.

Viburnum carlesii

Flowers of *Viburnum carlesii*

The tubular white flowers of *Viburnum carlesii* open in May from pink-red buds. The flowers are strongly aromatic with the spicy tang of clove. The flowering clusters are quite small and in some years are not so abundant. Fortunately, the broad ovate leaves of this Korean species are an attractive grey-green and additionally they turn bright red in autumn before they fall. The shrub has a relatively compact cupola form, becoming

Viburnum carlesii

Viburnum carlesii 'Aurora'

about 2m (6ft 6in) high. *Viburnum carlesii* 'Aurora' is one of the many cultivated varieties. The flowers of this cultivar remain pale pink, even when they have opened fully. With other forms, the flowers fade to white during the blooming period.

Viburnum dentatum var. dentatum

SOUTHERN ARROW-WOOD

The leaves of *dentatum* have serrated or toothed margins and are between 5-10cm (2-4in) long.

Viburnum dentatum var. *dentatum*

Viburnum opulus berries

In autumn, the leaves turn brilliant colours. The 10cm (4in) diameter clusters of white flowers appear between the end of May until July. These are followed in autumn by blue-black berries. The illustrated variety *dentatum* has strikingly thin leaves. It is one of countless varieties, cultivars, and sub species of this American shrub, that grows to about 4m (13ft) high and as much across.

Viburnum opulus

GUELDER ROSE

Viburnum opulus

The famous gardening philosopher, William Robinson, wrote in 1879: "We have searched the entire world for flowering shrubs, but none is more lovely than the guelder rose." Plant hunters since his time have continued the search but have not been able to better his assertion, because what shrub can surpass the guelder rose in its beauty? It has deeply lobed leaves and bears 10cm (4in) diameter clusters of white flowers, surrounded by a circle of sterile ray-florets. The berries turn red in August at the same time as the leaves also start

to change to burgundy. This beautiful shrub can become 4m (13ft) tall but often remains smaller. It can be kept to size through pruning. This very easily grown shrub can also be used as a windbreak.

Viburnum plicatum

JAPANESE SNOWBALL BUSH

Viburnum plicatum

The veins of the leaves of the Japanese snowball bush are so deeply sunken that the leaves look almost pleated. The leaves are about 10cm (4in) long and they change to brilliant red in autumn. The flowers emerge from light-green buds. Once the flowers are fully open, they are dazzlingly snow white. They are borne along the horizontally-growing branches in globular clusters. This shrub grows to about 3m (10ft) high.

Viburnum plicatum 'Mariesii'

JAPANESE SNOWBALL BUSH

This cultivar of the Japanese snowball bush varies considerably from its original parent.

Viburnum plicatum 'Mariesii'

Blossoms of *Viburnum plicatum* 'Mariesii'

Viburnum sieboldii

The flower clusters consist of creamy-yellow fertile florets at the centre with a ring of eye-catching, pure-white sterile flowers surrounding them. The clusters are borne along the entire length of the horizontal branches. Plant this outstanding shrub with its yellow-green leaves in a sunny position or in partial shade and give it plenty of space – it grows to 4m (13ft) across and 2-3m (6ft 6in-10ft) high. It thrives best in fertile, moisture-retaining soil.

Viburnum sieboldii

This tall Japanese *Viburnum* grows to about 5m (16ft 6in) tall and in May, it is festooned with clusters of white flowers. The red flower stems carry red berries later in the year that subsequently turn black. The broad ovate leaves have sharp points and are dark green on the upper surface. The only negative aspect of this shrub is its rather untidy, tall growth, resulting in it being less widely planted.

Weigela

Weigela

Weigela is a genus of very popular garden shrubs. They flower abundantly, usually from the end of May to the beginning of July, and can have a second flowering flush in later summer. They will grow in almost any normal garden soil, even under the least favourable circumstances. They can happily withstand the full sun, or partial shade.

When the shrubs of this genus become too large, they can easily be pruned. Do so immediately after flowering so that they will flower the following year because the buds are formed on the previous year's new wood. Pruning helps the shrub to form new branches. Older branches become thick and form fewer flowering shoots, so after several years, cut the oldest branches back to the ground.

Weigela 'Caméléon'

The name 'Caméléon' is apt for this shrub because its flowers change colour just like a chameleon. They emerge pure white from cherry red buds but as they become older, they become increasingly suffused with pink until they finally are dark pink. This shrub becomes about 2m (6ft 6in) high and similarly wide and it flowers abundantly.

For care see Weigela.

Weigela 'Caméléon'

Weigela 'Conquête'

Weigela 'Conquête' has large pink flowers, al-

Weigela 'Conquête'

most 5cm (2in) wide, making them the largest blooms of all the garden varieties of Weigela. The main flowering does not happen until June. This shrub has ample foliage and grows to about 2m (6ft 6in) high.

Highly recommended. For care, see Weigela.

Weigela coraeensis

Weigela coraeensis

The newly opened flowers are white with a pink blush that becomes stronger throughout flowering until the flower is completely red when it withers. The 2-3m (6ft 6in-10ft) tall shrub is adorned with these flowers in May to June. This species grows wild in Japan, where it can reach 5m (16ft 6in) high. For care, see *Weigela*.

Weigela florida 'Pink Princess'

Weigela florida 'Pink Princess'

Weigela florida originating from eastern Asia was the most cultivated species of *Weigela* for a long time. Many cultivated varieties were created but then the larger calyces of other species became more popular. The flowers of the *W. florida* hybrids are elegantly slim and more refined than the other garden varieties. *W. f.* 'Pink Princess' forms a fine rounded shrub, about 2m (6ft 6in) tall, that flowers extremely profusely in May to June, with laden clusters of bright carmine blooms. Very hardy. For care, see *Weigela*.

Weigela middendorffiana

Weigela middendorffiana

Yellow flowers are rare with *Weigela*. With *Weigela middendorffiana,* sulphur yellow flowers, with egg-yolk yellow patches in their throats, appear from May to June. The colour darkens throughout flowering until the flowers are eventually orange-brown. The flowers are borne on the ends of the branches, which have dark green leaves. The entire shrub, that can become 1.5m (5ft) high, gives a somewhat untidy impression. The rather coarse foliage of this species, from Japan and China, is one of the reasons why it is not among the more popular garden plants. For care, see *Weigela*.

Weigela praecox 'Floreal'

Flowers of *Weigela praecox* 'Floreal'

Weigela praecox is an oddity. This shrub, from China and Korea, is the earliest flowering of all Weigela – from the beginning of May. The pink flowers smell like honey, which is also exceptional, because otherwise only a few white-flowering *Weigela* are scented. *W. p.* 'Floreal' is a very rewarding cultivar, with pale pink flowers that emerge from carmine buds. These flower on upright growing branches, that can become 2m (6ft 6in) tall. For care, see *Weigela*.

5. Evergreen shrubs

Shrubs that keep their leaves in winter

Aucuba japonica

SPOTTED LAUREL

The first specimen of *Aucuba* brought to Europe from Japan in 1783 had variegated leaves. The natural green was speckled with golden yellow.

Today, the golden-yellow speckled varieties are the most eagerly sought after. These plants are particularly popular for those who want "effortless gardening". The evergreen shrub grows to about 3m (10ft) tall with leaves of 10-20cm (4-8in) and makes few demands for its care. Plant it by preference in partial shade, where the variegated leaves are at their best. The red berries, that are only carried on female specimens, remain all winter.

Aucuba japonica

Left: *Camellia* 'Chandler Elegans'

Aucuba japonica

Berberis julianae

BARBERRY

A hedge of *Berberis julianae* is quite impenetrable. This sharp-thorned shrub becomes

Berberis sargentiana

about 2m (6ft 6in) high. It has prickles on the branches and the leaves have sharp teeth.

This terrifying plant is softened in appearance with cheerful yellow blossoms in May, though these can also be suffused with red. Some of the leaves also turn red in autumn. The rest of the plant remains green. This hardy species will thrive in any type of soil.

Berberis sargentiana closely resembles *B. julianae,* but it loses more leaves in winter and has no red in its flowers. Its flowers are mildly fragrant and they are intensively visited by bees.

Berberis x *lologensis*

BARBERRY

Berberis x *lologensis* 'Mystery Fire'

This barberry is a natural hybrid that was discovered by Lake Lolog in Argentina. The person who discovered the plant found 1m (3ft 3in) tall open shrubs with the branches covered in yellow blossoms. Since then, many cultivars and varieties have been bred, including the abundant-flowering *Berberis x lologensis* 'Mystery Fire', that becomes about 1.5m (5ft) high and has upright branches that in May and June are completely hidden by flowers.

Berberis x *lologensis* 'Mystery Fire'

Berberis x *media*

BARBERRY

Berberis x *media* 'Parkjuweel'

The branches of his semi-evergreen barberry arch over as they grow. The shrub forms a low cupola about 1m (3ft 3in) high. The shrub is rather dull, except in autumn, when the leaves turn red and then some of them fall.

The most popular cultivar of *Berberis x media* is 'Parkjuweel', which varies little from the hybrid parent.

Berberis *verruculosa*

BARBERRY

Evergreen shrubs with attractive autumn colourings are rare. *Berberis verruculosa* is such a rarity. In autumn, some of its leaves change colour so that shining green is interspersed with scarlet. The cupped yellow flowers appear in May. For the rest of the year, this barberry is plain green. This shrub easily becomes 1m (3ft 3in) tall and as much across and it has spreading arching branches with sharp prickles. It can withstand shade.

Berberis verruculosa

Berberis verruculosa florets

Buxus sempervirens

Buxus sempervirens 'Elegantissima'

Buxus sempervirens

COMMON BOX

Box is probably the most widely planted shrub of all and one of the most important for gardens. It is the plant used most for creating hedges and is particularly suitable for creating partitions and the framework for herb gardens and box can also be formed to all manner of shapes using the art of topiary, such as globes, cones, and animals figures. There are even specialist companies that do nothing else than create and maintain topiary. If not trimmed, box will grow into a respectable shrub or small tree. In the Caucasus mountains, specimens have been found at least 16m (52ft 6in) tall. Box grows slowly though and can be easily kept under control by pruning and clipping. Do not leave this too long, because the shrub does not restore itself so easily on old wood. The best month to prune is August. In addition to the common box with its slightly elongated round leaves, there are numerous cultivars available such as *Buxus sempervirens* 'Planifolia', with relatively long leaves, and the variegated-leaf variety *Buxus sempervirens* 'Elegantissima', with cream leaf margins.

Buxus sempervirens 'Planifolia'

Camellia

CAMELIA

Camellias were grown for many years as sub-tropical plants in greenhouses and indoors as house plants. Once central heating became more or less universal, the air indoors was too dry for them and they lost their popularity.

More recently these plants have gained fresh approval since it has been realised that they can survive in the garden. Their popularity is helped by the fact that they flower very early in about February, making them much prized shrubs. This is all due to the New Zealand brothers Les and Felix Jury who bred varieties that are guaranteed to withstand frosts of up to minus 18°C. Where frosts more severe than this are experienced, camellias can still remain out of doors provided they are wrapped with insulation, such as rush mats, and hessian ; never use polythene.

Camellias originate particularly from eastern Asia, Indo-China, and Japan. Most of the approximately 250 species grow in the undergrowth of mountain forests, protected from the wind. The roots entwine themselves around rocks, on which a layer of humus from fallen leaves is formed. The forest floor is lightly acidic and evenly moist, but never drenched, because water always runs off. For those who can recreate these conditions, there will be much pleasure from this evergreen shrub. In any even, they cannot withstand having their roots permanently soaked. Camellias are really not suitable for places where the water table is high. The same is true of lime-rich soils, in which a camellia will wither away. Camellias can be grown in such unsuitable places in raised beds with an equal mixture of garden soil and peat.

Just as in the rocky forests, camellias grown with shallow roots and do not like to be disturbed or damaged. It is best therefore, not to hoe or dig beneath them. Equally, the soil must not dry out. Evenly moist soil is essential to prevent stunting growth or bud drop. Do not manure or otherwise feed plants in open ground because the chances of harming the plants is greater than their suffering from lack of nutrition. Allow fallen leaves to rot and add leaf compost each year if possible.

Plant camellias in shelter because northerly and easterly winds in particular are damaging. The leaves will be dried out by the wind, especially if the soil is frozen solid so that the roots cannot replace the moisture that evaporates.

Keep camellias out of the morning sun. The morning sun prompts the buds to grow when the cold roots cannot yet supply the essential moisture, causing the plant to dry out. The sun later in the day does not cause the same harm, although the shrub is better placed in partial shade to prevent the soil around its roots from drying out. Make sure though that there is ample light because camellias need plenty of light to flower abundantly. The flowering buds are formed in late summer and the plant requires sufficient light and warmth during this period.

There are more than 30,000 cultivated varieties of camellia. The cultivars featured here are all certain to withstand temperatures of minus 18°C, except when the other growing conditions are not suitable. With harsher frosts, the ends of the branches will die back. It is rare for the entire shrub to be lost.

Camellias grow slowly but steadily. Eventually, they can grow to several meters (yards) high, but for those with insufficient space, they can be pruned to an acceptable shape after flowering.

Japonica en cultivars

Camellia japonica

CAMELIA

Of the 30,000 cultivated varieties of camellia, there are 20,000 in which *Camellia japonica* has played a role. For centuries, this was the only species known in the West. Because there can be such a wide variation in the seedlings from one fruit, the range of cultivars is extremely wide. A few are described here.

Camellia 'Adolphe Audusson'

Camellia 'Adolphe Audusson'

The first flowers from this strong cultivated variety often appear in January. They are semi-double and fiery red, with a beautifully contrasting yellow central boss of stamens. The shrub grows strongly yet remains compact, bearing temperatures of minus 20°C. It is highly recommended.

Camellia 'Akashigata' syn C. 'Lady Clare'

Many camellias have both an eastern and a western name. People have bred camellias in China and Japan for more than a thousand years. After C. 'Akashigata' was introduced to Europe from Japan in the nineteenth century, it was called *Camellia* 'Lady Clare' but the original name is the only correct one and it is more appropriate for the anonymous Japanese breeder who has produced a shrub with slender branches that arch over somewhat. These bear remarkable, cupped, double blooms that hang down at an angle. These are pink-red, with a lighter fleck at their centre.

Camellia 'Akashigata'

Camellia 'Areshi'

The single-bloomed pink flowers of 'Areshi' appear from January to March.
The flowers are not abundant, so that each

Camellia 'Areshi'

flower can be individually admired with their eye-catching thick bunches of stamens. This cultivar was bred in Japan in 1877.

Camellia 'Ballet Dancer'

Camellia 'Ballet Dancer'

Camellia 'Chandleri Elegans'

The double cream-coloured flowers of 'Ballet Dancer' are peony-form. The tips of the petals have a touch of pink in them. The main flowering happens in February to March. The shrub grows with an open habit and has ample foliage.

Camellia 'Chandleri Elegans' syn *C.* 'Chandleri Elegans'

One of the best camellias is undoubtedly *C.* 'Elegans'. This shrub is compact but broad and it flowers abundantly in February with semi-double white anemone-form blooms that are pink-red.

Camellia 'Dr. Tinsley'

Camellia 'Dr. Tinsley'

The semi-double to loose peony-form flowers are white, suffused with an entrancing pink, that is stronger towards the petal margins. The shrub grows with an upright habit but is relatively compact.

Camellia 'Fleur de Pêcher'

The soft pink flowers appear relatively late, from the end of February. These looks fine against the dark-green shiny leaves and the shrub is hardy. Although this cultivar was registered by a British grower in 1920 and is one of the most rewarding of them all, it is almost never featured in books and is rarely available to buy.

Camellia 'Fleur de Pêcher'

Camellia 'Marguerite Gouillon'

of the petals is white, suffused with salmon-pink. This wonderful floral display occurs in February on a strongly-growing shrub, that expands outwards when it is mature.

Camellia **'Mathotiana Alba'**

Camellia 'Guilio Nuccio'

Camellia 'Mathotiana Alba'

Camellia **'Guilio Nuccio'**

The semi-double, large, pink-red flowers are a treat for the eye. They bloom copiously in February on this strongly growing shrub. The combination of good growth and lovely flowers, makes this cultivated variety one of the most adored camellias.

Camellia **'Marguerite Gouillon'**

The baroque flowers of this old cultivar are surprisingly striped with pink-red, the ground

The ice-white, double flowers of 'Mathotiana Alba' are not too resistant to rain and cold. This is why this old Belgian cultivar is mainly kept in greenhouses and conservatories. The shrub has an open growth habit with fine, large leaves, and long branches. It is sensitive to winds and therefore is best planted in a sheltered position against a wall or fence, where temperatures will not fall below minus 15°C.

Camellia 'Yukimiguruma'

Camellia 'Yukimiguruma'

Flowers of Camellia 'Yukimiguruma'

This is an old Japanese cultivar that grows fairly quickly and upright so that it easily becomes 4m (13ft) tall. The shining green shrub is decorated from February with single, white flowers, of which the yellow stamens are clearly visible.

Williamsii en cultivars

Camellia x williamsii

CAMELIA

About 1930, J.C. Williams crossed Camellia saluensis with *Camellia japonica*. The result was a breakthrough. *Camellia saluensis* is fairly hardy but has small flowers. *Camellia japonica*, which until then had been the parent of virtually every cultivated variety, bears large flowers but is not always so hardy. The hybrid, that was known as *Camellia x williamsii*, combined the good properties of both parents. The best three of all the many cultivars resulting from this hybrid are described below.

Camellia 'Buttons 'n Bows'

Camellia 'Buttons 'n Bows'

One of the new hybrids from the American, Nuccio, was introduced in 1985, resulting from *Camellia saluensis x Camellia japonica*. The funnel-shaped, double-flowers, are fashionably white suffused with apricot with pink on the outside. They tend to hang down somewhat askew on their rather floppy stems with healthy dark-green leaves.

Camellia 'Debbie'

Camellia 'Debbie'

Camellia 'Jury's Yellow'

One of the loveliest examples of camellia breeding by the New Zealand Jury brothers, is 'Debbie'. New flowers continually appear from January until well into March. These are pink, double, peony-form blooms. The leaves are slighter lighter than most other camellias. A strongly upright-growing shrub that is very suitable for training against a wall.

Camellia 'Jury's Yellow'

Camellias always seem to be white or red, with the occasional in between colour, such as apricot and pink. In 1976, the Jury brothers introduced an anemone-form camellia with yellow in it. The yellow is at the centre of the flower, that is otherwise white. This 'Jury's Yellow' became one of the most sought after camellias, because of this and its long flowering and growing well.

Other cultivars

The parentage of some cultivated varieties is no longer known, or so involved, that the plants cannot be assigned to a particular group. A few are now described.

Camellia 'Diamond Head'

Camellia 'Diamond Head'

A cultivar from New Zealand that eventually grows into a compact shrub of 2m (6ft 6in). This camellia grows well and bears attractive shiny, dark-green leaves. The large, semi-double flowers are bright red, with profuse bunches of yellow stamens.

Camellia 'Madame Martin Cachet'

Camellia 'Madame Martin Cachet'

A French cultivar from the end of the nineteenth century with peony-form pink-red flowers. These are borne in pairs that enclose the flimsy stems which droop under their weight. For all this, the shrub grows outwards to form a compact, attractive shrub, with shiny, dark-green leaves.

Camellia 'Ruby Wedding'

This is one of the new varieties from New Zealand. The robin-red flowers are double and peony-form. They appear from February amid dark green, shiny leaves. The shrub grows strongly upright.

Camellia 'Spring Festival'

Camellia 'Spring Festival' grows very upright to form a narrow shrub 2m (6ft 6in) tall. The flowers appear late in the season, often not until April.

They are evenly pink, almost double but with plenty of stamens still on show. This plant has a clear oriental character.

Camellia 'Ruby Wedding'

Camellia 'Spring Festival'

Cotoneaster microphyllus syn. C. integrifoliu

Cotoneaster microphyllus 'Cochleatus'

The botanical name for this *Cotoneaster* indicates its small leaves, that are only slightly more than 0.5cm (³/₁₆in) long. The shrub is low growing – not higher than 1m (3ft 3in) and it generally has a creeping habit. In the countries of the Himalayas, it is planted to prevent soil erosion on inclines. It is ideal for planting on slopes in gardens. The more compact variety, *Cotoneaster microphyllus* 'Cochleatus' is usually planted in gardens. This cultivar grows slowly as ground cover to about 50cm (20in) high. White flowers appear on the branches in May and June, followed by bright red berries. It is fully hardy.

Elaeagnus x ebbingei

OLEASTER

The most widely sold oleaster has to be the hybrid resulting from cross-breeding *Elaeagnus macrophylla* and *Elaeagnus pungens*. The barely noticeable flowers can be smelt in

Flowering of *Elaeagnus* x *ebbingei*

Leaves of *Elaeagnus* x *ebbingei* 'Gilt Edge'

Elaeagnus x ebbingei 'Limelight'

October at some distance. In mild winters, the leaves remain on the shrub but can fall in colder winters but the plant is hardier than Elaeagnus pungens. The oleander, *Elaeagnus x ebbingei,* is more suitable for a milder maritime climate. The shrub will grow to about 3m (10ft) high but can be heavily pruned. *Elaeagnus x ebbingei* 'Gilt Edge' is a variegated-leaved variety with warm-yellow leaf margins to its 10cm (4in) long leaves. *Elaeagnus x ebbingei* 'Limelight' has the yellow instead right in the centre of the leaf along the main vein, with the edges of the leaf remaining green.

Elaeagnus pungens

SPINY OLEASTER

Elaeagnus pungens

The brown, spiny branches of this oleander have thick, leathery leaves that are shiny and green with silver undersides. The plant grows to about 2m (6ft 6in) high and is often planted as part of a boundary where it can be left undisturbed and where its evergreen foliage will dampen the wind. This is the problem. Dry, freezing winds in winter will damage the leaves, which is why this oleander is really only suitable for coastal areas. The flowers in September and October would easily be overlooked but for their wonderful fragrance. *Elaeagnus pungens* 'Maculata' has elongated yellow flecks in the centre of each leaf. The margins always remain green.

Erica carnea

ALPINE HEATH, WINTER HEATH

Erica carnea 'Myretoun Ruby'

Immediately after the snow has thawed in the Alps, the alpine heath bursts into flower on the slopes. The strings of flowers on the short stems are a soft but deep pink. At lower altitudes, the heath blossoms in November or December, to encourage those who cannot wait for spring. It grows to about 20-30cm (8-12in) high. *Erica carnea* is usually known as winter heather, though some know it as snow heather. It grows in humus-rich soil between lime-rich rocks and scree, so that it can tolerate some lime, making it suitable for normal garden soil. After a severe winter, the leaves look very ugly. *Erica carnea* 'Myretoun Ruby' is just one of around a hundred cultivars. The flowers of this variety are dark pink. There are also cultivars with white, and red to lavender-coloured flowers.

Erica x darleyensis

DARLEY DALE HEATH

Erica x darleyensis

The hybrid resulting from crossing *E. carnea* with *E. erigena* flowers later than *E. carnea* between January and March. It grows to about 50cm (20in) high with upright branches that mainly bear whitish or pink flowers. Many cultivars have been selected from this hybrid with white, pink, or mauve flowers. This heath is less hardy than *E. carnea*. For care, see *Erica carnea*.

Euonymus fortunei

SPINDLE TREE

The evergreen spindle is mainly grown as a shrub or hedge. In this situation, it grows to about 1.5m (5ft) high but when allowed to climb against a wall, it can reach much higher.

Euonymus fortunei 'Sunshine'

Hebe albicans

The fully hardy variety can also be used as for ground cover. The original green species is rarely sold with the varigated leaved cultivars being more widely offered. These are usually the varieties that have golden-yellow flecks on the leaves that become cream in summer. The cultivar *Euonymus fortunei* 'Sunshine' has more golden-yellow than green in its new growth but the flecks become lighter during the year while the green becomes darker.

Hebe albicans

Hebe is not sufficiently hardy to be grown outdoors in winter except in coastal areas. The plants can survive many winters but one severe winter will finish off most of them. However, they can be purchased when flowering and it is easy to replace them. The various species and their cultivars have white, pink or blue flowers.

The New Zealand species *Hebe albicans* is one of the hardier Hebe species, capable of withstanding minus 15°C, provided it is planted in dry soil and sheltered from northerly or easterly winds. This shrub grows to about 50cm (20in) high and it bears clusters of white flowers on the ends of the densely-leaved branches in summer.

Hedera helix

COMMON IVY, ENGLISH IVY

Everyone knows ivy as the evergreen climbing plant. It is less well-known as a shrub. When ivy has reached its highest point, it undergoes a change to its top-most growth. These shoots do not have the adventitious rootlets, their leaves are not lobed, and they begin to flower

Flowering shrub form of *Hedera helix*

in September to October. The cup-formed flowers are visited by masses of bees and other nectar-feeding insects. By cutting off such a flowering shoot and propagating it, a rounded shrub about 30-50cm (12-20in) high can be created that has no tendency to climb and which flowers every year. These shrubs are sometimes known as *Hedera arborea* or *Hedera helix* 'Arborescens' but in reality it is just the flowering form of common ivy or one of its cultivars.

Helianthemum 'Rhodanthe Carneum'
syn. *H.* 'Wisley Pink'

Helianthemum 'Wisley Pink'

ROCK ROSE, SUN ROSE

The rock rose, or sun rose originates principally from southern Europe and Asia-Minor. Despite this, their are varieties that can survive northern winters. *H.* 'Rhodanthe Carneum' can withstand at least minus 15˚C. Plant this marvellous grey-leaved shrub where the soil will not become too wet in winter. Each pale-pink flower only blooms for a short time but from the end of June until the end of summer there are constantly new flowers opening. This shrub grows more or less as ground cover to about 40cm (16in) high. It is highly recommended as a plant for raised beds, against walls, and on dry, sunny slopes.

Ilex aquifolium

COMMON HOLLY

Common holly grows wild in western and southern Europe. The shining leaves have a serrated edge with sharp prickles. These are intended to prevent animals from eating the foliage, and when the holly grows too tall for this risk, the leaves cease to have prickles on them.

Ilex aquifolium in bloom

After the barely noticeable flowering in May to June, the berries start to turn red in September to October on the female trees. Holly grows initially as a shrub but can then grow on to form a tree of about 20m (65ft) high.

Through pruning, holly can be maintained as a shrub and it can be used to form an impenetrable hedge. In the wild, holly frequently grows as undergrowth so it able to withstand shade. It prefers loose, humus-rich soil but will grow in any soil provided it is not waterlogged.

There are many cultivars that are overwhelmingly shrub-form. Some of them are solely male, others purely female. Only female holly bears berries, but only when there is a male holly within flying range of the insects that fertilise the flowers. There are a few forms that do not need insects to fertilise them in order to form their fruit.

Ilex aquifolium 'Elegantissima'

This varigated leaved variety never bears berries because it is a male plant. The leaves are spiny with sharp prickles and their margins are butter-yellow to cream, with a centre that is green to grey-green.

Ilex aquifolium 'Elegantissima'

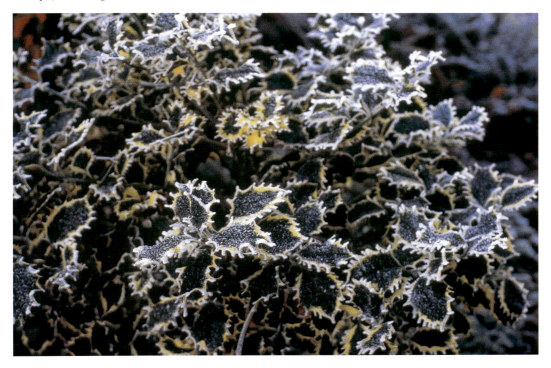

Ilex aquifolium 'Golden Milkmaid'

Ilex aquifolium 'Golden Milkmaid'

The spiky margins of the leaves of this unusual variegated variety are dark green. Along the vein in the centre of the leaf there is a golden-yellow patch alongside a light-green patch. As the leaves get older, these patches change colour to, respectively, butter-yellow and grey-green. Berries are formed on this female plant.

Ilex aquifolium 'Handsworth New Silver

Ilex aquifolium 'Handsworth New Silver'

This is a variegated cultivar with very good characteristics, such as attractive and exceptionally long leaves – up to 9cm (3^1/$_2$in) with very uniform white margins. The spiny leaves are borne on mauve branches. Bright red berries appear on this female plant towards the end of the year.

Ilex crenata 'Convexa'

BOX-LEAVED HOLLY, JAPANESE HOLLY

Ilex crenata 'Convexa'

At first glance, this holly looks like box, hence its name. The leaves are a similar size and shining colour green as box. The leaves feel thick and leathery to the touch though. The elliptical leaves are minutely scalloped, or crenated, hence the botanical name. The leaves of the cultivar are tightly packed together on the branches that form a shrub of about 1m (3ft 3in) with the occasional specimen growing to 2m (6ft 6in).

Ilex x meserveae

BLUE HOLLY

The blue holly was bred by crossing the common holly *(I. aquifolium)* with a creeping species from the Siberian Sakhalin and the northernmost island of Japan known as *Ilex rugosa*. This hybrid proved to be extremely hardy and this holly is planted in parts of Europe where common holly can only be grown with difficulty. This hybrid species also grows less quickly and has smaller leaves – about 5cm (2in) long – that can be described as blue-green with a certain amount of imagination.

Many cultivars have been selected of the blue holly, such as *Ilex x meserveae* 'Blue Angel', that grows very slowly to no higher than 3m (10ft). These are all female plants that bear the cheerful red berries on their own.

A similar attractive female cultivar with larger leaves that carries even more berries is *Ilex x meserveae* 'Blue Princess'.

Ilex x meserveae 'Blue Prince' is grown for its shining foliage and purple stalks because no berries are borne on this male cultivar.

Ilex x *meserveae* 'Blue Angel'

Kalmia latifolia 'Splendens'

Kalmia latifolia

CALICO BUSH, MOUNTAIN LAUREL

Kalmia latifolia flowers in May and June, with corymbs of double white to pale pink flowers. Each floret is about 2cm (¹/₂in) across. This species originates from the south-eastern parts of the United States where it grows in the shade of the mountain forests. In that climate, it grows to 10m (33ft) tall but in the cooler climes of Northwest Europe it is better to plant this *Kalmia* with more light, in not more than partial shade. This evergreen shrub will then grow to about 2m (6ft 6in) high. It only thrives well in distinctly acidic, moist and humus-rich soil. *Kalmia* is a close relative of *Rhododendron*.

Lonicera fragrantissima

Lonicera fragrantissima

Flowers of *Lonicera fragrantissima*

HONEYSUCKLE

The flowers of this winter-flowering, semi-evergreen, shrub honeysuckle have the strongest fragrance of all the winter flowers. For the first four months of the year, a succession of new, cream flowers appear on light brown branches which also have dark-green oval leaves, except when the frosts are severe, in which case they fall. This shrub, that originates from China, has no special requirements, is fully hardy and will grow to about 3m (10ft) tall and as wide across.

Lonicera nitida

HONEYSUCKLE

Lonicera nitida 'Maigrün'

This Chinese honeysuckle forms an ideal hedge. When regularly clipped, the stems will branch out to form a dense shrub with its elongated, dark-green leaves. In May, this shrub – that can grow to 2m (6ft 6in) high – has nondescript white flowers with a delightful fragrance. This honeysuckle is fully hardy, although the tips of the branches may suffer from frost burn. Plant it by preference where it is protected from bleak icy winds. *Lonicera nitida* 'Maigrün' becomes about 1m (3ft 3in) tall. Its foliage is a fresh golden-green. This cultivar is less susceptible to frost burn than the species form.

Lonicera pileata

Lonicera pileata

With its fresh-green leaves and spreading growth, *Lonicera pileata* is a rewarding ground-cover plant. This shrub only grows to about 30cm (1ft) high. In winter, the dark green leaves on its branches can act as a focal point for the garden in winter. Those who run parks departments are well aware of its excellent properties for use in public open spaces and they plant this species more and more. It deserves a place in the private garden too, if only for the fragrant pale yellow flowers in May that are eagerly visited by bees.

Mahonia aquifolium

OREGON GRAPE

Mahonia aquifolium 'Apollo'

The indestructible nature of *Mahonia* has made it a favourite with those responsible for planting public open spaces. Some parks are full of them, particularly where children play, because the leaves have prickles. The leaves turn bronze to red in winter, particularly after frosts. When the temperature drops below minus 20°C and especially if there is a cold, freezing wind, the leaves will be lost, leaving the shrub looking forlorn. In this case, cut the shrub back heavily in spring. *Mahonia* spreads outwards quite significantly and grows to about 1-2m (3ft 3in-6ft 6in) tall. From April, fragrant yellow flowers are borne in terminal clusters, or racemes. This shrub from the United States has many different cultivars that often have quite different foliage.
Mahonia aquifolium 'Apollo' scarcely grows taller than 50cm (20in) but is quite rampant in its horizontal growth. It flowers profusely and has attractive red foliage in winter.
Mahonia aquifolium 'Done well' has elongated spiky leaflets and grows upright at first

Mahonia aquifolium 'Donewell'

Mahonia aquifolium 'Green Ripple'

before arching over, reaching about 1m (3ft 3in) tall. Moderate flowering. The pattern of the veins stands out strongly with *Mahonia aquifolium* 'Green Ripple'. The broad leaves on the upright branches have virtually no stem. This cultivar flowers profusely, particularly in May. *Mahonia aquifolium* 'Undulata' is one of the simplest and yet the finest of the cultivars. The leaflets have wavy edges. It flowers abundantly.

Mahonia aquifolium 'Undulata'

Mahonia bealei 'Gold Dust'

Mahonia bealei 'Hivernant'

Mahonia bealei or *Mahonia japonica* 'Bealei'

Mahonia bealei

The experts cannot agree about this species or cultivar. Officially it is a cultivar of *M. japonica* and yet *M. bealei* is also recognised by some as a species in its own right, complete with its own cultivars. This particular cultivar sometimes starts to flower in February. The main flowering is in March to April. The elongated flowering racemes with yellow florets resemble the delightful fragrance of lilies-the-valley. During spring and early summer, they turn into white-frosted blue to blue-black berries. The leaves are extremely long, up to 40cm (16in), with nine to seventeen leaflets with prickles to each leaf stem. The feathery leaves are at the ends of the branches where they crown the growth. Treat this 1-2m (3ft 3in-6ft 6in) shrub as a forest plant in a clearing: ensuring humus-rich, moisture retaining (but not drenched) soil, and shelter, in particular from drying and icy winds that can seriously damage the foliage. *Mahonia bealei* 'Gold Dust' is very similar to *Mahonia japonica*, growing slightly less vigorously and with relatively shorter flower racemes of 10-20cm (4-8in). *Mahonia bealei* 'Hivernant' flowers from March with 35cm (14in) long flower racemes. In the course of the summer, these become copiously filled clusters of steel-blue berries, covered with a haze of white.

Mahonia x media

MAHONIESTRUIK

The parents of this hybrid are *Mahonia japonica (Mahonia bealei)* and *Mahonia lomariifolia*. There are countless selected

Mahonia x *media* (cv.)

Flowers of *Osmanthus* x *burkwoodii*

Osmanthus delavayi

The leaves of *Osmanthus delavayi* are more

Osmanthus delavayi

cultivars from this union that generally all resemble *Mahonia japonica (Mahonia bealei)*. See *Mahonia bealei* for care information. There are also variegated leaved varieties, that generally grow more slowly.

Osmanthus x *burkwoodii*

Osmanthus x *burkwoodii*

Flowers of *Osmanthus delavayi*

At the beginning of April, the air is filled with the heady fragrance of the white flowers of this hybrid (resulting from the cross breeding of *Osmanthus decorus* and *Osmanthus delavayi*). The flowers are a mere 0.5cm (3/16 in) long but they are clustered together. The leathery, dark green leaves and multi-branching growth of this shrub keep the shrub dense without pruning. It can eventually become 5m (16ft 6in) tall but is usually kept shorter by pruning. *Osmanthus* x *burkwoodii* grows slowly so that it only needs pruning once each year which is done immediately after flowering. The shrub will then flower abundantly the next year. It is an ideal plant for hedges. *Osmanthus* x *burkwoodii* deserves to be more widely planted than is the case, particularly in areas with a maritime climate where it is sufficiently hardy. Plant it where there is shelter from bleak winds. It prefers moist soil that can contain lime.

sensitive to wind damage than *Osmanthus* x *burkwoodii*. Plant this shrub of Chinese origin, which grows to about 2m (6ft 6in) tall, with ample shelter, so that it can survive the winters. White flowers appear in April that are strongly aromatic, rather like the blossom of *Daphne mezereum*. For planting position and care, see *Osmanthus* x *burkwoodii*.

Osmanthus heterophyllus

The white blossoms of *Osmanthus hetero-phyllus* smell wonderfully sweet. They bloom

Osmanthus heterophyllus 'Gulftide'

Osmanthus heterophyllus 'Variegatus'

in September to October. The great similarity of the leaves with those of the holly is quite striking and many will confuse the two species. The difference is that holly has its leaves alternately arranged on the branch while its imitator's leaves are opposed pairs. The other great difference in north-west Europe, is that *O. heterophyllus* rarely forms

berries in this part of the world. The blue berries are elongated and about 1cm (3/8in) long.

Osmanthus heterophyllus is fully hardy. It is not necessary to protect the foliage. It prefers lightly acidic soil but can withstand some lime. This species grows more rapidly than the other types of *Osmanthus*, reaching about 4m (13ft) high. It can readily be pruned and trimmed to form a hedge. *Osmanthus heterophyllus* 'Gulftide' is a cultivar with dense foliage. The green leaves are slightly arched with very sharp spines at the margins. The leaves of *Osmanthus heterophyllus* 'Variegatus' have broad white to pale yellow edges.

Photinia davidiana syn. *Heteromeles davidiana, Stranvaesia davidiana*

Photinia davidiana

In spring, it is as if the clocks stopped in August: the evergreen leaves of *Photinia davidiana* are interspersed with bunches of orange-red berries. The shrub appears to mock the seasons because the older leaves turn brilliant red in autumn whilst the younger foliage remains green. White flowers are born on corymb-like panicles, that look a lot like May. This shrub can grow to a 4m (13ft) high tree but usually remains lower and shrub-form. This is another species from the *Rosaceae* family, like May, which means it is susceptible to fireblight. For this reason, do not plant it in fruit growing areas.

Photinia x fraseri syn. *Heteromeles x fraseri, Stranvaesia x fraseri*

The foliage of *Photinia x fraseri* becomes copper-coloured and shiny in spring. This hybrid results from crossing *Photinia glabra*

This abundantly flowering *Pieris* has small white blossoms in April to May that look similar to those of bilberry: small, upside-down white vases. They dangle on their stems from the top of the 3m (10ft) tall shrub. It is surprising to note that the flower stems do not hang down themselves but point upwards, at a slant. This the main difference with *Pieris japonica*, that has drooping clusters of flowers. *Pieris floribunda* originates from the south-eastern parts of the United States but despite this, it is fully hardy and frosts of minus 25°C present no problem. For further information on care, see *Pieris japonica*.

Pieris japonica

Pieris japonica 'Debutante'

Pieris japonica 'Flaming Silver'

with *Photinia serrulata*. During the summer, the leaves become steadily greener. This shrub grows to about 2m (6ft 6in) tall and about 3m(10ft) across. It is only sufficiently hardy to survive winter near coasts. *Photinia x fraseri* 'Red Robin' is one of the many cultivars with striking red foliage. The leaves of 'Red Robin' emerge reddish-bronze but this cultivar is also not fully hardy, and is unlikely to survive frosts below minus 10°C.

Pieris floribunda

Pieris floribunda

In mild springs, *Pieris japonica* will start to flower in February. Otherwise, the shrub is fully decorated in March and April. The chalk-white flowers hang in terminal clusters. This shrub originates from the hills of Japan. In sheltered positions it will eventually grow to 3m (10ft) tall but most cultivars remain somewhat lower. Many cultivars have been selected from *Pieris japonica*, often with

Pieris japonica 'Forest Flame'

Pieris japonica 'Grayswood'

Pieris japonica 'Forest Flame'

vibrantly-coloured new foliage, that is brightest in April and May.

Plant all Pieris in a sheltered position out of the north-east wind, in partial shade or the full sun. The shrub will flower more abundantly in the sun, but there is then a risk of the soil drying out. They cannot withstand dried out soil, waterlogged ground or lime. They should be planted in lime-free, humus-rich soil.

Pieris japonica will withstand temperatures of minus 20°C, but the new foliage can be damaged by a moderate frost. This causes the plant to form new shoots and fresh leaves. Compact growth is best achieved by cutting back "gawky" growth after flowering.

Pieris japonica 'Debutante' is a very compact cultivar that forms a shrub about 1m (3ft 3in) tall. It has fairly large, white flowers.

Pieris japonica 'Flaming Silver' has been selected from 'Forest Flame'. In spring, its leaves emerge carmine coloured, with pink margins. Within a few months these turn grey-green with cream margins. It grows to about 1.5m (5ft) tall.

The new leaves of *Pieris japonica* 'Forest Flame' emerge shining red, changing through pink and cream to green. It is a vigorously growing shrub that reaches about 2m (6ft 6in) high.

Pieris japonica 'Valley Valentine'

Pieris japonica 'Valley Valentine'

Pieris japonica 'Grayswood' flowers early, mainly in March, with long strings of white flowers on single flowering stems. It grows to about 2m (6ft 6in) high. It is possible that this variety arose out of a crossing between Pieris japonica with *Pieris taiwanensis. P. j.* 'Grayswood' is less hardy than *Pieris japonica*. Most cultivars have white flowers, but those of *Pieris japonica* 'Valley Valentine' are pink-red.

Prunus laurocerasus

CHERRY LAUREL, COMMON LAUREL

The cherry laurel, or common laurel is one of the easiest shrubs to cultivate in the garden. The plant grows to 2-3m (6ft 6in-10ft) tall and at least 6m (20ft) across. The leathery, dark-green, and shiny leaves can be between 5 and 25cm (2-10in) long. The wide difference is caused by the origins of the plant. Those from the *Caucasus* bear large leaves, while the ones that originate from the Balkans have small leaves. Breeders have taken this opportunity to develop a wide variety of cultivars with differing shapes and sizes of leaves.
Plant the cherry laurel by preference in lightly

Prunus laurocerasus 'Camelliifolia'

Prunus laurocerasus 'Otto Luyken'

Prunus lusitanica

acidic soil. It can withstand more lime than *Rhododendron*. Its preferred position is partial shade, where the soil is less likely to dry out. Prune after flowering in April to May, when lengthy clusters of white flowers decorate the plant. Mature shrubs which stop growing can be rejuvenated by rigorously cutting them back. Some cultivated varieties need this treatment following severe winters, when many leaves and branches have been frost damaged.

Every part of this shrub is poisonous. When it is pruned or bruised, Prussic acid gas is given off. Do not allow cattle to feed on the prunings and make sure that children do not eat the berries that are initially red, then black.

Prunus laurocerasus 'Camelliifolia' has very different foliage. The leaves are fairly short and wide and crooked towards the rear, rather like those of camellias.

Prunus laurocerasus 'Otto Luyken' is the most widely sold cultivar. The shrub has spreading growth and grows about 1m (3ft 3in) tall. The dark-green, shiny leaves have pointed ends and are usually shorter than 10cm (4in). In May and June it bears 20cm (8in) long trusses of white flowers and can flower again in autumn.

Prunus lusitanica

LAUREL, PORTUGUESE LAUREL

In the wild, in Portugal and Spain, the laurel, or Portuguese laurel, can grow to 20m (65ft) tall. In north-west Europe, it grows as a shrub to about 10m (33ft) tall and as much wide. Although it can be heavily pruned, this plant is less suitable for the average garden. In parks, it forms dense "walls" of leaves about 10cm (4in) long that are as tough but less thick and leathery than the cherry laurel. The shrub

grows without problems in partial shade or full sun but can die back quite extensively with frost damage in severe winters. In such circumstances, prune back hard; the shrub will eventually recover.

Pyracantha

FIRETHORN

Pyracantha

Pyracantha is almost always planted against a wall so that it appears to be a climber but it will not climb or let itself be trained. The firethorn is naturally a broadly spreading shrub that grows to 5m (16ft 6in) tall and looks far better in a free-standing position than grown against a wall, The shrub is decorated in May and June with clusters of white flowers that develop into round bunches of berries. Only cultivars are grown in gardens and these are impossible to assign to one of the six species of wild firethorn. Depending upon the cultivar, the berries are orange, red, or yellow. They are eagerly eaten by birds, in particular by blackbirds.

The firethorn is very susceptible to disease and insect predation, especially when grown on a hot, south-facing wall. This can lead to brown patches on the leaves, premature leaf fall, and misshapen berries. Although the firethorn is an evergreen, its leaves are very much affected by frosts.

Rhododendron

RHODODENDRON

The around eight hundred species of rhododendron on earth are distributed throughout the temperate zones of the northern hemisphere, and in the south, through Asia and northern Australia. Tropical species, the majority of which grow in New Guinea, can withstand no frost and are not dealt with here. The rhododendrons in our gardens and parks originated from south-western China and the region of the Himalayas. The wild species were crossed with each other and the hybrids appear to grow and flower better than the botanical species. The hybrids have in turn been cross-bred and selected for their differences, that so many cultivars exist that people have lost count. A list of registrations in 1958 (which was not comprehensive) amounted to 10,000 cultivars and thousands more have been added since.

Care

This chapter deals with the evergreen cultivars and varieties that all need more or less the same care (see chapter 4 for *deciduous Rhododendron* or azaleas). They come from mountainous regions where the rocks are covered with a layer of fallen leaves that slowly decay. The roots establish themselves in this humus-rich layer, that is cool, acidic, and moist.

In gardens, rhododendrons spread their roots. Those in the top layer seek nutrition. This layer of soil must not contain any lime because alkaline soil is entirely unsuitable for rhododendrons. Where the soil is slightly alkaline, the top layer can be replaced with humus-rich, acidic soil. Wherever they are planted, rhododendrons benefit from an annual mulching about 10cm (4in) thick. Use compost, leaf mould, or peat substitutes. Only use wood chips and shredded bark in conjunction with well-rotted horse manure, because wood draws nitrogen from the soil in the rotting process.

The mulch layer not only raises the acidity of the soil, it keeps the roots cooler and the soil remains moister beneath the mulch. Regular mulching makes feeding with manure or fertiliser unnecessary. Rhododendrons can be harmed by over-feeding. Young rhododendrons in particular need protection from strong sun, because this heats the ground up too much and causes if to dry out. Once the shrub is larger, it casts its own shadow on its roots. Winter sun and frozen soil are a harmful combination. The roots are unable to draw moisture while the leaves are heated and moisture evaporates. Drying winds are liable to dry the plant out. This needs to be borne in mind when planting. Choose a position where the morning sun in particular will not shine too harshly on the foliage. When frosts are severe, the evergreen rhododendrons let their leaves wilt. This is perfectly normal. By reducing the moisture content in the leaves, the plant protects itself against frost. Once the frosts are gone, the leaves will restore themselves.

All the varieties described in the following section are fully hardy in Europe, with the exception of the extreme north and in mountainous areas, and of those examples where other indications are given.

Rhododendron 'Album Novum'

Rhododendron 'Album Novum'

A first-class cultivar from the Catawbiense group. Grows vigorously to about 4m (13ft) high and is extremely frost resistant. The mother-of-pearl with pink buds open in late May and the shrub flowers with pale pink blooms with yellow ochre to yellow-green interior spotting. For care see *Rhododendron*.

Rhododendron 'Alice Street'

Rhododendron 'Alice Street'

With pale yellow flowers and a mature size of 3m (10ft) tall, 'Alice Street' is one of the less refined examples from the *Wardii* group. It was bred from *Rhododendron* 'Diane' with pollen collected from *Rhododendron wardii* subsp. wardii. The abundant flowering in May makes up for its failings. For care, see *Rhododendron*.

Rhododendron annae

Rhododendron annae

RODODENDRON

To see the flowers of *Rhododendron annae*, it is necessary to look up. In the wild in the mountains of China, this species grows to 8m (26ft) tall and it can reach 4m (13ft) in cultivation where it has an upright habit. It is best combined with other shrubs. The magical flowers are white, sometimes suffused with yellow, with carmine stipples. The plant can withstand minus 20°C. For care, see *Rhododendron*.

Rhododendron augustinii

Rhododendron augustinii

The flowers of *Rhododendron augustinii* vary enormously. In the mountains of central and eastern China, the shrubs mainly produces pink flowers but pale blue examples can be found. The flowers are born in groups of two or three on the ends of the branches. With *Rhododendron augustinii* var. *chasmanthum* there can be up to five or six flowers to each group.

In garden cultivation, this shrub mainly spreads out and grows to about 2-3m (6ft 6in-10ft) high. It will withstand more sun than most rhododendrons and will flower more abundantly in sun than in partial shade. The flowers emerge in April to May. They are easily affected by late night frosts. The plant itself can withstand minus 20 ˚C. For care, see *Rhododendron*.

Rhododendron augustinii 'Electra'

Rhododendron augustinii 'Electra'

Rhododendron augustinii 'Electra'

The light blue of *Rhododendron augustinii* 'Electra' is very fashionable. The species was crossed with *R. chasmanthum* and the finest seedlings were selected. The offspring now have pride of place in many wooded gardens. This rhododendron grows quite upright to reach about 3m (10ft) tall, and it flowers profusely in April to May, particularly when planted in a sunny location. This is a marvellous plant for the water's edge but it is not sufficiently hardy for areas which regularly experience frosts below minus 20ºC. For further care, see *Rhododendron*.

Rhododendron 'Barmstedt'

Rhododendron 'Barmstedt'

This is a form from the *Yakushimanum* group that are hybrids resulting from crossing *Rhododendron* 'Sammenglut' with *Rhododendron yakushimanum*. The shrub will eventually grow to 1.5m (5ft) tall and 2m (6ft 6in) wide. The pink flowers open in May as round clusters on the ends of the branches. The centre of the flowers are pale pink to pink suffused with white. For care, see *Rhododendron*.

Rhododendron 'Boccia'

The pink flowers of 'Boccia' emerge somewhat crinkled from their buds in May. The entire blooming process gives an unkempt impression but the flowers eventually become fully open and cover the shrub in pink. This hybrid resulted from crossing *Rhododendron* 'Catawbiense Compactum' with *Rhododen-*

Rhododendron 'Boccia'

dron williamsianum and forms one of the varieties of the *Williamsianum* group. The fine leaves have been inherited from the second-named parent. This shrub spreads out particularly strongly and will eventually become 1.5m (5ft) tall. For care, see *Rhododendron*.

Rhododendron 'Bremen'

Rhododendron 'Bremen'

The cultivated varieties from the Forrestii group, such as 'Bremen', usually flower bright rose-red. It is an ideal plant for anyone who is fond of thorns. The flowers in May are borne in heavy clusters on this shrub, which when it matures is likely to be just a bit taller than you. The foliage after flowering is fine and dense.

The cultivated variety was bred from *Rhododendron forrestii* subsp. *forrestii* and *Rhododendron* 'Catawbiense'. For care, see *Rhododendron*.

Rhododendron bureavii

Rhododendron bureavii

Flowers are rarely seen on this species from China and it is the foliage which provides the main decorative value. The young leaves are completely covered with reddish-brown indementum or felt-like coating that disappears from the upper-side of the leaves. The coating remains on the under-sides. This is a slow-growing and compact shrub that matures at about 1.5m (5ft) high. For care, see *Rhododendron*.

Rhododendron calophytum

Rhododendron calophytum subsp. *calophytum* 'Pink Form'

The leaves of *calophytum* can be up to 30cm (1ft) long. They form almost a ruff-collar at the ends of the branches. They are crowned in April and May with clusters of pale pink flowers, each with a dark red patch in its throat. The flowers only bloom on mature shrubs, when they are fairly tall. They grow as a tree with bare trunk lower down and in parks can reach 10m (33ft).

The main attraction of the immature plants is their unusual foliage. For care, see *Rhododendron*.

Rhododendron 'Catawbiense Album'

This variety from the Catawbiense group is a strong grower that withstands the strongest frosts.

They thrive in the mountains of central Europe and Scandinavia and belong to the group with the widest distribution in the gardens of Europe. 'Catawbiense Album' flowers late, from the end of May to June. The white flowers

Rhododendron 'Catawbiense Album'

have a white haze and the outer petals have yellow-green stipples. For care, see *Rhododendron*.

Rhododendron 'Catawbiense Grandiflorum'

Rhododendron 'Catawbiense Grandiflorum'

Rhododendrons prefer to grow in cool soil, making them less suitable for pot and container growing. 'Catawbiense Grandiflorum' is such a strong plant that it is even sold in pots. It is essential for this rhododendron to eventually be planted in the ground because it grows to 4m (13ft) high and just as big across. The carmine-pink flowers appear in May to June and have orange-brown stipples in their centre. For care, see *Rhododendron*.

Rhododendron 'County of York'

Rhododendron 'County of York'

The buds of 'County of York' are full of promise: they are light green. In May, they open to reveal large, white flowers with an apple-green centre. They are clustered vertically along the branches towards the tips. *Rhododendron* 'Catawbiense Album' was the mother plant with pollen from *Rhododendron* 'Loderi King George' to make it fertile. The result is a fine shrub about 3m (10ft) tall. It is ideal for parks and large gardens. For care, see *Rhododendron*.

Rhododendron 'Curlew'

This miniature rhododendron is only about 30cm (1ft) high when fully grown. The elongated leaves remain on the shrub in winter. In May, relatively large lemon-coloured flowers that are about 5cm (2in) in diameter are borne. This hybrid results from cross-breeding with *Rhododendron ludlowii* and *Rhododendron fletcherianum* 'Yellow Bunting'. For care, see *Rhododendron*.

Rhododendron 'Curlew'

Rhododendron dichroanthum

Rhododendron dichroanthum subsp. *scyphocalyx*

Salmon pink and apricot are all the rage. This means that there is renewed interest in hybrids in which the southern Chinese species *Rhododendron dichroanthum* has played a role. The colour of these flowers varies widely, but is predominantly orange or pink.

Flowers of *Rhododendron dichroanthum* subsp. *scyphocalyx*

By cross-breeding with other cultivars, delightful in-between shades have been created. An additional benefit is that the shrubs resulting are rarely taller than an adult man so that they fit in an average garden.

Those are the blessings but there are also disadvantages: a rather unkempt growth habit, a small number of flowers per cluster and susceptibility to frost of some of the hybrids. Ask the supplier expressly for a cultivated variety that is reliably fully hardy. For care, see *Rhododendron*.

Rhododendron 'Festivo'

Rhododendron 'Festivo'

This *rhododendron* belongs to the Wardii group. The pollen came from *Rhododendron wardii* subsp. wardii. Who the mother was is unknown but some people are fairly certain it was from the Yakushimanum group and classify the hybrid, originating from 1986, as such. This is a shrub that grows strongly outwards but becomes only about 1m (3ft 3in) tall. It flowers abundantly in May. The pink buds open to reveal pale yellow flowers with rose red stipples. For care, see *Rhododendron*.

Rhododendron 'Flava'

Rhododendron 'Flava'

Although the name 'Flava' is not officially recognised, the plant which goes through life with that name is quite remarkable. It belongs to the hybrids of two of the preferred species: *Rhododendron wardii* and *Rhododendron yakushimanum*. The result is an excellent but slow-growing shrub that will eventually grow to 2m (6ft 6in) high. The pale yellow flowers, with red patches in their throats, bloom profusely in May. For care, see *Rhododendron*.

Rhododendron 'Goldjuwel'

The yellow, bell-shaped flowers with red throat patches, betray that 'Goldjuwel' originates from the Wardii group. *Rhododendron wardii* is an extremely variable species from which many different cultivars have been selected. 'Goldjuwel' flowers abundantly in May. The shrub after many years of slowly growing will eventually reach 3m (10ft) high. For advice on care, see *Rhododendron*.

Rhododendron 'Goldjuwel'

Rhododendron 'Kimberly'

Rhododendron 'Karin'

Rhododendron 'Karin'

'Karin' is one of the best cultivars from the Williamsianum group. The shrub flowers when still young and when mature is rarely taller than 1.5m (5ft). From the end of April, it is totally covered with an abundance of pink flowers that are suffused with red, with a paler centre. The leaves of this cross between *Rhododendron* 'Britannia' and *Rhododendron williamsianum* are extremely attractive, as with all the other members of this group. For care, see *Rhododendron*.

Rhododendron 'Kimberly'

The pale pink flowers of 'Kimberly' are clustered together in small groups at the end of the shoots on this compact shrub. Blooming starts in April and continues into May, provided the flowers are not surprised by a late frost. In company with other varieties of the Williamsianum group, 'Kimberly' has attractive foliage. It was bred by crossing *Rhododendron williamsianum* with *Rhododendron fortunei* subsp. *fortunei*. For care, see *Rhododendron*.

Rhododendron 'Mrs A.T. de la Mare'

This rhododendron belongs to the Fortunei group. The genes from *Rhododendron fortu-*

Rhododendron 'Mrs A.T. de la Mare'

nei are responsible for the somewhat unkempt growth habit of this shrub and its scarcity of foliage. The leaves mainly appear on the ends of branches, where in May, 'Mrs A.T. de la Mare' bears white flowers from soft pink buds. The centre of the uppermost petal is tinged with an apple-green fleck. This cultivar was bred from 'Charles Butler' x 'Halopeanum'. For care, see *Rhododendron*.

Rhododendron 'N.N. Sherwood'

Clear pink buds open to reveal pale pink flowers at the end of May or beginning of June. The centre of the flowers is golden-yellow. The

Rhododendron 'N.N. Sherwood'

shrub will eventually become 3m (10ft) tall. 'N.N. Sherwood belongs to the Ponticum group that share the characteristics of *Rhododendron ponticum* (see below). For care, see *Rhododendron*.

Rhododendron orbiculare

The leaves of *Rhododendron orbiculare* are oval, almost circular. The typical bell-shaped flowers bloom in groups of five to ten from the end of April but mainly in May. This Chinese species is so attractive that little improvement is possible. Yet there are a number of cultivated varieties derived from it. *Rhododendron* 'Temple Bell' flowers pale pink but not until mature, and has a scarcity of foliage (see *Rhododendron* 'Kimberly' for an interesting alternative). *Rhododendron* 'Elfin' has white flowers but is only sufficiently hardy to survive winters in a mild maritime climate, such as the south-west of England and Ireland.

Rhododendron orbiculare

Both the species and cultivars grow in cultivation to 1-2m (3ft 3in-6ft 6in) tall. For care, see *Rhododendron*.

Rhododendron 'Osmar'

Rhododendron 'Osmar'

The flower calyces of 'Osmar' open wide and cover this compact shrub with pale pink blooms. The buds and the striping on the outside of the flowers are darker pink, but the uppermost petals are stippled light brown. 'Osmar' was registered in 1989 with *Rhododendron williamsianum* and a hybrid of *Rhododendron williamsianum* as its parents. The shrub is usually 1m (3ft 3in) tall and never more than 1.5m (5ft). For care, see *Rhododendron*.

Rhododendron ponticum

Rhododendron ponticum

Rhododendron ponticum grows in the wild in southern Europe, on the Iberian peninsula, the Balkans, and the south-western parts of the former Soviet Union. The shrubs grows so well in the mild coastal areas in England, Scotland, and Ireland that it has become a nuisance in woods, estates, and parks. In cooler regions, it stays under control and does not become rampant.

The varieties from this group are well-known as shrubs in parks and on estates. They flower quite late, in June, and are mainly red to purple. For care, see *Rhododendron*.

Rhododendron 'Praecox'

Rhododendron 'Praecox' was bred from *Rhododendron ciliatum* and *Rhododendron dauricum* in the middle of the nineteenth century. Despite this great age, this is still one of the most desirable rhododendrons. The

Rhododendron 'Praecox'

early flowering, from March, obviously helps this popularity. This does, however, have its disadvantages: frost can damage the buds and flowers, so that this 1.5m (5ft) tall shrub does not flower abundantly every year.

Although this is officially an evergreen rhododendron, it loses some of its leaves each autumn. For care, see *Rhododendron*.

Rhododendron 'President Roosevelt'

Rhododendron 'President Roosevelt'

The real charm of 'President Roosevelt' is contained in its leaves that provide a sort of collar for the flowers. The leaves are three-coloured, with a normal dark-green margin. The centre of each leaf has irregular pale green flecks, surrounding yellow. The central vein is always yellow, and yellow patches can spread out from this central part of the leaf.

These attractive leaves can be admired on a shrub that grows to 1.5-2m (5-6ft 6in) high. Unfortunately it is somewhat susceptible to frost damage, so that it is really only suitable for coastal areas. It flowers in May. For care for this variety from the Ponticum group, see *Rhododendron*.

Rhododendron 'Rothenburg'

Not all the varieties from the Williamsianum group remain small. 'Rothenburg' grows to an impressive shrub of 3m (10ft) tall, and easily as wide across. Sulphur yellow flowers appear from the beginning of May that gradually fade

Rhododendron 'Rothenburg'

to white. Unfortunately, the flowering buds only develop on older plants. The attractive dark-green leaves eventually come to be borne only on the ends of the branches. This is an attractive shrub for parks and large gardens, when combined with other shrubs. For care, see *Rhododendron*.

Rhododendron 'Scarlet Wonder'

Rhododendron 'Scarlet Wonder'

Rhododendron forrestii has also been known as *Rhododendron repens*. This old, incorrect name means "creeping" and is an apt description for the plants from the Forrestii group.

The well-known *Rhododendron* 'Scarlet Wonder'(a hybrid from *Rhododendron* 'Essex Scarlet' and *Rhododendron forrestii)* stays lower than 1m (3ft 3in) and spreads out. Eventually, a low globe is formed that will be covered in bright red flowers in April and May. For care, see *Rhododendron*.

Rhododendron 'Sneezy'

This is a fairly recently created hybrid from *Rhododendron yakushimanum* with *Rhododendron* 'Doncaster'. This *rhododendron* belongs to the Yakushimanum group. This shrub will eventually grow to 1.5m (5ft) high, flowering with abundantly-filled clusters of blooms.
The outer edge is dark pink, that becomes lighter towards the heart of the flower. The upper petals is covered with burgundy flecks. For care, see *Rhododendron*.

Rhododendron 'Sneezy'

Rhododendron 'Spring Dawn'

Rhododendron 'Sweet Sue'

Rhododendron 'Spring Dawn'

The flowers of 'Spring Dawn' sit on the ends of the branches in May like bright red balls. The heart of each flower is flecked with yellow ochre to light brown. This shrub grows to about 3m (10ft) tall and it belongs to the Catawbiense group. For care, see *Rhododendron.*

Rhododendron 'Sweet Sue'

Rhododendron 'Sweet Sue' is one of the better known cultivated varieties from the Dichroanthum group. The flowers appear in amply-filled clusters on the ends of the branches in May.

This compact shrub grows to 1.5m (5ft) high) and it is completely festooned with the pink flower clusters in May. In contrast with many other varieties from this group, 'Sweet Sue' is hardy. For care, see *Rhododendron.*

Rhododendron wardii subsp. *wardii* 'Type Nymans'

Rhododendron wardii

Rhododendron wardii grows from the most far-flung corners of Tibet to the other side of China. It is therefore not surprising that the species has wide variety within it. There are pure-yellow flowering forms, but also cream to white, with and without red flecks in the heart of the cup-formed blooms. Once they were regarded as different species such as *Rhododendron astrocalyx, Rhododendron croceum,* and *Rhododendron litiense*. Today they are treated as a groups. *Rhododendron wardii* subsp. *wardii* 'Type Nymans', for example, with its red throat flecks, belongs to the Astrocalyx group. The bell-shaped flowers are suffused with pink. The shrub has elegant oval leaves, growing slowly to about 3m (10ft) tall and about 4m(13ft) across. It flowers in May. Plant this shrub in a sheltered position to prevent the flowers from being damaged. For further care, see *Rhododendron*.

Rhododendron yakushimanum

Rhododendron yakushimanum grows wild in the mountains on Yaku-shima, one of the Japanese islands. The species was only

Rhododendron yakushimanum x *Rh.* 'Corona'

described for the first time in 1921, and first cultivated in the 1930s. Since that time, the interest in the species has been tremendous, particularly as this shrub does not grow taller than 1.5m (5ft), an ideal garden size.
The species plants are covered with felt-like hairs. The new leaves emerge in an ochre cobweb. The upper-side of the leaf soon loses the felt covering, but the underside remains covered in a russet-coloured, felt-like coating. During hybridisation, much of the hair covering is lost. The undersides are usually

Rhododendron 'Loderi' x *Rh. yakushimanum*

remain fox red-brown. The more intensive the colour of the flowers is, the less woolly coating there is. The mainly pink flowers appear in voluptuous clusters, that fade during blooming to white. The hybrids illustrated here used, in the first instance that flowers in May, pollen from *Rhododendron* 'Corona' (a cultivar from the Griffithianum group) and in the second, *Rhododendron* 'Loderi' received pollen from R. yakushimanum.

Skimmia x confusa

Skimmia x *confusa* 'Kew Green'

This hybrid from *Skimmia anquetilia* and *Skimmia japonica* has flowers of both genders (male and female), that bloom in April. The shrub mainly spreads out, reaching 1m (3ft 3in) high, with some exceptions reaching 3m (10ft) tall. The leaves are strikingly light green. The plant has as few cultivation demands as *Skimmia japonica. Skimmia x confusa* 'Kew Green' only has male flowers, that are borne as cream bunches on the ends of the branches, in April. They have a wonderful fragrance but do not develop berries.

Skimmia japonica

Skimmia japonica 'Nymans'

Skimmia is one of the most popular ornamental shrubs. It remains low – maximum height 1.5m (5ft) but usually much lower – so that it is suitable for use in small gardens. The ornamental value of its shiny, evergreen foliage is added to by scented blossoms in spring and orange-red berries, that often remain on the shrub throughout the winter. The berries are only formed on plants that are both male and female, or on female plants when there is a male *Skimmia* close by.

Skimmia grows in any normal garden soil. Select forms that bear berries such as Skimmia japonica 'Nymans', or *Skimmia japonica* 'Veitchii'. The berries of *Skimmia japonica* 'Kew White' and of the fairly weak *S. j.* 'Fructo-albo' are white. Make sure there is a male *Skimmia japonica* in the vicinity, such as 'Rubella'.

Skimmia japonica 'Rubella'

Skimmia japonica 'Rubella'

The male cultivar 'Rubella' is very popular for gardens, even though it bears no berries. Late in summer, the shrub is already decorated with red-brown buds, that adorn the shrub throughout winter. They open in April to May to provide fragrant, cream-coloured flowers. It grows to 1m (3ft 3in) tall.

Trochodendron aralioides

Trochodendron aralioides

Foliage of *Trochodendron aralioides*

The flowers of *Trochodendron* have no petals. The stamens point outwards from the shoot tips like the spokes of a wheel. *Trochodendron* literally means "wheel tree". The evergreen leaves are borne in spirals, clustered together on the branches. Each leaf is about 10cm (4in) long.

In their natural habitat in the mountain forests of Japan, Korea, and Taiwan, the shrub grows to a tree of about 20m (65ft) tall. In Europe, it grows as an upright shrub to about 5m (16ft 6in) high. It is sensitive to frost and can only survive in very sheltered places, preferably near the coast. Plant it there, in neutral, moisture-retaining soil, in a sunny position or partial shade.

Viburnum x burkwoodii

In mild winters, this *Viburnum* evergreen retains its ovate, sparsely-toothed green leaves. Pale pink buds open in March to April to reveal white flowers, clustered together in rounded terminal corymbs that are about 5cm (2in) in diameter. The delightful fragrance of the flowers closely resembles vanilla. The flowers can be damaged by severe frosts, but this risk is relatively small. Sometimes flowering clusters appear on the shrub towards

Viburnum x *burkwoodii*

the end of the year. It grows to about 2m (6ft 6in) tall and 3m (10ft) wide and is fully hardy. Plant *Viburnum* in fertile, moisture-retaining soil but not in water-logged ground.

Viburnum davidii

The flower buds of *Virburnum davidii* can sometimes be surprised by a snow shower in March. The white flowers, in flattened terminal cymes, emerge in April to May. During the summer, ovoid blue berries are formed. The shrub originates from West

Viburnum davidii

Viburnum davidii

China. It reaches about 1m (3ft 3in) high and slightly wider. Plant *davidii* in a warm position to stimulate flowering and fruiting. It is only sufficiently hardy to survive winter in coastal areas, but there are hardier cultivars available. Make sure that these too are sheltered from icy and drying winds.

Viburnum henryi

This is a very slender, upright shrub, that grows to about 3m (10ft) tall with equally slender foliage. The leaves are about 12cm (5in) long but only 2-3cm (1in) wide. The leaves remain on the shrub throughout mild winters and its is only sufficiently hardy to be grown reliably in coastal areas. Protect it from icy and drying winds, and from the morning sun. White flowers are born on conical panicles about 10cm (4in) in diameter in May to June.

Viburnum rhytidophyllum

These 6m (20ft) tall shrubs are only suitable for parks and large gardens.
They get noticed in parks in winter because of

Viburnum henryi

Viburnum rhytidophyllum

their strange way of letting their 20cm (8in) long leaves wilt during cold weather. The tops of the leaves are dark green but the undersides have downy hairs which give the leaves a grey-green look. Fully hardy.

The leaves become erect again in spring and musty-scented, off-white flowers are borne in large umbel-like cymes that are 15cm (6in) in diameter. Large clusters of red berries appear in late summer, that change later to black.

Viburnum tinus

Viburnum tinus starts flowering at the end of February in mild winters, with copious clusters of fragrant white blooms on the ends of the branches. The leaves are strikingly shiny. The shrub will eventually reach 2-3m (6ft 6in-10ft) tall. This *Viburnum* is only able to survive winter in areas with a mild climate, such as coastal regions.

Even here, the foliage needs protecting from icy and drying winds, and the morning sunshine. It can be happily grown as a container plant in colder areas.

Viburnum rhytidophyllum with paper birch

Viburnum tinus

6. Conifers

Abies alba

SILVER FIR

Abies alba

The silver fir grows in the mountainous regions of Europe, from the Black Forest in Germany, through central Europe and to the southern mountains. Its perfect conical form grows to about 40m (130ft) tall with exceptional specimens reaching 65m (215ft). It makes good timber.

The needles are borne in two rows at the side of the branches. They are dark green and shiny, but light green on the new growth. The slender cone is about 10cm (4in) long.

The silver fir becomes far too large for gardens and it is rarely planted in parks. Despite this, there is a cultivar available that is fairly widely planted in gardens: *Abies alba* 'Pendula'. This tree creates a gawky impression with drooping branches, but it too will eventually grow to 10-15m (33-50ft) high.

Abies cephalonica

GREEK FIR

The horizontal branches of the Greek fir are closely packed together to create a dense tree. In the Greek mountains, they grow to 30m (100ft) tall, but when cultivated, they grow fairly slowly and form a 15m (50ft) unkempt-looking tree. Despite its southern origins, the Greek fir is hardy in all but the most northerly and colder mountainous regions of Europe.

Left: *Abies alba*

Abies cephalonica

Abies concolor

COLORADO WHITE FIR

Abies concolor 'Violacea'

The needles of the Colorado white fir create a woolly impression. The greenish purple cones are about 10cm (4in) long and 3cm (1½in) wide.

This species can occasionally grow to 60m (200ft) high on the North American west coast, from where it comes. They generally stay much shorter than this, but still reach 30m (100ft), making this attractive and robust large tree only suitable for large gardens and parks. *Abies concolor* 'Violacea' has green needles with a blue tinge. It is ideal for growing where the winters are "on-and-off", where the blue varieties of the Colorado spruce (*Picea pungens*) suffer from aphids. 'Violacea' becomes a really large tree.

There are also dwarf forms of Colorado white fir available:

Abies concolor 'Violacea'

Abies delavayi var. *forrestii*

Abies concolor 'Gable's Weeping' is a creeping form with somewhat stiff needles.
Abies concolor 'Igel' is a true enthusiast's plant, with its globular form that is covered with light-green needles.

Abies delavayi

Certain silver firs have striking blue cones, such as the renowned *Abie koreana* that is sold at almost every garden centre. *Abies delavayi*, that originates from western China has striking blue flower forms that later grow into smooth cones of about 8cm (3½in).

The edge of each needle is bent under. Seen from underneath, they are grey, with a prominent green central vein. Eventually this silver fir will become 20m (65ft) tall, often with a broad crown. It is hardy for north-western European winters.
The usual cultivated form available is *Abies delavayi* var. *forrestii,* that varies little from the species.

Abies grandis

GIANT FIR

Abies grandis

The long, flat needles of the giant fir remind you of the yew (*Taxus*), but with *Abies grandis*, they are on a giant of a tree. There are specimens that have grown to 100m (330ft) tall. They originate from the north-west of the United States. It is an outstanding tree for timber, and it is widely planted in Europe, particularly where the ground is wet. Despite its attractive conical shape, and hanging branches, the giant fir is almost never used as an ornamental tree because of its huge size.

Abies homolepis syn. *A. brachyphylla*

NIKKO FIR

Abies homolepis

Abies homolepis

The Japanese Nikko fir is mainly to be seen in special collections and arboretums, although it grows without difficulty and would not look out of place in a local park. The conical tree, of about 30m (100ft) creates an oriental atmosphere. The branches are coated right around with grey-green needles. Fully hardy.

Abies x *insignis*

Abies x insignis

This cross between *Abies nordmanniana* and *Abies pinsapo* grows into a broad cone that is eventually 30m (100ft) tall. The forked side branches are an attractive sight. They hang downwards from the trunk but the tips of the branches turn upwards.

Abies lasiocarpa

This species grows in the cold mountain forests from West of America to Alaska. The tree has a slender upright habit to form a column up to 30m (100ft) tall. In winter, the

Abies procera

NOBLE FIR

The noble fir can grow to 90m (295ft) in the forests in the south-west of the United States. In cultivation, it can easily grow to 25-45m (80-150ft) tall. Despite this, it is often seen in gardens because of the blue bloom on its needles.

Abies procera

snow has little room to settle on its relatively short branches.

In cultivation, the tree will grow to 25m (82ft) tall. This is far too large for the average garden, however, there are smaller forms, such as *Abies lasiocarpa* 'Compacta' that has plenty of blue in its mature needles.

Abies pinsapo

HEDGEHOG FIR, SPANISH FIR

The needles of the hedgehog, or Spanish fir, are borne in spirals around the branches. Not only do they have blue "chalk" stripes on their undersides in common with other firs of this genus, but they have them on the upper-sides too. This tree from the mountains of southern Spain grows into a broad cone that is eventually 30m (100ft) tall.

Abies pinsapo 'Glauca', that also has blue needles, grows less vigorously and is more suitable for larger gardens.

Abies pinsapo 'Kelleriis' has fine needles with a blue bloom.

Abies procera 'Glauca'

Araucaria araucaria

The cultivated form *Abies procera* 'Glauca' is usually selected for gardens, with its relatively modest 15m (50ft) height. For a true dwarf in a rock garden, choose the very slow growing *Abies procera* 'Blue Hexe'. This variety forms a low flat globe and is densely covered with blue needles.

Araucaria araucaria

CHILEAN PINE, MONKEY PUZZLE

The Chilean pine or monkey puzzle tree is planted for its curiosity value rather than its beauty. The entire length of its branches is covered with triangular-ovate leathery leaves that are sharply pointed. *Araucaria araucana* grows rigidly upright, with wreaths of side shoots that grow almost horizontal. The branches remain on the tree for about ten years but the bottom of the tree eventually becomes bare. Although this tree originates from South America, it can withstand winter in temperature coastal areas. Grows up to 12m (40ft).

Calocedrus decurrens

INCENSE CEDAR

The incense cedar always remains slender but it can grow to 45m (150ft) high. Although this tree originates from the south-west of the United States, it can survive winters in European coastal countries. It prefers to grow in moisture-retaining, fertile soil.

Cedrus deodara

DEODAR CEDAR

In parks in countries with a maritime or Mediterranean climate, this cedar from the Himalayas can reach 35m (115ft).

Calocedrus decurrens

233

Cedrus deodara

Cedrus deodara 'Aurea'

Cedrus libani

CEDAR OF LEBANON

Cedrus libani

Cedrus libani 'Comte de Dijon'

Elsewhere, the tree suffers too greatly with frosts. The tree initially forms a cone, then in later life (although sometimes rather earlier) it starts to spread outwards with horizontally growing branches.

Cedrus deodara 'Aurea' is an attractive form with golden-green needles. In areas where the temperature drops below minus 25°C, cultivars that have been specially selected for their resistance to the cold are planted, such as *Cedrus deodara* 'Karl Fuchs', or the creeping, blue cultivar *Cedrus deodara* 'Feeling Blue'.

No tree is mentioned as frequently in the Bible as the cedar of Lebanon. Palaces and temples were built with its timber, and it was also the most highly regarded timber for shipbuilding. By origin, it grows in a wide mountainous area around the Mediterranean. Rapacious building has taken its toll of the tree, so that today only relatively small numbers of the tree remain. The striking characteristic of this tree is the way the branches with their blue-green needles emanate from the main trunk in clear layers. The species is only sufficiently hardy to be grown in southern and north-western parts of Europe.

Cedrus libani 'Comte de Dijon' grows outwards very slowly to become a dense compact shrub of medium size.

Cedrus atlantica, the Atlas cedar (syn. *C. libani* subsp. *atlantica*), also known as cultivar *C. libani* 'Glauca Pendula' is usually grafted. The branches hang down like a veil with blue needles.

Cedrus libani 'Glauca Pendula'

Naalden van *Cephalotaxus harringtonia* (male)

Cedrus libani 'Glauca Pendula'

Cephalotaxus harringtonia (female)

Cephalotaxus harringtonia

PLUM YEW

Cephalotaxus harringtonia (male)

Needles of *Cephalotaxus harringtonia* (female)

A plum yew is always male or female. They can be easily differentiated during flowering. Outside this period, they both resemble an unkempt yew shrub, growing to a maximum 5m (16ft 6in) high. The needles are not spiky. *Cephalotaxus harringtonia* originates from northern China, Korea, and Japan, and it is fully hardy. It grows best in partial shade on moisture-retaining sandy soil. It does not like lime.

Chamaecyparis lawsoniana

LAWSON CYPRESS

The Lawson cypress originates from the mountains of California and Oregon on the west coast of the United States. In the wild, little difference can be discerned between the trees of this species yet in cultivation, the differences are so great that they are classified in separate groups. Lawson cypresses grow best in moist, slightly acidic soil but can withstand less favourable conditions. Drying winds turns the scaly needles rather ugly. For this reason, plant it with some protection. Then it will happily survive minus 25°C.

Chamaecyparis lawsoniana 'Aurea Densa'

This is the most rewarding dwarf form of Lawson cypress. The very compact foliage

Chamaecyparis lawsoniana 'Aurea Densa'

remains an attractive golden-yellow throughout the year. Initially the shrub grows irregularly but it eventually forms an oval shape no taller than 80cm (32in) and half that width.

Chamaecyparis lawsoniana 'Columnaris'

The slender and attractive cultivar 'Columnaris' is one of the best known conifers. Its upright columnar growth makes it a popular choice for coniferous hedges, particularly in gardens of new housing estates where the gardens are often no more than 7-9m (23-30ft) wide, and the desire for privacy is great. In the first few years, 'Columnaris' seems the ideal solution, but eventually even this slender conifer grows into a column that is 5-10m (16ft 6in-33ft) high with a width of 2m (6ft 6in). By taking out the tops, the characteristic form and the charm of this tree are lost. Cutting back the tree's width is a greater problem. Only new growth will regenerate after pruning.

Chamaecyparis lawsoniana 'Columnaris'

Chamaecyparis lawsoniana 'Ellwoodii'

The needles from the slender 'Ellwoodii' turn an attractive blue in winter. It is not surprising that this is a favourite of garden designers that happily sketch its shape in their designs for modern houses. Gardens centres sell them in their thousands with the story that it is a dwarf conifer. The owners discover how untrue this is only some years later for the tree grows quite slowly but will eventually reach 7-10m (23-33ft) high.

Chamaecyparis lawsoniana 'Globosa'

With its mature adult height of 1m (3ft 3in), 'Globosa' is a true dwarf cypress. The shrub grows more or less globular, with a flat crown. The branches initially grow upright but then hang down under the weight of the green needles.

Chamaecyparis lawsoniana 'Ellwoodii'

Chamaecyparis lawsoniana 'Globosa'

Chamaecyparis lawsoniana 'Lutea'

'Lutea' indicates the golden-yellow colour of the needles of this tree. The botanical name is quite appropriate, because this is the most yellow of the Lawson cypresses. The tree also remains an attractive colour when it is older.

Chamaecyparis lawsoniana 'Lutea' (left) with *l.* 'Naberi' (right)

Eventually, this tree will grow to 10m (33ft) but this will take many years because of the slow growth of this cultivar.

The branches spread horizontally and are often twisted like a spring with its needles pointing in every direction. The needles of immature trees can suffer from late frosts.

Chamaecyparis lawsoniana 'Minima Glauca'

'Minima Glauca' is a very slow growing dwarf form. In 20 years, if will become about 1m (3ft 6in) tall.

The needles are more green than blue. This shrub eventually achieves an irregular conical form with a definite top in contrast with

Chamaecyparis lawsoniana 'Nana Glauca', that is a broad-crowned dwarf, yet is often confused with 'Minima Glauca'.

Chamaecyparis lawsoniana 'Naberi'

The tips of the branches of this "old-fashioned" conifer are sulphur yellow. In the winter, the colour changes to a milky blue. The somewhat unrefined growth of 'Naberi' has led to a drop in its popularity.

Chamaecyparis lawsoniana 'Stewartii'

In summer, the ends of the branches of 'Stewartii' are golden-yellow. For this reason, it was one of the most popular conifers for a long time.
What's more, it thrives in almost any soil and is fully hardy. However, in winter, when conifers get noticed most, this tree changes colour to yellow-green. In addition, more compact conifers are now preferred.

Chamaecyparis nootkatensis

NOOTKA CYPRESS

On the west coast of Canada and the United States, the Nootka cypress grows to a narrow cone about 40m (130ft) high.

This extremely hardy conifer has branches that droop somewhat. The characteristic is most noticeable in the best known cultivated variety: *Chamaecyparis nootkatensis* 'Pendula' with which the branches hang like a dark green veil. This weeping variety grows to about 20m (65ft) high.

Chamaecyparis obtusa

HINOKI CYPRESS

In Japan, where the Hinoki cypress grows in the wild, this 40m (130ft) tall tree is as popular with foresters as it is with Bonsai enthusiasts. This large tree provides first class timber but also exists in dwarf form that are so popular for creating miniatures. Slow growing cultivars

Chamaecyparis nootkatensis 'Pendula'

Chamaecyparis obtusa 'Goldspire'

Chamaecyparis obtusa 'Crippsii'

are planted in gardens, such as the very popular *Chamaecyparis obtusa* 'Crippsi'. The golden variety with its strikingly fine divided and feathery foliage, takes 70 years to grow 20m (65ft) tall.

Chamaecyparis obtusa 'Goldspire' remains much shorter at no more than 5m (16ft 6in) high. It also remain quite slender, almost columnar. Yet for all this, it creates a soft impression. The outer scales are lemon yellow

in both winter and summer and stick out like curved eyelashes in front of the blue tinge of the older needles. Plant Hinoki cypresses in lime-free soil if possible.

Chamaecyparis pisifera

SAWARA CYPRESS

The Sawara cypress comes from Japan, where it is a popular commercial timber tree. In the damp valleys, it grows there to 40m (130ft) tall. In Europe, it grows more slowly, eventually reaching 25m (82ft). The species itself is rarely planted because of its unkempt growth but the many cultivated varieties are grown as ornamental trees.

Chamaecyparis pisifera
'Filifera Aurea'

With the most popular cultivated variety of Sawara cypress, the scale-like needles are strung together, with few side shoots. They

Chamaecyparis pisifera 'Plumosa Aurea'

create wire-like forms that hang down under their own weight. Those on the outside are golden yellow. The conifer grows as a shrub and can eventually reach 5m (16ft 6in) tall but because it grows extremely slowly – 2m (6ft 6in) in 20 years – it can be regarded as a semi-dwarf.

Chamaecyparis pisifera 'Plumosa Aurea'

The scaly needles of the varieties in the Plumosa group are spiky when young. The needles of the "false cypresses" (*Chamaecyparis*) take on one form before mature, and then change via an intermediate stage to their adult appearance. Many cultivars maintain the youthful form of needles even when they are mature.

With the Plumosa group, the cultivars keep the intermediate form of needle. 'Plumosa Aurea' has golden-yellow new growth that turns greenish yellow later in the year. It grows strongly to a conical shape, about 10m (33ft) high.

Chamaecyparis pisifera 'Filifera Aurea'

Chamaecyparis pisifera 'Plumosa Flavescens'

Chamaecyparis pisifera 'Plumosa Flavescens'

In summer, the green tips of 'Plumosa Flavescens' are sulphur yellow. In winter, they are more or less green. The low shrub grows into a broad cone or globe that is eventually about 1m (3ft 3in) tall and wide.

Chamaecyparis pisifera 'Sungold'

'Sungold' is from the same group as 'Filifera Aurea' but is more "wiry". With its very low, spreading habit, and tolerance of less favourable circumstances, this new cultivar has a potentially rosy future as a ground-cover conifer for parks and public open spaces. Some of the "wires" are golden yellow while others are light green, so that 'Sungold' creates a variegated appearance.

Cryptomeria japonica

JAPANESE CEDAR

Although the *genus Cryptomeria* consists of just the one (possibly two) species, there are more than 200 different cultivars – from 60m

Chamaecyparis pisifera 'Sungold'

Cryptomeria japonica 'Elegans'

(200ft) tall trees to the smallest dwarfs and bonsai. *Cryptomeria japonica* grows in the wild in China and Japan. In the latter country, this tree has been the most important tree for commercial timber for as long as anyone can remember. It grows best in damp ground, where it forms shallow roots. For this reason, it is often planted in volcanic regions (e.g. the Azores). The Japanese cedar grows to about 30m in Europe but it is the cultivated varieties that are usually planted.

Cryptomeria japonica 'Elegans'

The soft needles of 'Elegans' are spiky when immature and rather spread out along the branches. This bushy plant can grow to 15m (50ft) tall but it usually remains lower at about 5m (16ft 6in). The needles are green in summer and change to bronze or reddish brown in winter, depending upon how severe the frosts are. Not recommended for areas where frosts below minus 10°C persist.

Cryptomeria japonica 'Elegans Viridis'

Cryptomeria japonica 'Elegans Viridis'

This variety is very similar to 'Elegans', except that its needles remain a fresh green in winter and summer. It is hardy with the exception of mountainous areas and the far north.

Cryptomeria japonica 'Globosa Nana'

Cryptomeria japonica 'Globosa Nana'

The needles are typical for *Cryptomeria japonica* in that they cover the branch and all point in the direction of growth. 'Globosa Nana' is categorised as a dwarf but it grows vigorously and will eventually reach 2m (6ft 6in) high. The densely packed branches bend over slightly to form a compact globe or broad green cupola. Fully hardy.

Cryptomeria japonica 'Gracilis'

Cryptomeria japonica 'Gracilis'

The short shoots of 'Gracilis' are extremely slender and they blow about all over the place. They are covered with adjoining, short needles. Although 'Gracilis' can grow to 5m (16ft 6in), it can be considered a semi-dwarf because it remains a manageable size – under 2m (6ft 6in) –for some considerable time. It is green in summer and winter. Enduring frost of lower than minus 10°C will damage the foliage.

Cunninghamia lanceolata

The flexible yet strong leaves of this conifer are pointed.

Cunninghamia lanceolata needles

In China, from where *Cunninghamia lanceolata* originates, it grows to 50m (164ft) tall and is a very important tree for commercial forestry. In cultivation, 30m (100ft) tall is sizeable, because the tree usually remains lower than this. It will only grow in sheltered, moist places. A drying wind, especially an icy wind is disastrous for this tree, and will spoil the needles. The tree though will survive minus 25°C.

Cunninghamia lanceolata 'Glauca' is hardier and what's more has a blue tinge to its needles. This is the most popular cultivar of this species which is otherwise seldom seen outside arboretums.

x *Cupressocyparis leylandii*

LEYLANDCIPRES

The "x" in front of the botanical name indicates that this is a cross-bred, or hybrid species. In this case it is a crossing between species from different genera – *Chamaecy-*

x Cupressocyparis leylandii 'Castlewellan Gold'

paris nootkatensis with *Cupressus macrocarpa*. The result is a dark green, conical shape , that rapidly grows to its eventual height of 30m (100ft), which is far too tall for the average garden. This rapid growth persuades a lot of people to plant them as a hedge. In a few years, they are as tall as a man and from then on can only be kept under control with considerable effort. Trim them several times each year to keep the growth dense and green. They are fully hardy and will grow in any soil.

x *Cupressocyparis leylandii* 'Castlewellan Gold'

The tips of the branches of this cultivated variety have an attractive plume form and during summer, they become lemon yellow. The foliage turns green, or blue-green in winter. 'Castlewellan Gold' grows to a pointed column but does so much less rapidly than the normal standard Leyland cypress, reaching 6m (20ft) high in 10 years. It is not much troubled by wind, air pollution or salt, and is therefore ideal for use by the coast. Fully hardy.

x *Cupressocyparis leylandii* 'Gold Rider'

x Cupressocyparis leylandii 'Gold Rider'

This modern yellow form retains its golden colour is summer and winter. The tree grows to a conical column much less quickly than the green *leyandii*. Ideal for use on its own, or as a hedge provided it is regularly clipped for attractive dense growth.

x *Cupressocyparis leylandii* 'Silver Dust'

x *Cypressocyparis leylandii* 'Silver Dust'

'Silver Dust' is a remarkable variegated form of Leyland cypress. Some of the branches are blotched with cream, others are completely green, while many are a mixture, with cream patches contrasting sharply against the green. The cones too are similarly variegated. This slender columnar tree grows slightly slower than the standard Leyland cypress but will eventually become as tall.

Cupressus arizonica

ARIZONA CYPRESS

The majority of cypresses are not fully hardy in north-western Europe. Despite its origins of California and Mexico, the Arizona cypress

Cupressus arizonica 'Sulfurea'

Cupressus arizonica 'Sulfurea'

will survive winters in north-western Europe. There are small differences between the species but the real differences are to be found in the various cultivated forms, which differ widely. In the wild, the cypress can grow to 25m (82 ft) tall.

Cupressus arizonica 'Sulfurea' is a slow-growing columnar variety with yellow-grey foliage.

Juniperus chinensis 'Plumosa Aurea'

CHINESE JUNIPER

Juniperus chinensis 'Plumosa Aurea'

Juniperus chinensis 'Plumosa Aurea'

Juniperus chinensis grows whimsically – to 20m (65ft) tall – at Chinese temples. From the species that grows wild in China and Japan, cultivated varieties have been bred that remain must smaller, such as *Juniperus chinensis* 'Plumosa' that spreads outwards vigorously but rarely taller than 1m (3ft 3in). The branches of *Juniperus chinensis* 'Plumosa Aurea' grow upwards at a sharp angle, to reach about 2m (6ft 6in) high. The mature branches are covered with non-spiky, scaly yellow-green needles. The fruits are blue.

Juniperus communis

COMMON JUNIPER

Dry, desolate open heaths and commons that are grazed by sheep are ideal for the common juniper. It does not thrive in the shade, so that grazing sheep prevent woodland forming but they do not disturb the spiky juniper. They grow both prostrate and dwarf but usually become a medium-sized shrub, sometimes reaching 10m (33ft) tall. A lone juniper, the height of a man, can look like a person on a misty heath. *Juniperus communis* grows in open places throughout the northern hemisphere, from Greenland to North Africa. It cannot cope with waterlogged soil but is tolerant of lime, whatever previously held opinions may have been.

In its enormous range of distribution, the variety of habitats is equally wide, so that breeders have been able to choose from a wide range of cultivars for further selection.

Juniperus communis 'Hibernica', or Irish Juniper, grows to a striking pointed column about 5m (16ft 6in) high but it does so slowly. It has dense growth, with copious, non-spiky,

Juniperus communis 'Compacta'

Juniperus communis 'Hibernica'

Juniperus communis 'Suecica'

needles.The Swedish juniper, *Juniperus communis* 'Suecica' grows in many different forms in Sweden but is only offered for gardens as a columnar cultivar. This name is used for an extremely wide range of differing plants from small columns with pointed tops and non-spiky needles, to broad, multi-stemmed columns with spiky needles.

Juniperus x *media* 'Pfitzeriana Aurea'

PFITZER CYPRESS

Juniperus x *media* 'Pfitzeriana Aurea'

The most recent opinions suggest that the origins of this cultivar arise from a crossing between *Juniperus chinensis* and *Juniperus sabina*. The branches grow at an upward angle to form a very broad but low shrub that eventually is 2m (6ft 6in) tall. It is a sport, or naturally arising deviation of *J. x m* 'Pfitzeriana' that is the true Pfitzer cypress. This latter, green form is widely planted in public open spaces and churchyards because of its ground-cover properties and spiky growth. 'Pfitzeriana Aurea' has golden-green needles.

Juniperus procumbens

CREEPING JUNIPER, BONIN ISLAND JUNIPER

This Japanese species immediately spreads horizontally, covering a very large area. If not supported, it will reach no higher than 50cm (20in) tall. The needles are pointed and green, with blue-white stripes. In cultivation, no fruit is formed. A very satisfying ground-cover conifer that can be trained across walls and cover large stones, making it ideal for rock gardens.

Juniperus procumbens

Juniperus sabina

SAVIN

Juniperus sabina

Juniperus sabina 'Hicksii'

Savin grows wild in central and southern Europe and in the bordering areas of Asia, almost exclusively in mountainous regions with limestone. The mature shoots – of this 2m (6ft 6in) high but very broad shrub – have scaly needles. Dark blue berries, that are covered with a white bloom, ripen in autumn. Except for the very young berries, they are harmful if eaten. This is a very easy conifer to grow in almost any type of soil, provided it is not waterlogged.

Juniperus sabina 'Hicksii' is one of the most popular cultivated varieties with its blue-green scaly needles. Initially, the branches grow upright but as the plant matures, the tops of the branches bend to spread the shrub out. Becomes between 1.5-2m (5-6ft 6in) tall.

Juniperus squamata 'Blue Star'

Juniperus squamata 'Blue Star'

FLAKY JUNIPER

Juniperus squamata 'Blue Star' is one of the most popular junipers. It originates from another cultivar from the same species, 'Meyeri' but in contrast with that cultivar, 'Blue Star' is a dwarf form. It grows mainly outwards but so slowly that it will be many years before it has become 1m (3ft 3in) wide, and about half that height. It grows whimsically with short branches that have grey-blue spiky needles packed closely together.

Larix gmelinii

ASIAN LARCH

This is the first larch to regain its foliage in spring, specially the variety *Larix gmelinii* var. *japonica* that is sometimes known as the Kuril Islands larch after the islands to the north of Japan and east of Siberia.

This 30m (100ft) high tree is rarely seen outside tree collections. Late spring frosts can damage the newly emerged foliage.

Larix gmelinii var. *japonica*

Larix kaempferi

JAPANESE LARCH

Cones of *Larix kaempferi*

When the larch needles fall in November, the floor of the forest is brightened by the yellow debris. The needles slowly decay to form fine, acidic humus. One normally associates conifers with evergreens but larks have chosen an alternative winter strategy. They lose their

Cone of *Larix kaempferi*

leaves in autumn to avoid them transpiring moisture when the soil is frozen. Larches come chiefly from areas of cold climate. In the extreme north, they grow as shrubs.

In the forests of Europe, the European larch or *Larix decidua* is widely planted. Their resin is used to make turpentine. The Japanese larch closely resembles the European larch and because it is less susceptible to fungus, it is sometimes planted in preference. A cross between the two is also planted: *Larix x europlepsis*, or Dunkeld larch. All three grow to about 30m (100ft) tall.

The larch can create a fairy-tale atmosphere in a garden, especially towards the end of the year. Young trees can be pruned to form a thick deciduous hedge. Plant about five trees per metre/yard and clip and prune them to the required shape and size when their leaves have fallen. They are suitable for poor and acidic soil, although the European larch can withstand some lime.

Metasequoia glyptostroboides

DAWN REDWOOD

The dawn redwood is both an ancient yet very modern tree. For a long time it was known simply through fossils, until living specimens were discovered in western China in 1941. They resemble *Taxodium.*

The linear and flattened soft leaves emerge in spring light green. In autumn, they turn yellow, orange, and reddish brown before falling off, together with the young branches. The tree eventually grows to a column 40m (130ft) tall with a pointed top. Plant in moist soil, preferably at the water's edge. The base of the tree can quite happily stand in shallow

Metasequoia glyptostroboides

Microbiota decussata

This conifer closely resembles the juniper. It grows in the wild in the area around Vladivostok and is therefore absolutely hardy. This robust plant will grow anywhere, except in waterlogged soil.

Picea abies

COMMON SPRUCE, NORWAY SPRUCE

Picea abies var. *alpestris*

Leaves of *Metasequoia glyptostroboides*

water. The dawn redwood likes hot summers and therefore thrives best in southern areas in sheltered places. It is fully hardy.

Microbiota decussata

The spreading branches of *Microbiota* only reach about 50cm (20in) high, but they can cover a piece of ground 2m by 2m (3ft 6in by 3ft 6in).

Picea abies 'Diedorfiana'

Picea abies 'Inversa'

Picea abies 'Diedorfiana'

Picea abies 'Nidiformis'

This is the Christmas tree, not a pine as it is often described, but a spruce. The common spruce grows throughout much of Europe and it is widely planted elsewhere for its timber – deal. The tree grows dead straight upright and can become 45m (150 ft) tall. Eventually, it gets to look columnar because of the relatively short branches. If the trees are grown close together, eventually the lower branches will die off and only the uppermost branches will remain green. Spruce has lots of light needed to grow well. On

their own, they can withstand a great deal of wind.

Most spruces – especially the common spruce – grow well on moist, poor, acidic soil, with a pH value between 4-6. Unfortunately, such areas also have problems with acid rain. This precipitation containing acidic elements – caused by output from power stations, car exhausts, and even intensive animal husbandry – can damage huge areas of forest. The ground is made even more acidic, leading to the roots

Picea abies 'Ohlendorffii'

Picea abies 'Pendula Major'

being unable to gain sufficient lime and magnesium, so that they wither away. In small areas, such as gardens, this can be rectified by adding lime, or lime-based fertilisers to the soil. *Picea abies* var. *alpestris* comes from the Swiss Alps. Its grows slowly in a conical shape, with blue-bloomed green needles and hairs on its branches.

Many cultivated varieties have been selected from the common spruce that are suitable for gardens, such as *Picea abies* 'Diedorfiana'. This is a graceful, tall spruce with yellow-green young needles that subsequently turn dark green, so that the tree changes colour with the season: golden yellow in spring and dark green in late summer, autumn and winter.

Picea abies 'Inversa' is a widely used weeping form of about 5m (16ft 6in) high with the exceptional tree reaching 10m (33ft) tall. All the branches hang down to form a green column. It is popular in churchyards.

Picea abies 'Nidiformis', is the dwarf spruce and the most widely grown form of common spruce. It grows to about knee height but spreads outwards somewhat more to eventually form a flattened form. Very compact and well covered with foliage. Makes an ideal green focal point for a garden.

Picea abies 'Ohlendorffii' is a dwarf form that will eventually grow to 4m (13ft) tall and the same across but this takes many years to achieve. In the meantime, this spruce forms a densely branched globe or broad cone. Very suitable for gardens.

Picea abies 'Pendula Major' initially forms a small tree with drooping branches that completely hide the main stem. It eventually becomes a big tree with branches that slant downwards.

Picea asperata

DRAGON SPRUCE

Picea asperata

The dragon spruce is one of many forms of spruce from western China. The broad conical tree will eventually become 25m (82ft) tall. The needles are at first blue-green but they change to grey-blue. The needles are so attractive that this species is to be found in many parks and pinetums. *Picea asperata* 'Glauca' has much bluer needles than the species. It forms a perfect blue-grey cone of about 20m (65ft) tall. For care, see *Picea abies*, but the dragon spruce grows better in drier soil.

Picea breweriana

BREWER SPRUCE

Picea breweriana

The Brewer spruce was not discovered until the middle of the nineteenth century in the United States, even though this 20m (65ft) high tree has clear characteristics of its own. The branches point slanting towards the ground and the twigs on them point plumb downwards. These can be as long as 2m (6ft 6in) on older trees. The covering of blue-green needles (that are light green when new) is fairly sparse. Attractive specimens are only formed by propagating from seed. Grafted examples acquire a somewhat misshapen appearance. Given that the tree grows rather slowly for the first twenty years, it is only something for enthusiasts with ample patience. For care, see *Picea abies*, but the Brewer spruce prefers drier soil.

Picea glauca

WHITE SPRUCE

Picea glauca 'Conica'

Picea glauca 'Conica'

The white spruce originates from Canada and the north-west of the United States. Its needles are an attractive blue-green. For all this, the tree is rarely planted, because is grows fairly rapidly to 20m (65ft) high. For care, see *Picea abies*.

Picea glauca 'Conica' was discovered in Canada in 1904. The slow growth of this form makes it one of the most popular garden conifers. 'Conica' takes sixty years to grow 4m (13ft) high. When mature, it forms a perfect cone with a very dense mat of branches, twigs, and needles. The needles are light green in spring, turn light blue later and they can become somewhat suffused with a copper tone in severe winters. In dry, sunny positions, it can be affected by red spider mite. Otherwise it is robust and highly rewarding.

Picea mariana

BLACK SPRUCE

The black spruce grows to about 10 m (33ft) high in Europe with a conical form. Young trees are particularly attractive with their blue-green needles. In later life they become rather bare lower down and for this reason they are not ideal as ornamental trees.

Picea mariana 'Nana' on the contrary is extremely popular. It rarely grows taller than 50cm (20in), spreading outwards rather than upwards, with grey-green needles.

Picea meyeri

Picea meyeri

A conical tree that reaches about 20m (65ft) high. It originates from the Chinese mountains and is hardy in all but the coldest parts of Europe. It has beautiful, long, blue-green needles. For care, see *Picea abies*, but this spruce prefers drier soil.

Picea montigena

The long and particularly broad needles of this Chinese species are blue-green with an attractive bloom. The tree can become 20m (65ft) tall, with broadly spreading branches, that bend upwards at their tips. It is rarely

Picea montigena

Branches of *Picea montigena*

planted in gardens because of its irregular growth.

Picea obovata

There is little difference between this spruce and the common spruce, except for the greater extent of hairs on the branches of this species. *Picea obovata* grows in a belt from Finland, through Northern Russia, to Eastern Siberia, in a very climate.

Picea omorika

SERBIAN SPRUCE

The Serbian spruce once grew in large parts of Europe. It was driven back by the Ice Age to certain parts of the former Yugoslavia, where it grows on limestone. The Serbian spruce has the broadest needles of all European spruce species. In late spring, the new needles emerge with a blue bloom to them but they quickly turn green.

Picea omorika

The tree grows well in both acidic and alkaline soils and has been planted for commercial forestry since the end of the nineteenth century. When mature at about 30m (100ft) tall, the tree retains its attractive conical form and elegant, long curved branches. It grows best in relatively dry soil. For care, see *Picea abies*.

Picea omorika

Picea orientalis 'Aureospicata'

Blossoms of *Picea omorika*

Blossoms of *Picea orientalis* 'Aureospicata'

There are numerous cultivated varieties of the Serbian spruce, including dwarf, ground-cover, and weeping forms.

Picea orientalis

CAUCASIAN SPRUCE

Green needles, that are the shortest of all the spruces – less than 1cm (3/8in) long – cover the round branches of the Caucasian spruce. The tree can become 30m (100ft) tall and its is conical, with bowed branches. As with the other spruces, the cones hang under the branches. With the Caucasian spruce, the new cones have a striking mauve colour that later is suffused with purple.

The Caucasian spruce is ideal for planting in dry soil, where it will form a beautiful tree from an early age.
Picea orientalis 'Aureospicata' has unusual new yellow needles in spring that turn green during the course of the summer.

Picea polita

Picea polita

Picea polita will eventually grow to 25m (82ft) tall but it grows very slowly, so that it can provide ornamentation for a park or garden for a long time. The branches grow out sideways, like broad plumes, that some claim look like tiger's tails. The needles are borne right around the branches, except for a clear line on the underside; they are dark green and spiky. Creamy-yellow male blooms and pale

Needles of *Picea polita*

green female ones appear on the tree in late spring that turn into very smooth cones that have a slightly purple tinge to them. This tree grows on lava slopes in Japan. For care, see *Picea abies*.

Picea pungens

COLORADO SPRUCE

Needles *Picea pungens* 'Glauca Globosa'

The Colorado spruce grows best in clean air and a cool climate, in which aphids do not thrive. Fitful winters that never really become cold give aphids a chance to survive on this spruce. Plant the Colorado spruce therefore in a drier position then the common spruce. For further care, see *Picea abies*.

The species itself is rarely planted in gardens, because of its great height of about 30m (100ft). The most popular cultivars are the blue forms:
Picea pungens 'Glauca Globosa' is an extremely popular variety that is flat-topped and globular in shape, with blue-tinged needles.

Picea pungens 'Koster'

Pinus ayacahuite

The shrub grows very slowly to about 1m (3ft 3in) tall. *Picea pungens* 'Koster' is still sold as "the blue spruce" even though there are more modern blue cultivars than this one, that was first introduced in 1885 by the breeder whose name it bears. This conical tree can still be seen in the gardens of some older houses.

Pinus ayacahuite

MEXICAN WHITE PINE

Needles of *Pinus ayacahuite*

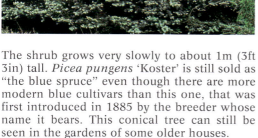

Pine needles are borne in clusters, surrounded by a sheath. Each sheath of the Mexican white pine has five to a maximum of eight needles. These are silver to blue-green and can be up to 20cm (8in) long. The cones are about 30cm (12in) long and they are often covered with resin. They hang on the undersides of trees, including young ones.

The Mexican white pine comes, quite naturally, from Mexico, but also from neighbouring Guatemala, and it is a true tropical tree. Despite this, it is possible to find specimens growing in Scotland. The tree only thrives in coastal areas or very sheltered positions inland. It grows to 30m (100ft).

Pinus cembra

AROLLA PINE, SWISS STONE PINE

This pine grows very slowly in the Alps and the Carpathian mountains, especially at high altitudes where exposed to the wind. Trees have been found in these conditions which have been estimated to be 2,000 years old. At lower altitudes, the tree grows fairly quickly to

Pinus cembra

about 25m (82ft). The upward growing branches form a regular cone. The blue-green needles are in clusters of five. This is a popular garden tree because of its uniform growth, attractive needles and indifference to the wind and poor soil. The woolly aphid or adelgids can seriously mar the appearance of this tree.

Pinus contorta

Pinus contorta var. *latifolia*

BEACH PINE

The beach pine is grown for its timber above all in the western parts of the United States. The species grows to 25m (82ft) high. The green, twisted needles are arranged in pairs. At the start of summer, the male blooms appear like yellow candles on the tree. There are a number of cultivated varieties that are suitable for the garden, such as the slow growing *Pinus contorta* 'Compacta' and the golden-yellow dwarf *Pinus contorta* 'Frisian Gold'. *Pinus contorta* subsp. *latifolia* or lodgepole pine is the most widely distributed form. It grows to about 35m (115ft) and is widely grown by commercial foresters.

Pinus flexilis

Pinus flexilis

LIMBER PINE

The limber pine could just as easily be called flexible pine. This pine from the west of the United States has branches that point crookedly outwards and are extremely pliable. The 5-8cm (2-3¹/₂in) long needles are arranged in groups of five that together with other sheaves of needles, form clusters of blue-green needles on the ends of the branches. The tree will eventually grow to 25m (82ft) tall but it does so slowly and this tree is suitable for the average garden.

Pinus mugo

DWARF MOUNTAIN PINE

The dwarf mountain pine from the mountains of central and southern Europe is a very variable species that has its needles arranged in pairs. This bushy pine rarely grows taller than 5m (16ft 6in) so it is not surprising that many hybrids and cultivars have been bred

Pinus mugo 'Zundert'

Pinus nigra

Pinus nigra 'Pierrick Brégeon'

Pinus nigra 'Pierrick Brégeon'

and selected for use in gardens. There are at least 100 globular varieties, with creeping and upright varieties in addition. The dwarfs are ideal for planting in pots or containers on a patio. They do not like acidic soil, so the pH level should be 6 or above. *Pinus mugo* 'Zundert' forms a compact shrub no larger than 80cm (32in) high. The needles are strikingly yellow in the winter but green again in summer.

Pinus nigra

AUSTRIAN PINE, EUROPEAN BLACK PINE

The black pine is widely planted to help stabilise sand dunes. It can withstand salt-spray in the wind and happily live on pure sand. Its natural habitat is the mountain areas of south-east Europe. In the wild there, it can grow to about 40m (130ft) tall but it often remains much lower because they can be extremely variable, with numerous forms from columnar to globular with many cultivars of great variety. The needles are arranged in pairs. The illustration shows a form with arched needles.

This cultivar from a hybrid that resulted from cross-breeding the black pine with the Japanese *Pinus densiflora* is very compact and has attractive long needles. The cultivar was introduced in about 1990 as a legally-protected form under the name 'Brepo'.
Because it grows so slowly, it can be planted even in a tub or pot for the patio. It will

happily survive wind and sun, and is able to withstand winter frosts in a pot. Planted in open ground, it belongs to the semi-dwarfs, because it will eventually grow into a 1m (3ft 3in) diameter globe.

Pinus parviflora

JAPANESE WHITE PINE

Pinus parviflora

In Japan, the Japanese white pine does not grow taller than 10m (33ft) but it often grows very much broader. In Europe, it generally forms a broad cone about 20m (65ft) tall. The pine cones remain on the tree for some years after they have ripened. They are highly ornamental, with their unusually wide, bowed scales. The grey-green bloomed needles are arranged in bundles of five. They are about 5cm (2in) long and bowed. The tree is fully hardy. *Pinus parviflora* 'Glauca' is an outstanding blue-green tree that eventually reaches 10m (33ft) tall. The bowed needles are borne on spreading branches that are "layered". 'Glauca' lends itself readily to bonsai treatment and practitioners of this art regard it highly.

Pine cones of *Pinus parviflora* 'Glauca'

Pinus peuce

MACEDONIAN PINE

Pinus peuce

The Macedonian pine usually remains an attractive blue-green, even on the undersides of its branches. It eventually forms a broad conical tree, about 30m (100ft) tall. It needs room to grow outwards of 20m (65ft) diameter. The 7-10cm (2½-4in) long needles are arranged in bundles of five. Resin drips from the young cones that hang down. The Macedonian pine grows rapidly in any type of soil and will stand firm if necessary against the wind.

Pinus ponderosa

PONDEROSA PINE, WESTERN YELLOW PINE
The mat-green needles of the Ponderosa pine are about 20cm (8in) long. They are arranged in threes and are attractively curled downwards. The branches too are slightly bent downwards. This pine from the West of the United States is more open than some pines and is therefore more transparent. It is fully hardy and can therefore replace less hardy long-needled pines in areas with cold winters.

Pinus ponderosa

Pinus pumila

Pinus pumila 'Glauca'

Pinus pumila 'Globe'

Pinus pumila

DWARF SIBERIAN PINE

Pinus pumila

The dwarf Siberian pine grows in parts of Siberia where there are 70°C of frost. It is also found high in the mountains of Japan. The tree has adapted itself to growing in these conditions, by not least of all, growing as a spreading bush. The dwarf Siberian pine does not need to grow any taller than 2-3m (6ft 6in-

10ft) because there are no other trees to compete with.

The twisted, grey-needles are arranged in fives. The true dwarfs are rarely sold. Several cultivars are understandably very popular.

Pinus pumila 'Glauca' is widely planted in rock and heather gardens because of its attractive blue needles. It is a spreading form that can grow to 2m (6ft 6in) tall. The red, male blooms, that are born at the ends of new shoots with their needles, are very eye-catching in late spring.

Pinus pumila 'Globe' closely resembles the previous variety but it always forms a globe up to 2m (6ft 6in) in diameter. The needles are even bluer than those of 'Glauca'

Pinus strobus

Pinus strobus 'Radiata'

Pinus strobus 'Summer Snow'

In the eastern parts of North America, the Weymouth pine grows to 50m (164ft) tall. Even though it will grow to 30m (100ft) it was a popular ornamental tree for both gardens and parks for a long time. It is a conical tree with horizontally-growing branches which have 5-12cm (2-4$\frac{1}{2}$in) long blue-green needles, that are arranged in bundles of five.

Currently, the Weymouth pine is rarely planted because it appears to be rather susceptible to a fungal disease.

Pinus strobus 'Radiata' is still planted despite a moderate susceptibility for the fungal disease. This is not surprising though, because it forms a wonderful, compact shrub with a flattened top, that rarely reaches 2m (6ft 6in) high. *Pinus strobus* 'Nana' looks identical to 'Radiata'. A third, very similar cultivar is *Pinus strobus* 'Umbraculifera'. The three names are often interchanged without any respect for the actual variety.

Pinus strobus 'Summer Snow' gets its rather strange name from the white tips of the young needles. It is a compact shrub that grows to about 2m (6ft 6in) tall and wide.

Pinus sylvestris

SCOTS PINE

Pinus sylvestris

In parts of Europe, the Scots pine is used to stabilise shifting sands where previous over-grazing by sheep has caused erosion of the top soil. In Britain it stands sentinel on top of hills in areas of heathland. The species grows from Siberia to Scotland and western parts of Asia. The Scots pine can survive in extremely poor soil, including almost pure sand. The tree is a valuable commercial timber specimen.

In the right position, the Scots pine can grow to 30m (100ft) but where it is exposed to the wind, it remains much more compact and often assumes a whimsical form. The striking feature is the orange-brown bark.

Pinus sylvestris 'Watereri' is the best cultivated variety to use as an ornamental tree.

Pinus sylvestris

Pinus sylvestris 'Watereri'

The twisted needles are arranged in pairs. The shrub, or low tree grows very slowly and then spreads more outwards than upwards. It only grows to 7m (23ft) tall after about 100 years.

Pinus tabuliformis

CHINESE RED PINE

The Chinese red pine grows conically at first but then its crown flattens out with much older trees. They can reach 25m (82ft) high but often remain much smaller and tend to spread outwards rather than upwards.

Pinus tabuliformis

Pine cone of *Pinus tabuliformis*

Trees of this habit can be seen at Chinese temples and places (including the Forbidden City in Beijing).

The shiny, green needles are arranged in bundles of two to three. They are about 10cm (4in) long and flop over.
The immature cones are ovoid and once ripe they are about 7cm (2½in) long. Although this species is fully hardy and has no specific

requirements, it is virtually only to be seen in special collections.

Pinus wallichiana syn. *P. chylla, P. excelsa , P. griffithii*

BHUTAN PINE, BLUE PINE

Pinus wallichiana

The Bhutan pine has a plethora of names in addition to its recognised ones: the weeping pine, Himalayan pine, but also *Pinus chylla, Pinus excelsa*, and *Pinus griffithii*. They all concern an attractive pine that originates from Afghanistan and the Himalayas. In that region, the 50m (164ft) high tree is important for its timber. In Europe, this wonderful ornamental tree rarely exceeds 20m (65ft).
The blue-grey needles are arranged in bundles of five and are evenly spread along the young branches. Eventually, they hang down to create a weeping effect that is accentuated by the horizontally growing branches bending downwards. When planted on its own, the lower branches remain on the stem. Although this tree is fully hardy in Europe (with the exception of the coldest regions), it is best to shelter it from icy winds.

Podocarpus nivalis

ALPINE TOTARA
Podocarpus is the southern hemisphere's equivalent of the yew (*Taxus*). The 100 species of this genus principally originate from tropical mountainous areas in the southern hemisphere. Most of them are not fully hardy and therefore unknown in northern Europe. *Podocarpus nivalis* is one of the few exceptions. This shrub, that grows to about 1m (3ft 3in) tall and 1.5m (5ft) wide, originates in the

Podocarpus nivalis 'Rockery Gem'

mountains of New Zealand and can withstand minus 25°C. Plant a male and female plant next to each other so that the red fruits will be formed. *Podocarpus* is not poisonous and therefore makes an alternative to yew (*Taxus*) in gardens with young children. It prefers moist ground and can be pruned and clipped as a hedge

Pseudolarix amabilis syn. *P. kaempferi*

GOLDEN LARCH

Pseudolarix amabilis

Pseudolarix amabilis

The pastel-green needles of the golden larch turn orange-yellow in autumn. This conifer makes an attractive 15m (50ft) high golden cone in a park or pinetum. The branches spread out and hang. Because the tree only looks attractive when standing apart, it needs a growing circle of at least 10m (33ft) diameter. The young trees in particular are prone to frost damage, mainly due to lack of moisture. Plant this tree from the eastern parts of China by preference in moisture-retaining soil where it is sheltered from the wind.

Pseudotsuga menziesii syn. *P. dounglasii, P. taxifolia*

Trunk of *Pseudotsuga menziesii*

OREGON DOUGLAS FIR
The trunk of the Douglas fir has cork-like, rough bark. Behind the bark is the "Oregon pine" timber that is commercially attractive. This is why this 60m (200ft) tall tree is so widely planted in commercial woodlands in Europe. It originates in the western parts of North America, where it is capable of growing to 100m (330ft). The needles are similar to those of yew (*Taxus*).

Sciadopitys verticillata

Sciadopitys verticillata

UMBRELLA PINE
The umbrella pine comes from Japan where it grows in moist mountain areas. The needles are arranged in wreaths of 10-30 to each twig.

Sciadopitys verticillata

Cone of *Sciadopitys verticillata*

Sequoiadendron giganteum

In reality, each needle consists of two needles that have joined together, lengthways. The needles are about 10cm (4in) long.

Provided growth is normal, a new wreath of needles is formed at the end of the branches each year. This 20m (65ft) high conifer grows extremely slowly. Despite this, it is only to be seen in parks and special tree collections, partly because the propagation sometimes produces deviations that do not have the attractive conical to columnar shape that is normal. The plant enthusiast will plant this species in lightly acidic sandy soil and protect it from drying and icy winds.

Sequoiadendron giganteum

BIG TREE, WELLINGTONIA

This massive tree is also known as giant redwood, and Sierra redwood. With its 135m (443ft) height and 12m (40ft) girth, the big tree lives up to its name. Specimens of these Californian giants that are no longer living, have been found to be about 3,000 years old. The tallest examples in Europe are about 50m (164ft tall. They were grown from seed that was brought to Europe in the middle of the nineteenth century. The huge conifer, with its reddish-brown bark, is a great attraction in parks and arboretums. The bark is so soft that you can bang your hand against it without hurting yourself. This resilient, thick bark protects the cambium from being damaged by the fires which regularly occur in its natural habitat. The big tree is neither the oldest or the tallest tree on earth. The tallest tree is the Australian Eucalyptus amygdalina with a maximum height of 155m (508ft 6in). The oldest tree found so far, was a dead example of *Pinus aristata* var. *longaeva* from the mountains of Arizona, of which the age was

Sequoiadendron giganteum

Trunk of a *Sequoiadendron giganteum*

Sequoiadendron giganteum 'Hazel Smith'

scientifically determined to be 4,600 years old. *Sequoidendron giganteum* 'Hazel Smith' grows rapidly and has better resistance to the one known problem in cultivation in Europe of this species: the honey fungus. In fact, the big tree grows better in Europe than in the United States. It can withstand frosts of minus 30ºC, and it grows rapidly regardless of soil and conditions, provided the soil is not strongly alkaline. Within a few decades, the big tree will live up to its name and tower above the tallest of the other trees in the park.

Taxodium distichum

Taxodium distichum

BALD CYPRESS, SWAMP CYPRESS

The leaves of the bald or swamp cypress fall in autumn, but before this happens, they turn a dazzling colours of orange to dark red. The tree's origins are the swamps and everglades of the south-eastern part of the United States but despite this it can survive in Europe in a temperature, maritime climate. In Europe, this tree grows to 40m (130 ft) high. In places where its roots grow in water, it forms aerial

Autumn colours of *Taxodium distichum*

roots, just like buttresses. The needle-like leaves are soft and the green of fresh summer grass. The tree can grow permanently in shallow water but it does just as well in normal garden soil, provided it is not too dry. Otherwise, the soil may be poor or fertile, acidic or lime-rich. This exceptional tree withstands almost any normal treatment and deserves to be more widely planted.

Taxus baccata

Berries of *Taxus baccata*

YEW

No tree is both so loved and so hated. Hated because of the toxicity of virtually the entire plant (the exception being the red seed aril). There are countless instances of cattle but especially horses being poisoned. It is much admired for its timber, that is exceptionally strong, pliant, and tough, but also as a shrub for the garden. In gardens, yew can be pruned and clipped to form a hedge or into intricate topiary forms. In contrast with many conifers, yew makes new growth in old wood when it is pruned, even, when necessary in the main trunk.

Yew prefers fertile, moisture-retaining soil but it will thrive elsewhere. If not pruned, it will grow to about 15m (50ft) high. The yew blooms almost non-stop in the spring and female plants bear rock hard seeds encased in a fleshy aril in the late autumn-early winter. These catch the eye because of the bright red colour of the fleshy aril. Birds are crazy about the fleshy seed cases that they ingest complete with the seed. The seed has the highest concentration of poison of the entire plant but because the seed is not digested by the birds it does them no harm. When they excrete the seeds, the birds help the tree to spread itself.

Only male plants exist of *Taxus baccata* 'Adpressa' so that no fruit are formed. The

Taxus baccata 'Adpressa Aurea'

Taxus baccata 'Adpressa Aurea'

shrub grows irregularly to about 6m (20ft) tall. The needles are not arranged at a right-angle to the branch, instead, they are at a slant. The needles are short, wide and dark green.

Taxus baccata 'Adpressa Aurea' grows in a similar way to 'Adpressa' but remains lower at a maximum height of 4m (13ft), though it is usually shorter. The ends of the branches have golden-yellow plumes of needles. Older leaves are yellow-green, with golden-yellow margins.

Taxus baccata 'Fastigiata' is known as Florence Court or Irish yew. The branches grow upwards to form columns. As the shrub broadens out, a whole forest of columns is formed. In cultivation, this variety grows to about 5m (16ft 6in). It has dark green needles. The shrub was discovered in Ireland and since then has been propagated by cuttings. There are only female specimens.

Taxus baccata 'Fastigiata 'Aurea' has all the

Taxus baccata 'Fastigiata Aurea'

Taxus baccata 'Semperaurea'

characteristics of Florence Court yew but with golden-yellow new needles. Taxus baccata 'Repandens' is a female creeping yew of less then 50cm (20in) height but it grows to 5m (16ft 6in) wide. *Taxus baccata* 'Semperaurea' remains golden-yellow all year. The shrub grows uniformly every time as wide as it grows tall, reaching about 2m (6ft 6in) in both directions. Seen from above, the needles remain golden-yellow but from below they are yellow-green. Occasionally, the needles only have yellow margins. This a popular and rewarding plant.

Thuja koraiensis

This rarely planted conifer is exceptionally

Thuja koraiensis

hardy. It comes, obviously, from Korea. The flattened shoots on the reddish-brown branches grow slightly pendant. The shoots are grey-green with a striking white bloom on their undersides. When the scales are pressed together, a definite almond fragrance is given off. The shrub usually becomes no taller than 2m (6ft 6in), because the plants sold are propagated from side shoots. If grown from seed, it will reach about 9m (30ft) tall.

Thuja occidentalis

Thuja occidentalis 'Smaragd'

Thuja occidentalis 'Smaragd'

AMERICAN ARBOR-VITAE, WHITE CEDAR

This western "tree of life" will thrive in wet soil, such as wet clay, where other conifers cannot survive. Once the others have been removed, Thuja occidentalis is then bought as a replacement. It is often sold as the "conifer for clay". Apart from wet soil, this conifer can also withstand more frost and grows rapidly, so that in no time, it can form a hedge as tall as a man. Little wonder that *Thuja occidentalis* is sold by the million as evergreen hedge, making it without doubt, the most widely sold garden conifer. This is a shame, because it does not do much for the garden. The foliage on the broad fan-shaped shrub is rather coarse. It can only be made attractive by regular pruning and clipping. Usually the reactions are too slow and this is done too late. Cutting back drastically to thick wood is not possible because this will simply result in large bald patches that will only recover very slowly. Where there is shade, there is no chance that the shrub will restore such bare areas. In cultivation, it reaches about 15m (50ft).

Thuja occidentalis 'Danica'

Thuja occidentalis 'Smaragd' as a hedge

Some cultivated varieties grow less aggressively and can be kept in sufficient check in the average garden.

Thuja occidentalis 'Danica' only reaches about 50cm (20in) high after twenty years. The globular form grows very slowly and is a fresh green. In winter, it becomes bronze-green. It can also be grown in a tub on a patio. Place it close to the house when there is severe frost.

Thuja occidentalis 'Smaragd', is synonymous with *Thuja occidentalis* 'Emerald'.

This superb cultivated variety will grow into a slender cone of several metres (10-13ft) high. It is closely covered with emerald green scales that retain their fine colour in winter.

Although 'Smaragd' grows much more slowly than the species, it makes a good hedge. It takes longer to establish than the species plants but it will form a denser hedge and be far easier to keep to the desired shape and size. This cultivar is recommended in place of *Thuja occidentalis* itself and the other rapid-growing varieties.

Thuja orientalis syn. *Biota orientalis, Platycladus orientalis*

Thuja orientalis 'Aurea Nana'

CHINESE ARBOR-VITAE

The eastern "tree of life" originates from the colder parts of Asia, such as north-eastern China. For all this, it is not as hardy in Europe as occidentalis, or the western species. Milder but moister maritime climates lead to the foliage of this species becoming unsightly. The branches grow like erect fans next to each other and will eventually, after growing very slowly, reach about 15m (50ft) high.

Thuja orientalis 'Golden Surprise'

The varieties that follow can cope with severe winters:

Thuja orientalis 'Aurea Nana' is a very popular golden-yellow, semi-dwarf Chinese arbor-vitae, Initially, it has globular or ovoid form to about 50cm (20in). After tens of years, a squat cone of about 2m (6ft 6in) is formed. The flattened branches grow almost vertical, like golden-yellow fingers alongside each other. The scales change in the course of the year from the summer yellow-green to orange to brown-yellow for winter.

Thuja orientalis 'Golden Surprise' resembles the previous form but it grows conically at an earlier stage. Its feathery foliage scales are arranged closely together. In summer they are yellow, especially at the tips. During the summer, they become gradually greener but then this magician changes once again for winter to orange-brown.

Thuja plicata

WESTERN RED CEDAR

The wood from the Western red cedar was highly regarded by the North American

Thuja plicata

Thuja plicata 'Rogersii'

Thuja plicata 'Zebrina'

Indians because of the oil it contained. The oil protects the timber from rotting. The Indians made totem poles and canoes from the timber. Nowadays, for those who prefer something finer than uPVC, the timber is used to make conservatories and greenhouses that will last a lifetime. The Western red cedar grows along the western coast of Canada and the neighbouring part of the United States. They grow extremely slowly and need to be at least 70 years old before they can be felled for commercial timber. The slender conical conifer can eventually reach 60m (174ft) high. The trunk can have a diameter of 4.5m (15ft). It is impossible to say how much of the timber from these trees sold in Europe is from cultivation, and how much is "grabbed" from natural forests. Because of its huge size when mature, the Western red cedar is rarely planted in gardens, although there are a few varieties which remain more compact. By rubbing the scales, a smell of pine-apple is exuded.

Thuja plicata 'Rogersii' is one of the dwarf forms that takes 25 years to reach a height of 1m (3ft 3in). In that time, it grows as an upright oval form. Later, the tree becomes conical, with more slender tips to the

Thuja plicata 'Zebrina'

Thujopsis dolabrata

branches. These are golden-yellow but bronze-yellow in winter. *Thuja plicata* 'Zebrina' reaches a respectable 15m (50ft) tall in cultivation. The conical tree is chiefly grown in parks and collections. The twigs are clearly green with yellow stripes.

Thujopsis dolabrata

HIBA

Thujopsis dolabrata

The needles of hiba are somewhat larger than those of *Thuja* but in other respects the two species are very similar. This conifer becomes about 20m (65ft) tall, growing to a broad cone, so that it requires plenty of room. When young, it remains bushy for a long time and is often planted in smaller gardens, particularly those with moist soil. Moisture is the one thing that this very hardy conifer requires to prevent its shiny green scaly leaves from drying out. Plant it where it will be protected from drying northerly and easterly winter winds.

Tsuga canadensis

EASTERN HEMLOCK

Tsuga canadensis 'Jeddeloh'

Hemlock likes moisture even more then the common spruce (*Abies*). The Eastern hemlock comes from eastern parts of North America where it grows to 25m (82ft) high. In north-west Europe, this tree needs the shelter of other trees to protect it from bleak winds. It usually grows much less tall in these circumstances and loses its conical shape. It is fully hardy.

Plant it in a position where it will be sheltered from icy winds, in damp, lightly acidic soil. The species is rarely propagated but there are many cultivars, including miniature forms, that are propagated by cuttings.

Tsuga canadensis 'Jeddeloh' is the best know cultivar. It was discovered in a churchyard in 1950. It grows slightly broader than it does high, looking like it has lost its top, and has bright green needles that are blue-grey on their undersides.

Tsuga diversifolia

NORTHERN JAPANESE HEMLOCK

In parts of northern Europe where the yew (*Taxus*) is not hardy enough, the extremely frost-resistant *Tsuga diversifolia* is grown as an alternative.

The needles of this Japanese hemlock are green from above but on their undersides, they are a fine chalky blue-green. The broad conical tree grows to 25m (82ft) in the wild, but in Northern Europe stays put at half that and often with a bushy or irregular form. It can withstand more dry, cold, and windy conditions than *Tsuga canadensis*.

Tsuga diversifolia

Tsuga diversifolia

Index

Acknowledgements

The author and publisher thank the following persons and organisations:

Kalmthout Arboretum (Belgium)
Poort-Bulte, Arboretum, De Lutte (Holland)
Trompenberg Arboretum, Rotterdam
Jeroen van de West, Siddeburen (Holland)
Bas Schooneboom, Groningen (Holland)
Arcen Castle Gardens, Arcen (Holland)
Botanical gardens of the University of
Patricia van Roosmalen, Rekem (Belgium)
Agriculture, Wageningen (Holland)
Pieter Zwijnenburg Jr., Boskoop (Holland)
Copijn, Utrecht
Schovenhorst Estate Pineta and Arboretum,
The Tree Foundation, Utrecht

Putten (Holland)
C. Esveld & Company, Boskoop (Holland)
Prof. drs. B.A. Bangma and mr. A.R. van
IJzinga
de Belder & Company, Essen (Belgium)
Veenstra, Haarlem
Eenum Arboretum, Smit & Company, Eenum
(Holland)
Plant Testing Institute for Tree Growers,
Boskoop, (Holland)
Hortus of Haren (Holland)
Ter Borgh Pinetum Foundation, Anloo
(Holland)
Intratuin Groningen (Holland)
Von Gimborn Arboretum, Doorn (Holland)
Jan Woltema, Niebert (Holland)